The Paradox of a Global USA

The Paradox of a Global USA

Edited by
Bruce Mazlish, Nayan Chanda, and Kenneth Weisbrode

Stanford University Press
Stanford, California 2007

Stanford University Press
Stanford, California

Library of Congress Cataloging-in-Publication Data

The paradox of a global USA / edited by Bruce Mazlish, Nayan Chanda, and Kenneth Weisbrode.
    p. cm.
  Based on papers presented at a conference held at the Yale Center for the Study of Globalization in 2003.
    Includes bibliographical references and index.
    ISBN-13: 978-0-8047-5155-1 (cloth : alk. paper)
    ISBN-13: 978-0-8047-5156-8 (pbk. : alk. paper)
    1. United States—Foreign relations—Congresses. 2. United States—Foreign relations—2001- —Congresses. 3. National characteristics, American—Congresses. 4. Globalization—Political aspects—United States—Congresses. 5. Globalization—Social aspects—United States—Congresses. 6. Americanization—Congresses. 7. Civilization, Modern—American influences—Congresses. I. Mazlish, Bruce. II. Chanda, Nayan. III. Weisbrode, Kenneth.
E183.7.P195 2007
303.48′273009045—dc22

2006028413

Typeset by Newgen in 10/14 Minion

Acknowledgments

This book arose out of a project co-sponsored by the Yale Center for the Study of Globalization and the New Global History Initiative (which operates under the umbrella of the Toynbee Foundation). We want to thank both organizations, and especially Haynie Wheeler of the Yale Center and Elaine Wyden, Executive Director of the NGH project, for their invaluable assistance.

The first step in the initiation of the project was a planning meeting, which drew mainly on resources in the New England area. Among those who were involved in that meeting were Alexis Albion, Sven Beckert, Nayan Chanda, Seth Fein, John Lewis Gaddis, Raymond Grew, Akira Iriye, Tina Klein, Bruce Mazlish, Rebecca McLennan, Elliott Morss, Frank Ninkovich, Dominic Sachsenmaier, Werner Sollors, and Bradley Zakarin. Their comments and interventions helped guide the further definition and development of the project. Akira Iriye continued to play an indispensable role in the subsequent efforts to promote the project, of which he was one of the original co-chairs, and is also a contributor to this volume.

At the full-scale international conference held at the Yale Center from October 30 to November 2, 2003, the following, in addition to the presenters whose work appears in this volume, were involved either in the preliminaries or in the conference itself in some fashion. Thanks are due to Michael Adas, Arjun Appadurai, Andrew Bacevich, Sven Beckert, Tom Bender, Charles Bright, Amy Chua, Neta Crawford, Seth Fein, Todd Gitlin, Neva Goodwin, Krishan Kumar, Lance Lindblom, Rebecca McLennan, Donald Miller, Elliott Morss, Balmurli Natrajan, Dominic Sachsenmaier, Wolf Schafer, Crocker Snow Jr., Mohammed Tamdgidi, William Uricchio, Elaine Wyden, and John Zogby.

Coming from many different backgrounds and affiliations, they helped ensure that the discussions were lively and useful. Others whose names may inadvertently have been left out are also to be thanked.

Special note must be made of the work, carried out in addition to his role as one of the co editors, of Kenneth Weisbrode in preparing the text for publication.

Support for the project was forthcoming from the Carnegie Corporation of New York thanks to Vartan Gregorian and from the Nathan Cummings Foundation in the person of Lance Lindblom. Their contribution, as they well know, was indispensable. Added to the provision by the Yale Center under its then-director, Strobe Talbott, of the conference facilities, all these grants made a wonderful meeting possible. It is hard not to gush in appreciation over the faith of these people in the project.

Lastly, appreciation is extended to Norris Pope, editor at Stanford University Press, who, in his usual graceful manner, saw this volume through the process of initial reviewing, then the approval of the board, and finally publication.

Contents

Foreword

Strobe Talbott

Globalization is as old as our species. It began when early bands of *Homo sapiens* wandered from their home valley, crossed a mountain, and came into contact with neighbors they had not even known were there. When not massacring those they encountered—or being massacred by them—our peripatetic ancestors exchanged information and goods. Over the millennia, imperialism—from the expansive realms of the Babylonians, Egyptians, Persians, and Greeks to the Pax Romana and the Pax Britannica—was a force for what we would now call globalization.

That term, however, is new. It was coined in the 1970s by European bureaucrats as they pondered the complex interdependencies of international trade and finance and conducted an experiment in supranational governance that is now the European Union. As the forces of globalization have accelerated over the past two decades, they have generated controversy. "Pro-globalization" pundits have bemoaned "anti-globalization" protests, as though the phenomenon were something to be for or against.

Moreover, "globalization," without a prefix, has become part of the vocabulary of the debate over the hard and soft power of the United States—and the direction of American foreign policy. Some have argued that, because of America's preponderance, "globalization" is a euphemism for "Americanization." Proponents of American unilateralism have proclaimed the United States to be the world's first "global nation," the legitimate champion of universal values, a modern—and benevolent—empire, and as such the enforcer of a Pax Americana.

In the context of American domestic politics, globalization is equally disputatious. Workers whose manufacturing jobs have moved overseas or whose service jobs have been "outsourced," along with politicians courting their votes, have depicted the United States as a victim of globalization.

In fact, globalization is, in itself, neither a positive nor a negative phenomenon; it is a reality, a defining aspect of the modern condition. Globalization, in its technological dimension, has made instant communications possible, with all the benefits that entails for such worthy causes as bringing medical treatment to remote areas and allowing scientists on opposite ends of the Earth to collaborate in research. But just as entrepreneurs, aid workers, and good ideas can cross borders and span the globe, so can terrorists, criminals, dirty money, and disease-bearing microbes.

Therefore, what is at issue is not whether we should support or oppose globalization but how we should respond to it as a reality, how we should manage it and its consequences. It is in that spirit that Bruce Mazlish, one of the giants of intellectual and cultural history, and his fellow contributors assembled this volume. They have provided a considerable—and timely—service in helping to integrate a field of academic inquiry that has tended to be balkanized. Teachers and students of economics, political science, sociology, and other disciplines have made heroic efforts to understand globalization as it applies to their own work. But too often, as Professor Mazlish notes, those specialties had brought to bear "their own preferred set of terms, their own references, their own central foci that are very much unlike those of other disciplines in the social sciences."

What is required is more collaboration across disciplinary and institutional lines. How appropriate, then, that this book should itself be the result of a partnership between the Yale Center for the Study of Globalization and the New Global History Initiative. The emergence of those two ventures in the past decade is itself an encouraging indication of how academe is responding imaginatively to the challenge of globalization. They have both found ways to reach well beyond the academy. For example, the Yale Center is the home of the *YaleGlobal* online magazine, widely—indeed, globally—recognized as the best publication of its kind.

In addition to serving as catalysts for interdisciplinary inquiry and international outreach on their own campuses in New Haven and Cambridge, the Yale Center and the NGH Initiative held a joint conference in the autumn of 2003. The chapters in this book are based on papers presented at that conference. They have since been updated and edited and now appear in print courtesy of Stanford University Press.

In keeping with the complexity of the topic, this book is a model of diversity in two respects. First, in substance, it draws from fields as diverse as history, religion, political science, and media studies. Second, while doing justice to the many important points of difference in perspective, analysis, and prescription, it brings together a variety of views and sets a high standard for civility of discourse. The result is a disciplined yet imaginative volume relevant to scholars, policymakers, and interested citizens of an increasingly globalized world.

Contributors

N. J. Demerath III, Professor of Sociology, University of Massachusetts Amherst

Akira Iriye, Professor of History Emeritus, Harvard University

Nicola Simpson Khullar, completing the Ph.D. program at Annenberg School for Communication, University of Pennsylvania; Managing Editor, *International Journal of Communications Law and Policy*

James Kurth, Professor of Political Science, Swarthmore College

Bruce Mazlish, Professor of History Emeritus, Massachusetts Institute of Technology

Roberta E. Pearson, Professor of Film Studies, Director of the Institute of Film and Television Studies, University of Nottingham

David Reynolds, Professor of International History, University of Cambridge

Ian Roxborough, Professor of Sociology and History, State University of New York at Stony Brook

Martin Shaw, Professor of International Relations and Politics, University of Sussex

Strobe Talbott, President of the Brookings Institution and Founding Director of the Yale Center for the Study of Globalization

Ian Tyrrell, Professor of History, University of New South Wales

The Paradox of a Global USA

1 Introduction

Bruce Mazlish

IN AUGUST 2001, during a vacation in Maine, I was thinking about a paradox. The United States of America, the country most strongly fostering globalization in the economic terms of the free market, is on many counts pursuing other policies that are antiglobal in their essence. Thus, the most powerful actor on the global stage seems resolutely determined not to live in the world it is helping to create through globalization.

Questions kept bounding forth: What are the roots in America's past that might explain this paradox? What are the pulls and the pushes toward and away from the country's participation in the new global society? What are the parts of globalization that America embraces and rejects? And what changes have occurred in the relationship of attraction and repulsion? Answering such questions meant going deep into the American past while also achieving a better understanding of globalization and its history than seemed readily at hand. This was exactly the task undertaken for the past decade by some of my colleagues and me under the heading of the New Global History (NGH) Initiative.[1] Could the questions about the paradox and the historical inquiry into present-day globalization fruitfully be brought together?

At Yale University in 2001, there was a newly created Center for the Study of Globalization. Its director was Strobe Talbott, former deputy secretary of state in the Clinton administration. We had talked earlier about a possible collaboration between his center and the NGH Initiative. I shared my reflections with him and asked whether this might be a proper topic for our joint efforts. He replied in the affirmative.

Then came September 11, 2001. The events of that day highlighted the importance of the project. America was made poignantly aware that it was, like it or not, part of the global society it was helping to bring about. That event pushed the George W. Bush administration into a partial reversal of its position of disengaging from the world, put forward when it first took power. Now it found itself deliberately on a path to what many have called "empire." In turn, our project was no longer merely a scholarly inquiry. It took on tones of urgency and political significance. It is in this overall context that the authors represented in this book set out to fulfill their assignments.

The Yale Center for the Study of Globalization and the NGH Initiative held a joint conference that ran for three and a half days, from October 30 to November 2, 2003. About thirty scholars and policy people participated, with about a third presenting papers, a similar number commenting on them, and the remainder participating in the general discussion. The framework was provided by the NGH Initiative and its previous work.

The NGH Initiative starts from the contemporary phenomenon of globalization, seen as a process, and seeks to understand it from an interdisciplinary, historical perspective. The starting point for the initiative resides in a number of basic facts of our times: a step into space, with its view of "Spaceship Earth"; satellites, making instantaneous communication possible; multinationals; human rights; nuclear weapons; environmental problems; and so forth. These factors, and others like them, transcend national boundaries, though not doing away with the nation-state, and interrelate with one another in unprecedented synchronicity and synergy. One result is a proposed new periodization, a "global epoch," which some date from the 1950s, others from the 1970s.

1

In field after field, efforts have gotten underway in the past few decades to grapple with globalization. Economic historians early on sought to reduce the phenomenon to the expansion of markets. International relations people either disregarded it at first or tried to tuck it into their field in terms of their concerns with governance and security. Sociologists and anthropologists emphasized the roles of social relations and of culture, respectively. Some crossovers took place, for example, by combining the perspectives of international relations, religion, and sociology. Policymakers and planners, of course, recognized the subject as important and tended to approach it from a practical and instrumental viewpoint.

What stands out is the use of disciplinary scissors to cut up the topic into arguably appropriate pieces. The diverse students of globalization tend to exist as if on separate planets. Open any journal of economic history, international relations, sociology, or anthropology, for example, and you will find scores of articles on globalization, but they always have their own preferred set of terms, their own references, their own central foci that are very much unlike those of other disciplines in the social sciences.

Where in all of this do we find the discipline, per se, of history? The fact is that Clio, the muse of history, seems to have been a latecomer. Most history is rooted in national history, which discourages an interest in globalization. We must add, of course, that so are all the other social science disciplines, whose origins date in general from the late eighteenth century in the West, at the time when industrialized national and nationalistic societies began to dominate the scene. It is not, therefore, that history is unique in being challenged by the emergence of present-day globalization, requiring its practitioners to rethink some of its most basic conceptions; its uniqueness lies in the fact that the very organization of the field in the last few centuries has been pronouncedly in terms of the nation-state. Much of history's activity, in fact, during this time has been to serve the state and provide an ideological past and a sense of identity confirming its exemplary nationhood. American history has been a shining example of this sort of service.

Yet history, particularly American history, has experienced the globalization currents that have been foaming around the nation-state. To touch briefly on what is more developed in Chapter 2, the first series of shocks took the form, after the end of World War II, of a retreat from the Eurocentric view that had hitherto prevailed. World history gradually became a recognizable and acceptable subject. Somewhat ill-defined and with an unclear research agenda, it nevertheless tries to use a wide-angle lens that sees more than just national histories. Its preferred subjects are civilizations and empires, or else less formally arranged groups of people subject to transcending forces such as disease or climate change. At its outermost reach, it often uses the synonyms "global" and "universal" for "world."

This is a stretch, but in the right direction. This direction was further developed by what is best called global history, where the particular strands in world history that are concerned with what can be called globalization are singled out for study. In global history, one could go back to the hunter-gatherers thousands of years ago and their drifting across the globe, and then to more recent concentrated bursts such as the Silk Road, the age of discovery in the Renaissance, or more contemporary instances such as the nineteenth-century British Empire. Such work places the present phase of globalization in proper perspective.

One result has been that American history has not been immune from globalization. Increasingly, American historians have been urged to place their country's origins in a globalizing frame, first shaped in the fifteenth-century discoveries; in the economic movements of the eighteenth century, especially slavery and the plantation system; in an Atlantic setting; and so on into the imperialism of the nineteenth century and the world wars of the twentieth century. A "revolution" has been hovering over American studies, preparatory to plunging them into the world of globalization.[2]

This is the situation surrounding the paradox at the core of this volume. The world's most powerful global actor *is* slowly becoming aware that, from its beginning, it has been part of the rest of the world, that now it is a primary actor in helping to create a globalized society, and that it needs to adjust to life in it. This awareness, I am arguing, is mirrored in the state of the discipline of history, forced to readjust its nationalist image and to see itself in a broader context. Neither the country nor the discipline is entirely happy—in fact, often quite the opposite. It is not only "traditional" societies that are uneasy about facing the upsetting processes of globalization but also the so-called most advanced nation in the world. In this context, history is the one social science that potentially can take a holistic view of what is happening, transcending the boundaries of economics, sociology, anthropology, and so forth. Thus, history, having been part of the problem, can now also see itself as an emancipating force.

2

What is the globalization of which we speak? The first point to make is that it is a highly politicized term, invoking much passion and making "cool" scholarship difficult. The next thing to say is that it is a very complex and complicated process, manifesting itself differently over time. The last thing to add in this preliminary pass at its definition is that it is a contested term. Though I will offer a number of different definitions, the essential definition of globalization lies exactly in its contestation, the arguments that swirl about its nature and meaning.

As I have noted, historians of globalization see it as having moved through various phases over time. Accepting this as true, some historians (among whom I number myself) have sought to focus on the study of present-day globalization. Defined as emerging in post–World War II developments, this globalization requires us to put forth a new periodization: ours is a "global epoch." As suggested earlier, it also presents us with dating problems: when does it manifest itself in recognizable terms? The 1950s? The 1970s? The 1990s?

But what is this "it," globalization? A few preliminary references can help us here. In conventional economic and political discourse, globalization equals the extension of the free market. To accept this definition as globalization *tout court* is, however, to accept the artificial boundaries of the existing disciplines. It is to embrace the view that, in actuality, economics is divorced from, for example, politics and culture. It is to buy into the very neoclassical ideology that serves to buttress the free market and to promote the self-interested drive of certain countries, a group in which the USA is *primus inter pares.*

Other definitions are needed. A typical one from international relations focuses on the global public domain. Thus, one scholar says, "I define the new global public domain as an institutionalized arena of discourse, contestation, and action organized around the production of global public goods. . . . It differs from anything in the past that might resemble it in its dynamic density, and by operating in real time."[3] The author argues in a sophisticated manner that it is the interplay of economic and political actors that make for this newly conceived domain, thus joining the discourses of the economic and political disciplines.

"Transnational" (instead of "multinational") is a preferred term in both international relations and sociology. Along with "cosmopolitanism," it is often used instead of the term "globalization." Yet sociologists have been pioneers in studying the globalization phenomenon in its own terms. With their focus on social relations, they offer the following as a typical definition of globalization: "a process of increased density and frequency of international or global interactions relative to local or national ones." In this instance, its causes are identified as "the increased power of global capital markets; the rise of new information and communication technologies; and the rise of a new hegemon which creates the conditions for increased trade."[4]

This introduction is not the place for a full discussion of the multiple definitions and meanings of globalization. Those given are simply to indicate the range of disciplinary efforts—a tasting, so to speak. One historian offers a very simple definition, given with one foot in world history. In this view, globalization is "a progressive increase in the scale of social processes from a local or regional to a world level."[5] Moving on from this terse statement, we can tentatively emphasize that at the heart of globalization is the transcending of established boundaries and borders of time, space, and territory, an increasing interdependence and interaction of peoples and, my own favorite, an emerging consciousness of what is happening—that is, an awareness of the global community that is being created and an interest in shaping that emergence in certain directions.

Within history, an interdisciplinary research agenda can center around specific elements, some already mentioned, in the coming about of present-day globalization: the step into space of the human species, satellites and their resultant communication possibilities, the compression of space and time, multinational corporations and nongovernmental organizations operating across national boundaries, nuclear meltdowns and military threats doing the same, and environmental impacts on a global scale. A host of other factors are ripe subjects: human rights, the United Nations, world music, global consumerism, and so forth. The result is a globalization that must be studied holistically. To do this is, in fact, the assignment of the NGH Initiative, joined with all the other efforts in various disciplines.

3

In studying globalization, we must always be aware that it is a process (not a thing) that is neither teleological nor deterministic. These are canards frequently leveled against it. Though there are strong currents pushing in the direction of some form of globalization, that form, indeed its very existence, is very much in play. There have been previous surges and retreats in globalization. One frequently remarked upon is the decline of globalization as the British Empire spawned rivals in the late nineteenth century. Another is the era of protectionism that set in at the time of the Great Depression in the 1930s, a development that itself added to the severity of the economic malaise. There is a whole set of scenarios that could be set forth as to how present-day globalization could falter, stumble, and perhaps come to a halt. Similarly, even if globalization largely continues in its present path, what shape, or rather shapes, it will take is by no means determined. In fact, this book is a disquisition on one part of that exact problem.

Contingency and human agency, along with natural causes (e.g., climate, ecology) and unintended consequences, must be the watchwords of anyone trying to understand globalization (as indeed any other aspect of history). So, too, must an awareness of the different evaluations that attach to the process be constantly in mind. For some it brings liberation, for others a new kind of servitude; for some a broadening of horizons, for others a destruction of stability and traditions. Occurring in many forms, anti-globalization is a constituent part of globalization.

With all this understood, I want now to turn to a part of the origins and then to a part of the results of globalization. Though the Cold War is touched on briefly in a number of the chapters in this book, not one of them is devoted to the subject. Yet that is the necessary condition for the emergence of the USA as the global hegemon at the beginning of the new millennium. This is, of course, hardly a new conclusion. Numerous books and articles have detailed how the Soviet Union and the USA, for a number of decades, each sought to make its version of a "one world" dominant. Much of American foreign policy was devoted to the containment of its Soviet opponent, a policy that resulted in the support of many unsavory regimes so as to keep them out of the camp of the greater tyranny, as it was viewed, and that had numerous side effects. Prime examples are Vietnam and Afghanistan, with the latter producing American-supported *mujahideen* who later turned their weapons against their patrons in a resultant surge of global Islamism.

Thus, the Cold War is a necessary background for our understanding of the paradox at the core of our book. It is not in itself, as traditionally treated, a part of that paradox. Hence, it does not have a separate chapter in this volume. If it were to have had such a treatment, it would have been in terms of the way the Cold War served as one of the factors in the coming of globalization per se. The emphasis would be on the production of nuclear weapons, guided missiles, satellites, the step out into space, and other such factors heralding the emergence of present-day globalization. In other words, the Cold War would be treated as a factor of globalization rather than mainly as a topic in international relations.[6]

I also want to mention a result of globalization that is taken for granted by many of the contributors to this volume but has not been given a chapter to itself. It is the subject of global society. That some sort of global society has been emerging is integral to the paradox in which America, the creator, turns its back on its creation while also trying to shape it in its own image. Mostly, the shape of society desired by many, especially idealistic, students of globalization (among whom I number myself, as a pragmatic idealist) goes under the heading of global civil society. It stresses institutions whose aim is justice and peace, such as the International Criminal Court and the UN, and talks optimistically about global consciousness and global identity.

At its best, global civil society is treated as both a vision and an emerging reality of sorts.[7] The vision, however, must never be confused with the reality, which is a mixed bag of imperfect actors, such as nongovernmental organizations (NGOs), and the complex, confused world that is depicted for us by toilers in the heated field of international relations. Yet there is no question that the vision has power—it becomes an actor, so to speak, in the globalization process—a power that is seen as threatening to both "traditional" societies and "advanced" societies such as the USA. Here is the crux of the great struggle today over questions of nationhood, sovereignty, religion, "settled" boundaries, and the transcending power of globalizing forces. Here is where we find our particular paradox played out in terms of the foremost economic globalizer (though this can be exaggerated; there are other globalizing powers), which happens also to be, potentially, the greatest threat to globalization as tending to a global civil society.

The global, it must be recognized, is always local. Virtual space seems to call this statement into question, displacing place. So it does to a limited extent. But overwhelmingly it is the local where the processes of globalization are grounded both in political and phenomenological terms, that is, daily lives. For example, the global free market may call for unlimited movement of capital, and, in theory, labor. In practice, protectionists clamor for restrictions, and nationalists claim restrictions on immigration. Global civil society may hold out the vision of the transcendence of particularistic ties, but the still-existing national and traditional definitions of these connections generally prevail. In short, globalization is a struggle, an often harsh conflict, whose outcome is always uncertain.

This struggle hovers over the chapters that follow. Up to now I have been suggesting a framework for the treatment of the paradox of the USA and globalization, viewing it as a local happening within the broader process of globalization. This is the "logic" behind the book. The chapters will try to fulfill some of the expectations behind that logic, to describe and analyze some of the ways in which the USA has both played a role in and reacted against emerging present-day globalization. The chapters will deal with both pushes and pulls, with the forces of attraction and repulsion. The results will not be uniform but a mix of productive agreements and disagreements around core concerns.

I

The chapters in this book are organized into three main groups. Following this introduction, there are two chapters discussing the nature of globalization and its possible equation with Americanization. Then there are two chapters focused on the USA and its historical past. These are followed by four chapters that are more concerned with present U.S. policy and attitudes. One of these chapters is on religion and another on media, both viewed as cultural elements of globalization. These are followed by a chapter on the military and then a penultimate one on the effects of 9/11, especially in regard to the question of American empire. All the chapters take up part of the paradox that is central to this book. At the end, not unexpectedly, I try my hand at a conclusion. Such is the overall structure of the book. Now, I offer some idea of each chapter—not an abstract but an interpretation and a comment on it—and how it contributes to the whole.

Martin Shaw starts from the basic insight that political changes were always crucial to globalization. Where so many others have stressed economics, he emphasizes the nation-state as an actor even as it must now be seen in the transcending terms of globalization. Foremost in this regard is the USA. Giving thought to the role of the Cold War in making America the contemporary hegemon, Shaw presents his discussion in the form of a meditation on the term "global" and its valences, ranging from world to global history. His own elegant approach is as a historical sociologist. Emphasizing that a transformation has taken place from the previously dominant international system, he accepts that a "rupture" (my word) of sorts has occurred and argues that social scientists must adjust their theories accordingly. Where others have stressed the role of NGOs, Shaw takes the broader subject of a world *political* system as the theater for America's role in the "new world order."

A minor paradox stands behind our larger paradox in Akira Iriye's chapter. For many Americans, globalization equals Americanization, which they see as a good thing. For many non-Americans who nevertheless accept the equation, globalization as Americanization is a threat, destroying local cultures and identities as well as economies. A little reflection in this regard suggests that Americanization can be perilously close to imperialism. Iriye is highly sophisticated in his analysis of Americanization, showing how it has changed over time: he tells us that in the first half of the twentieth century, it did place its stamp on globalization in a pronounced and mostly benign manner, especially if one accepts its equation with modernity. By the second half of the century, this was no longer the case, with the Cold War being the defining difference. Realists triumphed over idealists, for example, pushing the international interests in justice and peace to the side in favor of "national" interests. Yet the rhetoric, as well as some of the reality, of justice and peace continued to sound, leading to the paradox of Americanization broadening into globalization, but with a disparity between the two.

Where Shaw defined globalization in terms of a developing political system, Iriye's understanding of globalization is one centrally concerned with peace, justice, and international cooperation. Though this echoes Shaw, it introduces a subtle difference, connecting to a vision of global civil society, which, for Shaw, is only one possible outcome. Both, however, clearly see the advantages of moving from a traditional international perspective to that of a global one.

In the next two chapters, the historical past is examined from differing but complementary angles. We can see these chapters as variations on a common theme: the ambivalence of American nationalism. Originally, the theme was to have had three variations: Michael Adas was to have contributed a chapter titled "Wary Vanguard: Sources of American Attraction and Resistance to Globalization" to this section. Indeed, he made a presentation at the conference itself, using an extensive outline. Unfortunately, personal considerations kept him from submitting a complete essay for the volume. The outline, however, was so full and suggestive, and his presentation contributed so much to the ideas of the other participants, that we are going to take the unusual step of summarizing it here. What Adas did primarily was to stress the contradictions in the relations between the USA and the rest of the world. Like Iriye, Adas examines some of the ways Americanization became globalization, emphasizing free markets and democracy. From the beginning, however, the colony-nation was ambivalent. Against the image of America as the beacon of light, the city on a hill, that "city" also saw itself as exceptional and against entangling alliances. It tended toward Manichean views—good and evil sharply separated—and was deeply Puritan and religious. From the beginning, it also showed an inclination to unilateral interferences, invigorated by a "can do" attitude. A parochialism and isolationism rooted in the past persisted and grew in the present, fostered by a sense of mission. The commercialized media reinforced Americans' sense of superiority, uniqueness, and ignorance of other societies. Even when proclaiming global rules and aims, the USA was hypercritical about its own behavior and frequently flouted them. Local politics tended to cloud over global citizenship. No wonder then that resentment grew over globalization as Americanization, especially in the Muslim world, Africa, and Latin America. For large numbers of people in these regions, the American version of globalization looked remarkably like an American empire.

David Reynolds focuses on the nineteenth century but looks both backward and forward. He argues that the USA is a product of one phase of globalization, in the eighteenth century, with the British Empire and the slave trade figuring prominently in its formation. Though at first reaching only to the Mississippi River, the new nation, driven by technology, had continental aspirations "from sea to shining sea." Such a large territory was threatened by forces of dissolution—the Civil War made real the possibility of the country breaking apart—and needed desperately to establish an identity for its pluralistic immigrants. This identity, Reynolds argues, was achieved by antithesis. This could take the form of not being black, communist, and so on; not being this "other" lay at the heart of American nationalism. By the twentieth century, the nation, itself a product of earlier globalization, was "producing" globalization through the export of its products and also of its culture, emphasizing rugged individualism. Defining globalization as "integration by expansion," Reynolds sees a "historically distinct" phase emerging from the U.S. experience. Thus, he offers another version of Iriye's treatment of Americanization and an alternative to Shaw's emphasis on the political (instead stressing the technological), while being in agreement with both that present-day globalization should be seen as a new phase in a process stretching over at least three centuries. And, like Adas, he sees persistent features, even as there is change, in the American character.

Ian Tyrrell seems to work in the opposite direction from Reynolds, emphasizing the departures from global society. He explores them in terms of such elements as American exceptionalism, evangelism, and patriotism. Thus, he analyzes extensively the claim to exceptionalism in the eighteenth and nineteenth centuries, aligns it with the anticolonial tradition in American culture, describes the way evangelism internally inoculates the USA against evil through moral uplift while also reaching out into the world externally, and then shows how patriotism becomes the glue holding together a disparate population. America, he contends, is exempt in its own mind from class analysis and becomes so first by embracing the frontier myth and then the myth of equal opportunity. Nevertheless, there were and are ideals rooted in American exceptionalism—for example, those of freedom, liberty, and democracy—that could serve as a model for others and hence come to play a globalizing role. Though more an ideology than a historical fact, according to Tyrrell, American exceptionalism can be seen as a pull to globalization as well as a push away. In sum, he sees the USA as a prime participant in what he calls an "uneven global integration."

Taken together, Tyrrell and Reynolds (as well as Adas) offer a contrapuntal treatment of the way the USA has played an ambivalent tune in regard to the attractions and repulsions that mark its engagement with globalization. The gaze of these scholars has been mainly on the historical past, though they adumbrate the way that past persists into the present.

The last four chapters of this book, as remarked earlier, while often also glancing farther backward, are mostly concerned with the more recent past. Though in the previous chapters religion has figured as a subtext, N. J. Demerath III takes it as his main text in his chapter, claiming it as central to any account of globalization. Treating religion as a matter of imports and exports—a nice balance to the usual focus on economic goods—Demerath builds on his study of fourteen nations an extensive analysis of religion as both promoting globalization and opposing it. Surprisingly, however, he treats religion in America as more a matter of import than export, starting with the Puritans and continuing with present-day immigration that has made the country more Christian, though no longer of the established kind. Even more surprising, he insists that globalization is dependent on increased secularization—it is, in fact, a precondition. Yet, globalization seems to lead to greater religious conflict. Thus, American religion is also an ambivalent phenomenon. Though wide-ranging, much of Demerath's chapter is devoted to evangelical and Pentecostal Christianity. He looks at the way this kind of religion authorizes aggressive American policies. Differentiating cultural globalization from structural, or economic, globalization, he argues that the assumption that the former is preceded by the latter is false. (I would argue that the sharp division between religion and economics is itself false.) In any case, religion, acting as both a brake and a lubricant to the globalization process, brings people of different religions into possible conflict as well as contact. In the end, the chapter leaves us with the problem of globalization bringing about heightened religiosity that then spreads to the political arena.

Culture, though linked to economics and politics, is the central factor in Demerath's account. So it is in the chapter by Roberta Pearson and Nicola Simpson Khullar. Their topic is the role of media in globalization and specifically America's "cultural imperialism," that is, the spread of its culture across the globe. In this revisiting of the theme of Americanization, Pearson and Simpson Khullar frame their treatment in terms of the "culture industry" (Adorno is not mentioned, but it was originally his idea), noting the domination of six transnational media corporations (three American) and the way in which they promote globalization when it benefits them but stifle it when it seeks to enter their home market. One result, germane to our overall theme, is that America is largely shut off formally from foreign influences, yet those influences can be traced in the early history of film, with Hollywood first borrowing from the Italians, then thrusting its own wares on the world, and only in recent times again borrowing, especially from the British. Again, the chapter sounds the note of import-export, dealing, however, more with the influence of European, especially British, media on American films and TV rather than vice versa and with the crisscrossing of culture and economics in the spread of globalization.

Ian Roxborough defines globalization as "a diffusion of cultural norms and as increased transnational economic integration" and reminds us that it does not happen on its own but must be underpinned in large part by the political and military weight of a dominant power or powers. The ability to project military power globally is a measure of success. He handles this issue in terms of American strategic doctrine, its basic concerns being identification of the enemy, the creation of ordering institutions, and the capacity to "control the periphery." In these terms, Roxborough addresses the central paradox of the volume: the U.S. role in and resistance to globalization. As he tells us, U.S. military doctrine insists on a unique projection of force globally that allows for no real rival. Plans call for this supremacy to be maintained far into the future. The Cold War had one clear enemy: the Soviet Union. When it was vanquished, the Manichean need took the form of a search for a new principal enemy, with China the prime candidate, but then was derailed by the rise of Islamist radicalism. The result was a need for two different strategies and forces. In the case of terrorism, however, the enemy was a nonstate actor; this has called for an effort in local control on a global scale and thus intimations of empire. With much comparison to Great Britain as a previous global hegemon, Roxborough's is a rich treatment of our topic—I have hardly touched on the details—that raises forcefully the question of whether politics dictate the military policies or vice versa. The challenge, of course, is to study how they intertwine, along with the cultural and economic forces at play.

With James Kurth's chapter, we come to grips directly with America's most recent past and 9/11. Where Roxborough sees empire as an unintentional outcome of military doctrine, Kurth argues that "some kind of empire was a necessary condition for the globalization of a century ago" (p. 148), and, not unexpectedly, of this "American Century." Kurth claims that the American Empire, however, is unique in history in that it has no significant challenger. On another front, Kurth and Roxborough can be seen as entering into contention: For the former, the professional military are by disposition and tradition "nationalists" and thus in tension with the policymakers who are "globalists." In the latter camp, Kurth places both neoconservatives and neoliberals. Secretary of Defense Donald Rumsfeld's efforts to overset the traditional military with his Revolution in Military Affairs must be read as part of the American turn to global and imperial purposes. Unfortunately, it does not seem to work against the new enemy, radical Islam, and its terrorist strategies and tactics. This face of Islam is, Kurth argues, a natural reaction to its situation as a "loser" in globalization. In a dialectical relationship to American-inspired globalization, radical Islam becomes the prime case for antiglobalization. In Kurth's view, by ignoring the "local," America's reach for empire is doomed to failure. Globalization, a world revolution, is left in a quandary. The morass in Iraq may come to represent "an end to any kind of globalization at all," with American empire itself a fad. Such seems to be Kurth's black-hued conclusion. However, we must ask whether in conflating globalization and empire (which means the USA), as he apparently does, Kurth here is ignoring the holistic nature of globalization and its many players and factors.

II

Each chapter must be read for itself. In my account of them, I have given an interpretation of sorts rather than an abstract or summary. Where possible, I have sought to indicate the agreements and disagreements explicit or implicit in the chapters, to draw out the flavor of the actual and potential dialogue. Though all the authors seem to accept the existence of globalization as a major break of sorts in history, and, not surprisingly, exhibit a willingness to look at both the USA and globalization in terms of the paradox of pushes and pulls, attraction and repulsion, they sometimes differ greatly in choosing the aspects on which to center their attention. The same is true in regard to their attitudes toward the overall subject.

The authors come from a variety of disciplines: history, political science, international relations, media studies. This partly explains the differences of emphasis that they place on their analyses of globalization. Fortunately, a common language rather than a rhetoric of discipline has mainly prevailed, honed further by the exchange of views both during and after the 2003 conference. It can also be said that the writers, and the other participants at the conference, were selected with an eye to representation and an awareness of political inclinations. These ranged from liberals to conservatives and neoliberals to neoconservatives, with a few falling outside this spectrum. Whatever their politics, however, all are committed to the service of scholarship and respect for the views of others.

The topic itself, with its focus on the USA, would seem to carry an implicit contradiction to the idea of globalization. It might be felt that an air of Anglo-centrism hovers over the enterprise, made stronger by the fact that the writers come from only four countries—America, Australia, Canada, and Britain—though other countries were represented among the participants. Surely it would be interesting to have had papers from Chinese, Indian, Middle Eastern, and Latin American scholars. It is nice to think, however, that scholarship is global and that the results probably differ little (although political judgment might vary). In fact, I would argue, the subject of study is best seen as a "local" instance of the globalizing challenge displaying "universal" features.

Nevertheless, it must be acknowledged that the USA is not any local example but the most powerful player on the contemporary global stage. As such, its solution to its particular paradox is of greater-than-ordinary importance and will have the broadest possible ramifications. Moreover, as suggested, its struggles are those of all countries in the global epoch in which we live. How does one deal with the globalizing process as the world moves from a nation-state orientation (though still persisting strongly) to a more global one? How to handle questions of sovereignty and security? Of economic interdependence of an unprecedented sort, and the need for protection of one's workers and economic sectors such as agriculture or business? Of the threat of global terrorism?

Or is the USA, in fact, unique in both having and dealing with the paradox of pushes and pulls to the degree that we have seen outlined in all of our chapters? Is the very nature of the American identity, rooted in its "exceptional" history and experience, basically in conflict with a movement to global identity? Or in putting things this way am I succumbing to the Manichean insistence on either-or, black and white, when the real question is how to reconcile a national identity with a global one? The chapters that follow will help us in answering such questions.

2 The Political Structure of a Global World: The Role of the United States

Martin Shaw

THE HUMAN SCIENCES, in which we may include history, the humanities, and the social sciences, are very much a part of what we study. Our problems are to a significant degree those of the age in which we live. Our concepts, however we develop them, are those of the society we study. Our work attempts to explain the past but also to understand contemporary predicaments. In a fast-moving world, each half-century brings fundamental change, each decade major new alignments. Academic study responds to these challenges, for the most part indirectly, and they constantly reshape our agendas. We had hardly absorbed the epochal changes of 1989–91, resulting from the end of the Cold War, before we had to grapple with the new challenges of the world after September 11, 2001.

The issues of this volume appear to be shaped by this historical conjuncture. The apparently fundamental new perspectives of "globalization," which became increasingly dominant in the 1990s, have hardly been worked through in social and historical knowledge. And yet already they seem to be made problematic by the new polarizations of the post-9/11 environment. Understandably, scholars in the United States are particularly aware of these changes, but their colleagues in Europe and the rest of the world also experience them, if in different ways. Thus, in a political sense, the dominant liberal-democratic version of globalism that prevailed in the 1990s had already begun to be eclipsed in the years after 2001—in the United States by American national reassertion, elsewhere by a new vogue for critiques of American imperialism. These new trends have come together, indeed, in a new academic interest in empire, a central concept for both proponents and critics of American power.[1]

If history and social science are to transcend intellectual fashion, however, we need to stay a while with the "global" perspectives that still need further exploration. There are, of course, relatively easy ways to reconcile globalization and empire. Globalization has been mainly understood as primarily economic, technological, and cultural in nature; for many of its theorists, the state remained the nation-state. On this understanding, we have a world that is economically and increasingly culturally globalized but that remains politically and militarily in a preglobal state. The undermining of the nation-state, a powerful theme of the first wave of 1990s "hyper-globalizers,"[2] was always exaggerated, as "global-skeptics" maintained.[3] Hence there is no insuperable contradiction between economic-cultural globalization and political-military empire; in the formula of one Marxist, the new imperialism protects a global market that suits American interests.[4]

This chapter does not accept such a resolution. Before 9/11, the globalization literature had already transcended the debate about the undermining of the state, recognizing, as David Held and his colleagues proposed in a magisterial survey, that "global transformation" (their preferred term) was always multilayered, as much a political and military as an economic and cultural process.[5] Such "transformationists" recognized that political change was as much a driver as it was a consequence of wider social change. This interpretation helps to make sense of the novelty of the situation at the end of the twentieth century: what was new was not just the Internet or globalized stock markets but also the sense of the opening of the world, the collapsing of political divisions, following 1989's remarkable ending of the Cold War confrontation. Any theory that neglected such dimensions was clearly one-sided, although given the predilection of many social scientists for interpretations of an economic and technological nature, it is not surprising that they were widely developed in the 1990s.

In this chapter, I start from this basic insight—that political changes were always crucial to the global—and explore the understanding of global transformations historically. Looking at the global in this way means that we can also look at the evolving role of the United States in these transformations, gaining perspective on the present conjuncture. I explore these issues from the point of view of historical sociology, a discipline that has been widely used to explore the interactions of states and social forces but has not yet generally examined the significance of global change.[6]

World History and Global History

There are many reasons for thinking that human history should be understood in a common, worldwide framework. It is generally accepted that *Homo sapiens* spread across the world from singular origins in Africa. Extensive and repeated migrations diffused cultural forms across continents and oceans tens of thousands of years ago. In the largest historical sense, therefore, human communities were always interconnected, but for long periods many were—for all practical, day-to-day, and year-to-year purposes—separated from one another. Some, like historic European and New World civilizations, developed in complete ignorance of one another; others, like China and Europe in our medieval period, were aware of one another's existence but developed mainly limited, occasional, or indirect interactions.

World history, in the sense of a single story of human society with frequent and regular interaction, is therefore a relatively recent development in the largest story of humankind. Theorists of the world-system, who have pursued these questions most energetically in historical sociology and international studies, have been divided over its dating. Immanuel Wallerstein originally saw it as a modern phenomenon, coincident with the worldwide expansion of markets through European world-empires.[7] Others have pushed the world-system back 5,000 years.[8] Though this debate is important in its own right, for our current purposes it is sufficient to conclude that world history, a single stream of interaction, is a creation of the period of great civilizations and that its modern form has developed over the last few centuries.

Should we distinguish global from world history? Many have implicitly answered no, tracing globalization back through the same world-integrating developments of the last half-millennium that (for others) constitute the formation of a distinctive "world" history. However we define the terms, clearly there are important relationships between earlier phases of world integration—especially the history of modern empire, migration, and trade—and contemporary "globalization." Even those who use the latter term mainly to refer to changes in the late twentieth and early twenty-first centuries, like Anthony Giddens, nevertheless root global change directly in the longer historical processes of modernity.[9]

However, we should ask whether the spread of the term "globalization" is more than just a fashionable renaming of old tendencies. The word, first recorded in the 1960s, was used on a modest scale in the 1970s and 1980s and became a "buzzword" only in the 1990s. It followed, and superseded, other terms like "postmodernity" (developed in the 1980s) and "post–Cold War" (early 1990s) that also tried to account for the general change in social, cultural, and political conditions that was taking place in the last part of the twentieth century. It is indicative that while "postmodern" ideas developed in the period prior to decisive political change and "post–Cold War" ideas developed in the immediate aftermath of political change, "globalization" concepts spread most strongly as the political upheaval settled down. The only one of these three ideas to indicate a positive—rather than merely "post"—content, the significance of the global's increasing dominance of mid-1990s interpretations seems to be that it represented the sense of the emergent world's social realities, after the immediate upheaval following the end of the Cold War.

It is obviously possible to ignore this sense of a "new" global reality after the Cold War and, in adopting the concept, read it back into earlier periods, indeed centuries. However, a more fruitful strategy is to explore the meanings that attach to the concept and utilize these as a way into a historical interpretation of late–twentieth-century "globality." It makes sense to discuss our "global world" as distinct from the preglobal world that preceded it. In this sense, global history needs to look beyond world history.

The Meaning of the Global

"Global" is clearly a multilayered concept, and we need to explore the various dimensions of its meaning in general usage and in the social-scientific literature. I have suggested that these are threefold.[10]

1. The first substantive meaning is connected to the literal meaning of the word, belonging to the globe. Here "global" means *connected with the natural habitat of humankind*. The understanding of the world as round is a fundamental tenet of distinctively modern thought. In recent decades, moreover, images of the world from outer space have enabled us to visualize the planet's global aspect more concretely than ever before. This understanding has been powerfully reinforced by many new insights into relationships between human social activity and the natural environment as a whole that have developed in the late twentieth century. Thus, the environmental literature is paradigmatic of global social science in its disregard for—or relegation to secondary status of—national boundaries.

2. Even more widespread, and more directly connected to the technological, economic, and communications mainstreams of the globalization debate, is a

concept of the global as *the quality of being involved in the worldwide stretching of social relations.* In this concept, global social relations are relations that spread easily across the world, again increasingly disregarding national boundaries. Whereas the environmental concept of the global stresses the connection between human activity and nature, this concept is defined by transformations of human relations themselves, in which the changing relation to the natural environment is only one part. According to Giddens, for example, the transformation of time-space relations means that social linkages are not merely spread over long distances but also intensified, leading to instantaneous worldwide connections. For him, "globalization can . . . be defined as the intensification of worldwide social relations which link distant localities in such a way that local happenings are shaped by events occurring many miles away and vice versa." [11] For many, what is also involved is the spread of a supraterritorial dimension of social relations. [12]

Both the environmental and the time-spatial concepts of the global give it a content beyond the simple meaning of "world." The environmental concept indicates that an important dimension of common global consciousness is our recognition of the physical habitat that we share. However, in some versions, a primacy of nature is proposed: human activity is seen as a problem for the planet. This interpretation of the global can lead, then, to the subordination of human society to the physical environment. Compared with this, the spatial, or time-space, concept is more sophisticated. However, accounts that emphasize spatial stretching say too little about the *content* of global relations. In this view, global relations are essentially more instant, long-distance versions of preglobal relations, with the new dimensions that speed and density bring to interconnection. Insofar as changed qualities of relations are recognized, they are seen as consequences of these essentially technical changes in the mechanisms of social life.

The global quality of social relations, in both these accounts, is seen as the result of cumulative changes in people's relations with one another and their physical environments. In essence, society has been globalized not because human beings thought or acted globally but, because in pursuit of other ends—profit, power, communication—worldwide connectedness has developed. Of course, there is a large measure of truth in such an account. Whatever it is, the global aspect of social relations has not developed simply or mainly because most people had very clearly defined, specific global aims and intentions. If it had, we would understand it much more easily and would hardly need to argue so much about its meaning. So we must accept that the environmental and spatial accounts indicate important dimensions of the meaning of "global." But have they grasped its core?

3. Although the meaning of "global" is embedded in the largely spatial relations described by these partial concepts, the more developed usages of the term involve more than those concepts describe. By "global," we mean not just transformed conceptions of time and space but the new *social meaning* that this has involved. I propose that we understand this as the development of a *common consciousness of human society on a world scale*. We mean an increasing awareness of the totality of human social relations as the largest constitutive framework of all relations. We mean that society is increasingly constituted primarily by this inclusive human framework rather than by distinct tribes, civilizations, nations, or religious communities, although all of these remain in increasingly complex and overlapping ways within global society.

Social relations become global, therefore, when they are significantly and systematically informed by an awareness of the common framework of worldwide human society. Society becomes global when this becomes its dominant, constitutive framework. Awareness of a common framework in human society is not new, of course: this idea has been one of the driving forces of modernity. The distinction between global and preglobal is therefore that, with the development of global relations, the understanding of human relations in a common worldwide frame comes to *predominate* over other, more partial understandings.

It may be properly asked, of course, how far this is in fact the case. How far has a global society actually come into existence? How far does the global definition of society prevail over other definitions? When and how did this happen? The answer that this chapter proposes, in contrast to mainstream globalization literature, is that this final layer of the meaning of "global" has emerged principally through political developments that have begun to make global state institutions and global politics meaningful.

Global State Formation and Global Politics

If contemporary globalization represents something new in the twenty-first century world,[13] its novelty cannot lie in the spread of world markets, in the opening of world communications, or even in the creation of a common world culture. All of these trends, although powerfully reinforced in recent years, were well established in earlier historical periods. What has changed much more dramatically than any of these in recent times are the political conditions in which society, economy, and culture develop. It is to these changes in political relations, broadly understood, that the new, strongest sense of the "global" most coherently relates. Two main axes of political change are reflected in global consciousness: state integration and popular political mobilization.

At the beginning of the twentieth century, the major states were mostly national empires, largely authoritarian in their relations with their peoples—democracy was still emergent in only a small core of Western states. Relations between the major and minor centers of state power were all actually or potentially mediated through war, and indeed the major imperial nation-states did come to catastrophic war with one another in 1914–18 and 1939–45.

At the beginning of the twenty-first century, in contrast, the core of the world political system is an increasingly integrated complex of national and international state institutions. These are increasingly, if still very problematically, accountable to national and even to some extent international publics—democracy has been deepened in Western states and is emergent elsewhere. Relations between state centers are still, in many cases, actually or potentially warlike, but *within* the extended Western core, war has been abolished in favor of institutional negotiations of interest. The global layer of state institutions, centered on the UN, represents a legitimate framework within which all state power is exercised. Taking these developments together, there is an emergent global network of state institutions, a Western-global state at the center of the still anarchic relations of states worldwide.

Popular political mobilization has changed in ways that are part cause and part consequence of the state-level changes. In the first half of the twentieth century, social movements sought to transform national states. Despite the formal internationalism of the socialist parties, the communist revolutions of the first half of the century were nationally centered movements leading to new, more extreme kinds of authoritarianism in Russia, China, and elsewhere.

In the second half of the century, the most important popular movements have been those that have transformed authoritarian national states into democracies. The democratic revolution against Stalinism—from Berlin's 1953 uprising, through Budapest 1956, Prague 1968, and Poland's *Solidarnosc* to the 1989 movements that ended the Cold War—was a powerful model. In the 1980s and 1990s, similar movements ended authoritarian, pro-Western, Cold War regimes from the Philippines to South Africa and from South Korea to

Indonesia. Meanwhile, the knock-on effects of these democratic movements at the centers of states have been movements for national independence in peripheral regions, from Bosnia and Kosovo to East Timor and Aceh. In the bloody, even genocidal wars that have often resulted, groups of oppressed and victimized people have often appealed to Western states and the UN, invoking legitimate global values and norms and stimulating international state formation in turn. So the latest phase of democratic revolution is *global*-democratic, linked to the development of global state networks.

In both respects, the historical transformations have been multistaged. Although contemporary globality, at both the state and popular levels, is a post-1989 phenomenon, it would not have been possible without the even more profound transformations that took place after 1945. Globality did not emerge seamlessly from economic and technological processes, as the more naïve forms of globalization theory suggest. As Bruce Mazlish points out, "globalization was carried out by the very form, the nation-state, that is now under attack . . . by present-day globalizing forces."[14] Indeed, it was the catastrophe of the world war—the working out of the contradictions of the interimperial state system—that led to the demise of most of the national empires, not only those of defeated Germany and Japan but also (after further struggles) those of Britain and France, and the emergence of a global world order.

So if many nation-states have lost autonomy, as globalization theorists have suggested, the more fundamental loss was their control of military power—the core of sovereignty and legitimate state power—not the late–twentieth-century mutation of economic management capabilities that they had mostly acquired only after 1945. The paradox of the late–twentieth-century world, which ramifies to this day, is of course that within the bloc structures of the West and the Warsaw Pact, the core unit of statehood remained the nation; indeed, the nation-state form proliferated in the postcolonial world and even more after the demise of the Soviet bloc in 1989–91. State integration has been *international* in a cooperative sense, a more or less voluntary pooling of sovereignties.

Thus, although effective state institutions have been increasingly integrated—through military alliances (the North Atlantic Treaty Organization, United States–Japan, etc.), through economic institutions (the Organization for Economic Cooperation and Development, the General Agreement on Tariffs and Trade/World Trade Organization, etc.), and in Western Europe through tighter political and legal integration (the EU), as well as through extensive bilateral relations—the locus of formal legitimacy and popular accountability has remained almost exclusively at the national level (the only partial and so far not-very-significant exception being the European Parliament). Thus, state power has two faces: institutional linkage and democratic autonomy. One image of this combination is the single military organization combined with nineteen different political strategies that NATO presented during the Kosovo intervention in 1999.

Effective state integration was largely confined to the blocs during the Cold War and, ironically (in view of the ideology of socialist internationalism), was much more meaningful in the West than in the Soviet bloc. Indeed, a core reason for the failure of the Soviet model was precisely the coercive character of its integration. The reach of today's global state networks is still highly uneven: while some Western-centered economic institutions are becoming universal in military–political terms, many larger non-Western states remain more like classical national empires. China and Russia may be entering the World Trade Organization, but their military institutions remain autonomous, their modes of rule over outlying regions are quasi-imperial, and they are at best semi-democratic. Many smaller postcommunist states, on the other hand, have seen democracy and integration into Western and global institutions as a means of protecting newly gained national autonomy.

At the heart of all these developments, of course, lie fundamental contradictions, for example, between international independence and national sovereignty and between Western power and global legitimacy. Although these elements are behind contemporary globality, they are far from simply global in character, still less recognized as such by all states or social actors. Indeed, recognition of the global in the political sense is paradoxically weaker at the very center of the global world, in the United States, than in many other places.

The United States and Global History

I have written this story so far without mentioning the United States except in passing. Although it has formal coherence presented in this way, some of the dynamics are clearly weakened by the omission. For the United States has not been just one nation-state among many that make up the Western core of the emergent global polity. It has obviously been central to the story—so central that, as we have noted, the same history has been fairly plausibly written as one of American national power. How then do we account for this role of the United States while maintaining the broader global narrative?

Before the twentieth century, the United States, although a rapidly strengthening society and economic power and the center of technological development, was only one among a number of major states. The United States was from its origins an imperial state, in the relations between colonists and indigenous peoples in its expansion across most of North America and in its increasing commercial and political dominance in Latin America too, as other chapters in this volume discuss.

The emergence of the United States as a world political force was clear during and after the First World War, but the country remained one among several great powers. While the United States played a central part in the postwar settlement, it did not achieve a clear dominance; and as that settlement fell apart, the Nazi German and Japanese empires sought supremacy in Europe and Asia, respectively. The United States became dominant in the world only by defeating these challenges in the Second World War. It is possible to view the consequent subordination of Europe—defeated Germany and victorious Britain alike—and Japan to the United States as the creation of a new kind of world empire, spreading U.S. dominance to the former European colonial worlds. However, this is an unhelpful reading as the Western-dominated world system thus created was one in which the autonomous revival of Europe and Japan was nurtured, leading to the complex system of Western and global governance in which the United States is seen as *primus inter pares* rather than an imperial hegemon.

The new debate about American empire reflects, of course, the developments of the last decade in which the United States became today's "sole superpower" after defeating its one remaining rival, the Soviet Union, in the Cold War.[15] However, that victory was more than the result of the vaunted military supremacy of the United States and the economic might that underwrote it. It reflected the superiority of the Western system of power—and not just of democracy over totalitarianism but of internationalization over empire. The Achilles' heel of the Soviet bloc was the quasi-imperial domination of the Russian communist elite over states and societies in the "satellites." A major secret of the Western bloc's success, in contrast, was that, despite American dominance (especially in military matters), it was a more or less consensual partnership of states and societies in which nearly all gained in security and wealth. The West offered a model of internationalization that was not forced and, despite manifest inequalities, offered real benefits to allies and friends.

The central paradox, then, is that contemporary "globality" is a development of the post–Cold War, Western system of power that emerged through the half-century since 1945 so that globality and American centrality have become intertwined. For some, this is proof that globalization is a mere reflection of American empire and that its cultural phenomena are no more than Americanization. However, if the above account is accepted, global change has always been about more than that. Although its origins lie in the world of 1945, when the United States was simply dominant throughout much of Europe and Asia, and although today it appears that the United States is simply dominant once again, the emergent global world has had a momentum of its own that the United States has hardly been able to control.[16]

I have emphasized that globality has been centered on the complex of national and international state institutions that both constitute the political West (North America, Western Europe, Japan, and Australasia) and frame its military, political, and economic dominance worldwide. The United States stands at the center of this Western-global state conglomerate, and the bilateral linkages of other nation-states to Washington are often as important as relations in formal international organizations. And yet the structure of internationalized state power is much more than what is at its center. The European Union may have originated in what Geir Lundestad perceptively called "empire by integration,"[17] but it represents not only a powerful economic bloc, whose currency now rivals the dollar, but also an alternative model of international integration through institutionalization and law rather than alliance and bilateral linkages of national centers.

The core states of the EU may appear as "old Europe" in the eyes of former secretary of defense Donald Rumsfeld, but his preferred "new Europe" (Poland and other former communist states) looked just as firmly to the EU for its economic future as it did to the United States and NATO for its military security. Linked in many international institutions, both militarily and economically, the United States, the major European states, and Japan cannot escape their now-structural interdependence. Moreover, each of these institutional contexts has its own logic that constrains the individual national centers. Even the UN is thoroughly embedded as the legitimate center of world politics in a way that comparisons with the League of Nations fail to grasp.

Clearly, it is conceivable that this messy, even ramshackle structure of global political institutions and relationships could break apart, and it has certainly been tested in recent times (a point to which I shall return). However, it is reinforced by the processes of economic and cultural "globalization," which are often seen as independent of states but are in fact the outcomes of state actions. The United States was, of course, the major originator of these processes (as it was of the UN system itself). Economic globalization, in the form that became recognized in the 1990s, would not have been conceivable without the Bretton Woods system that laid the foundations of an open international economy, or indeed without the later phase of American economic liberalization in the 1980s that pulled the rest of the West behind. Of course, there are powerful forces in United States politics that have looked to gain the benefits of economic globalization without the burdens of political globalization. Take, for example, the fast-growing web of international law: the United States promotes the development of international commercial law and its embedding in national jurisdictions while trying to hold back the development of international criminal law and its international enforcement. Over decades, it seems likely that the effects of international legal development in both areas will be cumulative and mutually reinforcing. The kind of de-linking that many American politicians seek to achieve may not be a feasible long-term option.

Regressive Globality: Contemporary American Power

If globality is now a *structural* condition of the world polity and economy, reinforced by cultural integration (which I have not discussed), then the historical possibilities, short of catastrophic collapse, are different kinds of global order rather than the dissolution of a global world. In this light, we should interpret the radical interventions of the George W. Bush administration in world politics since 9/11 as attempts to reconfigure the global world. The historical sociologist Michael Mann, writing of nation-states, proposes that they "crystallize" in many different ways as their various institutions interact in power networks with organized social interests outside the state. His theory of "polymorphous crystallization"[18] is particularly useful in grasping the apparently conflicting, changeable forms in which global power networks are mobilized.

We may begin by emphasizing that, because of their unique structural location in the emergent global power networks, American leaders have always sought to mobilize the networks in particular ways, although these have changed with historical circumstances. During the Cold War, the United States preferred to manage its relationships in Europe through the formal military–political institutions of NATO, in which American generals typically commanded while civilian political management rotated among Europeans. The core military–political Western relationships with the Soviet bloc, however, were managed bilaterally between the United States and the Soviet Union, as were many relationships with pro-American regimes in the non-Western world.

In the early post–Cold War period—despite much discussion of "security architecture" and the relative merits of NATO, the UN and other institutions devoted to managing European and world security—mobilization in crisis situations was typically through ad hoc coalitions, such as that organized by George H. W. Bush in the 1991 Gulf War, in which United States leadership was legitimated by the UN. Only in former Yugoslavia, where Western European armies were already involved, did the United States eventually mobilize NATO. In almost all cases of military intervention, however, there has been a combination of bilateral relations, coalitions, and formal international organizations.

In responding to 9/11, the George W. Bush administration extended the preferred American mode of mobilization. In the first phase of the "war on terrorism," Bush constructed a remarkable but loose worldwide coalition, incorporating China, Russia, and India, as well as states like Pakistan whose immediate cooperation was needed for operations in Afghanistan. The role of the core Western alliance was downgraded in this phase, with the United States seemingly preferring bilateral linkages with European states to NATO mobilization. In view of subsequent events, it is perhaps important to note that European support for the United States in this phase was strong. Germany, for example, may have been much attacked by the United States for its position regarding the Iraq War in 2003, but its soldiers have died in Afghanistan and it has provided the only legal convictions to date for the 9/11 attacks.

The "war on terrorism" involved a particular kind of global power network. I have called this kind of crystallization "regressive globalism"[19] for several reasons. First, it prioritized coalition-making with authoritarian and semi-authoritarian states, legitimizing their repressive, antiseparatist campaigns in places like Chechnya, Kashmir, and Tibet alongside the U.S. campaign against al-Qaeda and the Taliban. Second, although the campaign gained formal UN backing, it marginalized legitimate international institutions in favor of this *ad hoc* alliance. Third, the campaign prioritized war over justice and global legitimacy, overlooking the opportunity to bring terrorist criminals to trial before an international tribunal and interning captured enemy combatants in a way that was internationally illegitimate.

It is clearly plausible to define the Bush administration's kind of globalism as "imperial" in character. Bush has accentuated the dominance of the

United States within the larger Western system and has bothered too little, in some phases at least, about the niceties of cooperative relationships with partners in Europe, provoking predictably negative responses from some. He has created informal U.S. protectorates in Afghanistan and Iraq with echoes of earlier European (and in the former case, Soviet) imperial ventures in these same places. However, on neither dimension has the imperial mode of power projection been very successful. By late 2003, as the conference that produced this book was taking place, Bush was already making concessions to secure wider Western participation in his increasingly troubled Iraq project. The number of U.S. casualties in Iraq began to threaten his reelection prospects. It was becoming less likely that the unilateral U.S. military overthrow of dictatorship would be repeated in other "rogue" states like Iran, North Korea, or Syria. As Mann put it, the Bush empire was "incoherent," its military power outpacing its political, ideological, and even its economic power.[20] Even in this "imperial" power projection, the Bush administration had to frame the overthrow of the Saddam Hussein regime within an internationally legitimate rationale. Hence, indeed, the ill-fated focus on "weapons of mass destruction," which presented no obvious direct military threat (even if they existed, which now seems not to be the case), and the manifest failure to convince most friendly governments of, or to sway broad international opinion on, this action.

The position of the British government in this crisis has been particularly revealing of the structures of global power and the strains that the Bush strategy has placed on them. Prime Minister Tony Blair appears to have acted on a general strategic imperative to maintain the strength of the British and European alliance with the United States. Although his cabinet, party, and public were unconvinced of the case for war, he prioritized the strategic connection above all other considerations and has paid a serious political price for this. Without this British stance, the United States would have been isolated among the permanent members of the Security Council, and the political (not military) support received from other states of some importance (such as Spain and Italy) might also not have materialized. Because the United States would almost certainly have gone to war in Iraq anyway, Blair's policy may have averted an even more acute split between the United States and all its major partners in global power networks and may have facilitated the partial postwar healing of the divisions that were caused by the war. On the other hand, it is just as conceivable that if Britain had joined the opponents of war, the dynamics of international opposition would have had an impact on the domestic debate and slowed down or even halted the drive to war. However, this kind of counterfactual discussion is not our real concern here.

Although it is easy to represent this crisis as a clash between national self-assertion and less mobile global institutions, Blair's stance ensured that this division would be blurred. The United States remained, however loosely, within the framework of global legitimacy, and of course its determination to overthrow the Iraqi regime aroused support from many Iraqi exiles determined to achieve a more open and democratic Iraq (thus connecting with the other side of the global political transformation that I identified earlier). Moreover, the postwar situation pushed, as we have seen, toward compromise. The United States had made only weak preparations for the administration of Iraq and was forced to adapt *ad hoc* to various postwar challenges that were mostly very predictable, incorporating ideas and practical input from the NGO sector that largely embraced different global values. The Bush administration and its international opponents were also obliged to come together over the political framework of the new Iraq, with the UN legitimating the new governing council that the United States established.

The conclusion we can draw from this crisis is, therefore, that while the Iraq War has tested much of the messy agglomeration of institutions and relationships that constitute the infrastructure of contemporary globality, it has not decisively ruptured them. The crisis has indeed exposed the inadequacy of current global institutions and political frameworks and should prompt us to consider alternative ways of embedding global frameworks in world society. It has also sharpened awareness of choices between different global futures; an interesting straw in the wind is that some formerly "antiglobalization" activists are now reshaping their ideas toward "reforming" globalization.[21] The global world is a reality, and citizens, as well as governments, are faced with the huge but inescapable challenge of reshaping it to more adequately meet their needs.

3

Globalization as Americanization?

Akira Iriye

"SO LONG AS ONE has faith in the American ideals, opportunities open to him," wrote Mbonu Ojike, a Nigerian scholar and politician, of his experiences in the United States in the 1940s. He encountered harsh racial discrimination, but he also met many who remained true to the American ideals. It was on account of their friendship and their commitment to those ideals, he concluded, that "one can almost always say, 'I have two countries: my native land and the United States of America.'"[1]

Globalization may mean for every person in the world to be able to say, "I have two countries: my native land and the United States of America"—except for those Americans who may identify with only one country, their own. There is a tension between these two positions. For the rest of the world, globalization involves Americanization, but it does not mean giving up their local identities, so the two terms are not interchangeable. For many Americans, on the other hand, to be globalized *is* to be Americanized, and Americanization *is* globalization, so it is not always clear how they will respond when globalization comes to entail more than Americanization.

If ever there was a time when Americanization was, or at least appeared to be, tantamount to globalization, that would have been at the turn of the twentieth century. The term "Americanization" had made its appearance toward the end of the nineteenth century, when globalization of goods, capital, and technology was a well-recognized phenomenon. Published in 1902, W. T. Stead's *The Americanization of the World* was one of the first attempts at understanding the phenomenal expansion of American influence throughout the globe. Arguably the most famous passage in the book is actually a quote from Fred

Mackenzie, a reporter for *Daily Mail*: "The average man [in England] rises in the morning from his New England sheets, he shaves with 'Williams' soap and a Yankee razor, pulls on his Boston boots over his socks from North Carolina, fastens his Connecticut braces, slips his Waltham or Waterbury watch in his pocket, and sits down to breakfast. There he congratulates his wife on the way her Illinois straight-front corset sets off her Massachusetts blouse, and he tackles his breakfast, where he eats bread made from prairie floor . . . tinned oysters from Baltimore and a little Kansas City bacon, while his wife plays with a slice of Chicago ox-tongue." To such daily utensils and food originating in the United States, Stead adds other lists. In the manufacturing of electrical appliances, for instance, he notes that a British firm "has imported American managers, American machinery and American methods" in order to compete with U.S. products. But American influence was not confined to material things. Far away in the Middle East, the author notes, "from the slopes of Mount Ararat all the way to the shores of the blue Aegean Sea American missionaries have scattered . . . over all the distressful land the seeds of American principles." An increasing number of "Armenians and other Orientals issue forth from the American schools familiar with the principles of the Declaration of Independence and the fundamental doctrines of the American Constitution."[2]

If the term "globalization" had existed in 1902, Stead might have used it to characterize what he was writing about. He might have said that various parts of the globe were becoming rapidly interconnected through new methods of transportation and communication and that American commerce, industry, and ideology were giving the interconnected world its unique character. There was a decisive American input into the process of globalization, he might have noted, and, therefore, globalization and Americanization were becoming interchangeable. Many Americans would have endorsed such a view. In his famous oration on President Ulysses S. Grant, delivered in Boston in 1898 just after war came with Spain, Senator Albert J. Beveridge declared, "Our institutions will follow our flag on the wings of commerce. And American law, American order, American civilization, and the American flag will plant themselves on shores hitherto bloody and benighted, but by those agencies of God henceforth to be made beautiful and bright."[3] A bit of jingoistic hyperbole, the speech nevertheless contained many ideas similar to Stead's. For Beveridge and others who shared his view, the world was going to be transformed through American goods and ideas. The more the globe changed, the more Americanized it would become—and Americans would make sure of it.

The writings by Stead, Beveridge, and countless others at the turn of the century suggest that they were fascinated by two aspects of the global transformation—which many of them saw as Americanization—that was going on. One was more mechanical, physical, material; the other more spiritual, mental, ethical. Changes taking place in the first areas were much easier to perceive than those in the second, and for this reason much was written about the possible implications of the former for the latter. A British sociologist, L. T. Hobhouse, for instance, published his widely read *Morals in Evolution* in 1908. The book was one of many that sought to consider the implications of modern commerce and technology for the future of the world. "With the improvement of communication and the growth of commerce," he wrote, "humanity is rapidly becoming, physically speaking, a single society—single in the sense that what affects one part tends to affect the whole." The question was whether such physical proximity had a spiritual aspect. As a philosopher, Hobhouse recognized the ethical dimension of the coming into closer contact of "races and classes who are not prepared by their previous history to live harmoniously together." Nevertheless, he believed that "ethically as well as physically, humanity is becoming one—one, not by the suppression of differences or the mechanical arrangement of lifeless parts, but by a widened consciousness of obligation, a more sensitive response to the claims of justice, a greater forbearance towards differences of type, a more enlightened conception of human progress."[4]

Shared consciousness of obligations, sensitivity to justice, acknowledgment of diversity, and belief in human progress—the items enumerated by Hobhouse were among the most enduring features of what he and others took to be the spiritual transformation of humanity that accompanied physical globalization. Virginia Woolf put it differently when she wrote (in 1924), "on or about December, 1910, human character changed." The change was as much psychological as physical and could be seen in the destruction of traditional social relations. The sound of "breaking and falling, crashing and destruction" was everywhere.[5] Though Hobhouse described the process of generation and Woolf that of destruction, they were both sensitive to the moral dimension of the global transformation. Stead, Beveridge, and others believed that the United States was taking the lead in defining this dimension and in helping the world transform itself spiritually as well as physically. A contemporary of Hobhouse and Woolf, Woodrow Wilson, would confirm that leadership when he led the world to a new international order based upon certain universal values.

It must be recognized, of course, that neither Wilson nor most of his contemporary exponents of Americanization believed in racial equality, and they would have failed Hobhouse's test of spiritual globalization if that meant accepting all races and classes living "harmoniously together." Indeed, as historian Norman Naimark and others have noted, interracial tensions became exacerbated in the age of globalization, and ethnic cleansing—exemplified by the Turkish massacre of Armenians during the Great War and the Nazi segregation and murder of Jews in the 1930s and 1940s—was to become a major blot in twentieth-century history; neither the U.S. government nor its people did much to put an end to such practices.[6] Spiritual globalization lagged far behind material globalization, and, by the same token, Americanization of the world was much more notable in the spread of goods, services, and capital than of universal values and moral standards. To that extent, one could even argue that globalization and Americanization were quite alike. To stop there, however, would be to ignore the significance of developments and ideas exemplified by Ojike's observations. For it is possible to argue that the idea of humanity's becoming "a single society," in Hobhouse's words, never disappeared but steadily gained influence in the subsequent decades. In the aftermath of the Great War, expressions like "a single-world community" and "a world melting-pot" became commonplace, and there was a clear American input into such vocabulary. While disappointed that the Wilsonian utopia made up of democratic states never came to fruition, Americans in various walks of life—businessmen, intellectuals, missionaries—joined their counterparts elsewhere in believing that a global community was emerging in which people all over the world shared a common culture.[7]

Even during the 1930s, the idea of a world community linked together by some universal principles never disappeared. As Dorothy Jones argues in her book, *Toward a Just World*, precisely because the world appeared to be reverting back to anarchy characterized by military aggressions and interethnic atrocities, there were redoubled efforts to define common standards of justice and humanity.[8] Victor Klemperer, a German scholar of French literature and linguistics who, because he was Jewish, suffered from all kinds of discrimination and indignities, wrote at the end of 1938: "At the very moment modern technology annuls all frontiers and distances (flying, radio, television, economic interdependence), the most extreme nationalism is raging. Perhaps a last convulsive upspring of what is already a thing of the past."[9] In thus contrasting technological and economic globalization to political and emotional parochialism, he was in effect continuing the same quest for meaning that Hobhouse had articulated thirty years earlier. Like the latter, Klemperer believed that, ultimately, forces of globalization would make extreme nationalism "a thing of the past" so that the technological annulment of "all frontiers and distances" would eventually bring about a more mentally interconnected and tolerant world. Ojike expressed similar optimism on the basis of his own experiences in the United States. Though the realities of world conditions and domestic developments in many countries were otherwise, there also grew a determination—in the United States, Britain, and elsewhere—that the world crisis that led to another global war must be overcome in such a way as to bring about a more just international order. Many spoke of the construction of "one world" (which was the title of a book written by Wendell Willkie in 1942 after his trip around the globe) as an objective that must be achieved if humankind were to be spared another global conflict, and, while such an idea may have seemed fantastic in the middle of a ferocious war, President Franklin D. Roosevelt and Prime Minister Winston Churchill endorsed the vision in the Atlantic Charter, enunciated in the summer of 1941. The reunified and reintegrated world that the declaration envisioned was to be based on certain universal principles (best exemplified in Roosevelt's "four freedoms") that expressed American values. To those who espoused such a vision, it must have been self-evident that what could bring about "one world" would be forces of Americanization.[10]

When, in 1941, Henry Luce published his famous essay, "The American Century," predicting that the twentieth century would come to be known as the period of unparalleled U.S. influence in transforming the world materially and spiritually, most readers would have agreed, not just in the United States but elsewhere. It can be argued that it was precisely because of the ongoing Americanization of the world that Germany, Japan, the Soviet Union, and other countries that opposed such a development entered into an anti-American alliance. Although the tides of globalization appeared to have been reversed during the world economic crisis that had ushered in a period of managed currencies, regional autarkies, and preferential tariff agreements, all of which combined to disconnect different parts of the globe, by the late 1930s the United States was once again championing the cause of liberal trade policies, something that the Axis powers bitterly opposed. The Second World War, then, was a struggle between forces of globalization-Americanization on one hand and of world partitioning on the other. (That the Soviet Union's leadership wavered between these two positions can be seen in its decision first to side with Germany and Japan and then with the United States and its allies. Even so, Moscow never accepted the equation between globalization and Americanization, as was to become clear after the war.)

When the Second World War ended with the Allies' resounding victory, it might have seemed that globalization and Americanization were approximating each other more than ever. American goods, capital, and human resources had decisively defeated countries that had stood in their way, and American ideas and values were now to be imposed on the defeated countries and spread to the rest of the world as well. In reality, however, while the decades after 1945 did indeed entrench American influence everywhere, that did not prove to be the same thing as the globalization of the world, a process that picked up momentum in the second half of the century. In fact, the equation of globalization and Americanization, a theme in early–twentieth-century history, became highly problematic in the postwar decades.

For one thing, the geopolitics of the Cold War kept the world divided, despite the fact that powerful forces continued to push for globalization. Instead of an Americanized "one world," what emerged in the immediate aftermath of the Second World War was, in the words of David Reynolds, "one world divisible."[11] The relationship between globalization and the Cold War is an intriguing one that is, however, beyond the scope of this chapter to discuss in detail. The United States vigorously promoted economic globalization (through the Bretton Woods system, the European Recovery Program, and the Organization for Economic Cooperation and Development, for instance), and in many instances it remained true to Wilsonian visions: by pushing energetically for the democratization of Germany and Japan, by supporting decolonization in Asia and Africa, and by undertaking educational and cultural exchange programs with most countries in the world. At the same time, however, by giving top priority to the struggle against the Soviet Union and its allies, the United States was willing in many instances to move in the opposite direction; it worked out security arrangements all over the world where strategic and political considerations took precedence over its other goals. One could argue, of course, that waging the Cold War against closed societies was part of the U.S. globalizing mission, but it cannot be denied that neither the strategy of massive retaliation nor the support of authoritarian regimes simply because they were perceived to be anticommunist was compatible with the idea of Americanization that had, during the first half of the century, been interchangeable with that of globalization. Americanization in the strategic, geopolitical realm was not necessarily the same thing as globalization. After all, preparing for a third world war that might have annihilated the globe was quite a different proposition from promoting transnational interconnectedness.

The bottom line may have been the fact that in the United States, as well as elsewhere, the state (consisting of policymakers, bureaucrats, the military, law enforcement officials, the courts, etc.) was growing more and more powerful so that Americanization often implied the expansion of the nation's geostrategic interests rather than material culture or idealistic visions. One can see this, for instance, in the fact that, whereas in 1900 there were only about 220,000 federal employees (including the armed forces), or one such official for every 350 citizens, the scope and functions of the state began to grow rapidly after the 1930s: by the midpoint in the century, the American state comprised more than three million civilians and military, or nearly one federal employee for every 50 citizens.[12] Although the enormous expansion of the state's power and authority was due as much to domestic socioeconomic problems that needed governmental responses as to external crises that called for a strong system of national defense, geopolitical considerations inevitably came to dominate the nation's approach to international affairs. We can understand the growing influence of "realism" in postwar U.S. thinking as a parallel phenomenon. "Realism" posited the supreme importance of "national interest," seemingly oblivious to Wilson's argument that U.S. national and international interests were, or should be, interchangeable. During the Cold War, the interests of the United States and its allies came first, whatever that might imply for international interests.

But globalization must, by definition, have to do with international interests—concerns like peace, prosperity, and justice. During the Cold War, the United States pursued these objectives some of the time but not necessarily all the time. Interesting examples of the tension between globalization and Cold War geopolitics can be seen in the debate on exchange programs that took place within philanthropic organizations such as the Ford and Rockefeller Foundations. Educational and cultural exchanges had been undertaken by these and other private organizations since before the war, and they had been very much part of the process of Americanization-globalization. After the war, as historians Frank Ninkovich, Walter Hixson, Volker Berghahn, and others have shown, the government became interested in making use of these programs as a weapon in the Cold War, defined at times as a struggle for "hearts and minds" throughout the world.[13] That complicated the foundations' tasks, as they would inevitably experience a tension between more traditional internationalism and what may be termed "Cold War internationalism" in their grants policies. For instance, in an April 1951 internal memorandum of the Ford Foundation, the staff were torn between two different objectives: on the one hand, "[the] conduct of political (psychological) warfare and other activities designed to combat Communist threats to peace, freedom and the West," and, on the other, "[the] advancement of international understanding in ways designed to . . . enhance recognition and acceptance of the social and political measures necessary for achieving democratic goals in a closely interdependent world." Another staff memorandum, written in May, supports this latter definition of the foundation's mission by stating that it should aim at helping remove "the basic conditions (e.g., poverty, disease, racial discrimination, ignorance, colonial exploitation, etc.) which create a climate conducive to conflict."[14] The Korean War, which broke out just after these words were jotted down, had the effect, for the time being, of forcing this and other philanthropic organizations to consider how best to promote the nation's geostrategic objectives. In the process, the gap widened between economic, technological, and cultural globalization on one hand and the expansion of U.S. geopolitical interests on the other. One might say that global community and American empire were becoming less and less synonymous.

Under the circumstances, it is not surprising that postwar globalization began to be promoted by forces other than U.S. geopolitical calculations. In the process, globalization came to mean something other than, or at least much besides, Americanization. While American economic and cultural influence continued to spread, many other actors besides the United States entered the picture and often went far beyond the latter in promoting global interconnectedness.

We can see this development, for instance, in the spectacular growth in the number and range of activities of international organizations after the Second World War, which was surely one of the most important developments in the story of globalization. Not only did those organizations bring scores of countries into daily contact with one another, but they also generated a sense of transnational solidarity. They dealt with global as well as local issues, and some of them, such as the World Health Organization, became truly international agencies and affected the lives of millions of people. In addition to such intergovernmental agencies, the number of international nongovernmental organizations increased by leaps and bounds, especially after the 1970s. They, too, connected distant regions of the world through their humanitarian and other activities. Postwar globalization cannot be discussed apart from their activities.[15] Although the United States supported, even initiated, many international organizations, it also stayed aloof from them when it saw them as detrimental to its interests. To the extent that such organizations were agents of globalization, then, they could not be equated with Americanization.

In the meantime, multinational enterprises, which began to make their appearance at the turn of the twentieth century, also grew in number and scope in the second half of the century. Paralleling the phenomenal rise of international nongovernmental organizations during and after the 1970s, multinational businesses, too, rapidly increased in these decades, establishing connections among capital, labor, and markets all over the world. Technology from the United States, capital from Europe and Japan, and labor from Asia and Latin America were often combined to produce goods and services more efficiently, and these were in turn marketed through distributors in the Middle East, Africa, and elsewhere. Some of the multinationals had more wealth than independent countries, and unlike sovereign states, they were "extra-territorial" and thus freer to move across national frontiers. They, too, were promoters of globalization. While U.S.-based enterprises (such as General Motors) were among the richest and most globalized of multinational enterprises, more and more firms of non-U.S. origin came to join them, establishing something akin to a global corporate culture (exemplified by their leaders' annual gatherings at Davos, Switzerland) that was not identical with American culture.

Nongovernmental organizations and multinational enterprises are nonstate actors, and their growing influence suggests an important theme in recent history: the challenge to an international order dominated by sovereign states. At a time when states were becoming more and more powerful, nonstate actors were defining their own world order, even threatening to undermine the state-centered international system. And they were more conducive to globalization than independent states in that states' interference in the process would be checked when nonstate actors promoted their own agendas through interacting with one another. (For this very reason, those upholding the sovereign rights of nations or adhering to the sanctity of the notion of national interest vehemently opposed activities by nonstate actors, especially by international nongovernmental organizations. In their view, globalization, if promoted by such organizations, should not be allowed to impinge upon national rights and interests. Recent attacks on nongovernmental organizations by some in the United States suggest that, in their view, globalization is not only not interchangeable with, but even antithetical to, Americanization.)

The development of regional communities such as the European Union added more complexity to the relationship between globalization and Americanization. Regionalism could have militated against globalization; that was exactly what happened during the 1930s when autarkic blocs threatened to divide the world into exclusionary groupings of states, each under a hegemonic power. After the Second World War, however, regional communities developed as a way of promoting economic integration and political interdependence among neighboring countries without, however, turning them into closed systems. Much of the impetus for such a development came from the United States, and to that extent regionalism, globalization, and Americanization were mutually compatible. At the same time, however, in certain instances—the establishment of the European Court of Justice, for instance—regionalism went far beyond Americanization. Or, it might be better to say that regional communities were pushing visions of Americanization beyond what the American people were willing to undertake.

In the last decades of the century, globalization came to embrace many new phenomena and to face many new challenges. Environmental issues provide a good example. Concern with protecting the natural habitat from encroachment by man has long existed, but it did not become an international agenda until the twentieth century, when some nations began exchanging treaties for the protection of certain categories of migratory birds, fish, seals, and whales that were considered to be in danger of extinction. Because of the two world wars, however, it was not until after 1945 that serious efforts began to be made to develop a comprehensive international strategy for natural conservation. The problem became more urgent because, in addition to the already industrialized nations whose economies grew spectacularly after the war, scores of new states were created, virtually all of which were determined to undertake development as part of their nation-building agendas. The implications of economic development and growth for the ecological system, the term that gained wide currency in the 1960s, were clear, and the problem of how to balance growth and environmental protection became a key concern of nations. Their voices coalesced in the 1972 Stockholm conference on the environment, the first truly international gathering devoted to the issue. From this time on, environmentalism was a global undertaking. Just as economic and technological globalization was establishing connections among all parts of the Earth, there developed a global awareness about the serious consequences of such a development. (The United States was not always among the more aware or supportive of this aspect of globalization, as best illustrated by its refusal to join other countries in entering into an agreement—the so-called Kyoto Protocol of 1997—that would bind them to reduce carbon dioxide emission with a view to curbing global warming.)

As a final example of the scope of globalization broadening beyond what had been perceived in the age of Americanization, we may consider the idea of cultural diversity as well as visions of intercivilizational tolerance and dialogue that entered the vocabulary of international relations in the second half of the twentieth century. Earlier in the century, when globalizing trends were considered virtually synonymous with Americanization, it might have made little sense to discuss issues like the relationship between Western and non-Western civilizations (except in hierarchical terms) or the need for a dialogue among different civilizations. Even Hobhouse, despite his sensitivity to the steadily expanding space for multicultural and multiracial interactions that was far ahead of his time, did not envisage the parallel development of civilizations as the norm. In the age of imperialism and power politics, civilizational discourses were limited to those who were either racial purists (such as Alfred Thayer Mahan and Karl Pearson) or racial fusionists (like some Japanese thinkers).[16]

All this was to change in the second half of the twentieth century. When the United Nations Educational, Scientific and Cultural Organization (UNESCO) declared, "Since wars begin in the minds of men, it is in the minds of men that defenses of peace must be constructed," the organization was envisaging the coming of a new age in which culture, not power, would determine the development of international relations. Because culture shaped "the minds of men [and women]," the world's religions and civilizations would have to be brought together for mutual understanding. The fact that most of the newly independent nations were non-Western meant that they would not accept a Western definition of the world but insist upon civilizational diversity. Globalization, as it developed in the last quarter of the century, steadily began to accommodate forces of diversity so that "the global" and "the local" came to be seen as two sides of the same coin. While technological and commercial globalization proceeded apace, local cultures became more and more assertive. They did not necessarily oppose globalization but insisted that material globalization accommodate local spiritual traditions. The twin theme of globalization and diversity was a subject of fascinating discussion at many international gatherings, such as the conferences on "dialogue among civilizations" that UNESCO sponsored in 2001, 2002, and 2003. It is clear from the discussions at these meetings that dialogue, not confrontation, among civilizations had the support of a large number of countries that sent their delegations. They were promoting the vision of a globalized world in which differences were tolerated and understood, where accommodation and not collision among civilizations would pave the way for a better future.[17] The globalization that is envisaged here may find empathetic echoes in the United States, but it nevertheless would be a far cry from the culturally more monolithic idea of Americanization.

In tracing the growing disparity between globalization and Americanization, it would perhaps be superfluous to refer to such negative aspects of global interconnectedness as the spread of communicable diseases or transnational terrorism that have obviously little to do with Americanization. The increasing ease with which people establish contact with one another—through air travel, telephone and facsimile exchanges, electronic communication—has facilitated the dissemination of diseases and also of terrorism and weapons of mass destruction. It may be said that terrorism first became a global, not just a local, phenomenon in the 1970s. In the very same year that witnessed the convening of the Stockholm conference on the environment, 1972—that was also the year of the Strategic Arms Limitation Treaty, marking the beginning of the long road toward the ending of the Cold War—a group of Palestinian terrorists attacked Israeli athletes participating in the Munich Olympics, and the incident instantly became worldwide news. In order to express their grievances over a local issue, the terrorists went on an international forum and made their appeal through a worldwide network of mass media. The Munich attack, as well as many subsequent incidents of terrorism, were global undertakings, financed from various sources across nations and perpetrated by members of international organizations. Likewise, such diseases as AIDS and SARS became global phenomena, both in that they quickly spread to many parts of the world and in that they became a matter of concern to people everywhere.

The point of mentioning all these facets of globalization is to remind us that they cannot be all equated with Americanization. Some, such as terrorism and disease, are obviously examples of global but not American developments. Others, such as environmentalism, have been pursued often more vigorously outside, rather than by, the United States. Still other developments, such as international organizations and regional communities, more often than not began through American initiatives but have since become much less identifiable with, and even considered antithetical to the interests of, the United States.

This last is an interesting phenomenon. Frequently, the United States has taken the lead in institutional globalization, be it a world organization such as the League of Nations or a regional community like the European Union. Just as frequently, the Americans have turned away from, even against, it. Political internationalism as espoused by Woodrow Wilson was a typically American idea. He wanted to bring all countries of the world together so as to safeguard the peace. He wanted such principles as the open door and arms control to be vital aspects of the new international organization. His own people rejected them, so the world order that might have been Americanized was notable by American absence. The United States tried again, under Franklin D. Roosevelt, and for most of the second half of the twentieth century, the nation supported the United Nations, often acting on its behalf to maintain the peace. If the global institution was not interchangeable with the United States, its many committees and affiliates, such as the Security Council and the International Monetary Fund, reflected American influence and embodied American values. At the same time, however, during the long Cold War and also in the post–Cold War era, the United States was willing to ignore the world organization or to consider it primarily as a means for promoting its own interests. Globalization and Americanization diverged when, at the beginning of the twenty-first century, some American officials and politicians even came to view the United Nations and other international mechanisms as anti-American. The nation had taken the lead in promoting nuclear arms control, environmentalism, and human rights, but it began to distance itself from international agreements that would bind all countries, such as the Mine Ban Treaty, the Kyoto Protocol, and the International Criminal Court. Whether or not these instances mark U.S. unilateralism or something else, it would be difficult to deny that, at this level, globalization has little to do with Americanization.

Thus far we have considered aspects of the global transformation that cannot be equated with Americanization. There is another way in which globalization and Americanization may be compared: to consider the transformation of American society and people in the age of globalization. Even as the nation spread its goods, ideas, and influence abroad, it also steadily transformed itself, in a sense becoming more and more globalized. Actually, even at the turn of the century, when Stead wrote about the Americanization of the world, the nation was not free from foreign influences. Stead's Englishmen and -women may have begun to become thoroughly Americanized, but their American counterparts were not entirely self-sufficient. They were even then consuming cultural products imported from abroad. As Kristin Hoganson has pointed out, the bourgeois American home after the Civil War had become more and more cosmopolitan, making use of furnishings and decorations that came from Europe, Asia, and elsewhere.[18] In one area, classical music, America was being Europeanized rather than the other way around. Stead noted, for instance, that while he was in Chicago "[few] things struck me more . . . than the attention which was paid to music, and the popularity of high-class music. Some people say that the Americans owe this to the large infusion of Germans."[19] This last point is corroborated by the recently completed study of German influence on the American musical scene by Jessica Gienow-Hecht.[20] As for American values and ideals, Daniel Rodgers's *Atlantic Crossings* amply documents the two-way exchange of ideas across the Atlantic.[21] He shows that American social and political reformers at the turn of the century were eager to visit European cities and attend European conferences to obtain new insights into such issues as urban planning, welfare policy, and labor relations.

Since then, the infusion of foreign goods and ideas into the United States has not stopped. In part this is because of the coming of huge numbers of people, whether as permanent immigrants or temporary sojourners (businessmen, students, tourists). In part, too, foreign influences have been brought back by Americans traveling abroad. More recently, the process of globalization has resulted in the influx of imports that are at competitive advantages over domestic products. Most of the daily necessities that Stead mentions as having been produced in the United States would today seem to be made abroad. As for values and ideals, Warren Cohen notes in his *The Asian American Century*, there will soon be as many Buddhists in the United States as Jews.[22] The fact that together Buddhists and Jews constitute 5 percent of the nation's population is a sign of its globalization. They, and hundreds of other religious and ethnic groups, have significantly added to, and altered, what Americans eat, wear, and even think about.

Thinking about oneself and about the world may be the most fascinating aspect of the question regarding globalization and Americanization. Do Americans today think more globally than, let us say, a hundred years ago?

Fifty years ago? Writing in 1867, Henry James noted, "it seems to me that we are ahead of the European races in the fact that more than either of them we can deal freely with forms of civilization not our own, can pick and choose and assimilate and in short . . . claim our property wherever we find it."[23] He was not necessarily being cosmopolitan; he was celebrating the contributions made by the nation's immigrants to its culture. Still, he was making an interesting point about American attitudes toward "civilizations not our own." They would seem to have fluctuated between tolerance and rejection, but to the extent that a sense of interrelatedness with the rest of the world has been a persistent strain of American society, it may be said to owe a great deal to education. In 1912, a Hungarian-born novelist, Arthur Holitscher, published an account of the United States after he spent several months touring the country. Among the things that struck him most was the educational system. The American school, he noted, "is not an institution in which the children will be stuffed full with all manner of erudition, nor on which they will need . . . to become adults. It is an instrument with whose help the children of America . . . will be made into world citizens."[24] Without a close examination of what was being taught at schools at that time, and especially without comparing the textbooks that were widely used, it would be impossible to determine whether Holitscher was justified in hinting that in the United States young people were being taught to think globally.

We have better evidence from today's textbooks and school curricula to gauge the extent to which the American schools prepare their students mentally and psychologically for a globalizing world. The picture is rather mixed. On one hand, there is much support nationwide for history education. In 1988 the Bradley Commission on History in the Schools, headed by Senator Bill Bradley, published a report emphasizing that history "belongs in the school programs of all students . . . because it provides the only avenue we have to reach an understanding of ourselves and of our society." In the same spirit, the Senate passed a law in 2000 to establish a "Teaching American History Grant Program," making funds available for projects and conferences that brought together history teachers and professional scholars so as to promote a close working partnership between them. The National Council for History Education (NCHE), established in 1990, has been at the forefront of private organizations to promote the same objective.[25] At the same time, however, much of these efforts has focused on the teaching of U.S. history, with the result that the teaching of world history has tended to lag behind. That is unfortunate. As a statement by the NCHE notes, "An education in history prepares youngsters to understand not only their own society but other societies and civilizations around the world." The fact that the NCHE has attracted a membership of over 5,000 who share such a perspective is encouraging, but, on the other hand, it has thus far been able to persuade only thirty-three states to establish state councils on history education, suggesting that there is a long way to go.

The idea has always been around that, in order to better understand oneself and one's society, it is imperative to know something about other times and other places, but it seems to have been asserted with greater intensity than ever before toward the end of the twentieth century as forces of globalization made the overcoming of intellectual parochialism an urgent imperative. For instance, in the 1984 edition of a widely used textbook, *Modern History* by Carl Becker and Kenneth Cooper, the authors explicitly state, "All history is our history in one sense . . . because we are all human and have much the same desires, passions, hopes, and aspirations. Human nature, which makes history what it is, is much the same whatever the period of history you may be studying."[26] Although the term "globalization" was not in general use when this textbook was published, the authors wrote about "global interdependence" when discussing the post-1945 world. Ten years later, *National Standards for History* was completed. This was a joint production of academic historians and school teachers intended to provide the minimum "standards" for the study of history in the schools. The book stressed the importance of studying history in order to see "one's connectedness with all of humankind." In justifying the teaching of world history at the elementary and secondary levels, the authors stated, "an understanding of the history of the world's many cultures can contribute to fostering the kind of mutual patience, respect, and civil discourse required in our increasingly pluralistic society and our increasingly interdependent world."[27] A history teacher in Philadelphia agrees and says that it is "vital to gain historical perspective on a variety of civilizations outside our own country, including not only Europe, but also Asia, Africa, and Latin America. Knowing the history of basic world processes—from disease transmission through trade and migration to cultural contacts—becomes essential."[28] Despite such awareness of the need to teach students not just the history of the United States but of other societies and civilizations, the majority of the nation's schools seem to be inadequately prepared to do so.

On the other hand, for those teachers and pupils willing to study world history, excellent textbooks have been published. When, during the academic year 2001/2002, a new "advance placement" (AP) world history program was introduced to some schools, *Teacher's Guide: AP World History* was published, listing a number of recommended textbooks. It may be assumed that these books are read by the nation's top students who are interested in history. In one of the books on the list, *The Earth and Its Peoples*, the authors (Richard Bulliet, Pamela Crossley, and others) are quite self-conscious about their determination "to write the best global history we could." They do so by stressing "the common challenges and experiences that unite the human past." While recognizing civilizational diversity, they want the student to gain an appreciation of how different cultures and people have become interconnected. The past, in their words, follows "a particular trajectory: from sparse and disconnected communities reacting creatively to their individual circumstances through ever more intensive stages of contact, interpenetration, and cultural expansion and amalgamation; to a twenty-first century world situation in which people increasingly visualize a single global community." Terms like "interpenetration," "amalgamation," and "global community" suggest the authors' sensitivity to contemporary trends, scholarly and nonscholarly, that seek to understand both individual and national experiences as aspects of globalization. The book's final section is titled "The Perils and Promises of a Global Community, 1945 to the Present." Here the discussion of the emergence of "an almost universal culture" is coupled with a statement about "new assertions of difference in religious movements, struggles for ethnic autonomy, and distinctive adaptations of modern industrial life to local values and traditions."[29] That would seem to be a plausible framework in which to understand the seemingly conflicting forces that shape the world today.

There is still a long way to go before the majority of school students are taught to gain a sense of global diversity and interconnectedness, but to the extent that strenuous efforts are being made in that direction, Holitscher's optimistic vision may be said to be still applicable today. Only if school education can nurture a sensitivity to the rest of the world, the widening gap between Americanization and globalization will be made narrower.

To sum up, globalization and Americanization were virtually interchangeable propositions at the beginning of the twentieth century. Both American goods and American ideals were spreading to all parts of the world, establishing connections and paving the way for the emergence of a single global community. During the course of the century, Americanization and globalization came to diverge, both because the United States became a receptacle of foreign goods and ideas and because globalization came to include many features that were not all generated, or even welcomed, by Americans. As the process of globalization became more and more global, America tended to grow more and more local. That, however, was an unfortunate development, if only because the sense of distance between the globe and the United States would make it difficult to undertake collective endeavors through cooperation.

We have seen such an unfortunate development during and in the aftermath of the Iraq War, when the rest of the world has appeared to be overwhelmingly opposed to, or at least skeptical of, the U.S. military action. But the problem lies deeper than disagreements in the geostrategic realm. Numerous foreign observers have expressed their dismay that American society and people appear to be less concerned with the nation's image in the world, indeed less solicitous of other countries' views, than at any time in the last half-century. This is not the America that Americanizes and therefore globalizes. It is an America that withdraws to itself, disconnects itself from the globe. Foreigners still cling to the idea of an America that they can admire, and the fact that they continue to want to emigrate to the United States indicates that most of them retain Ojike's faith in what the nation stands for. Nevertheless, the psychological distance between the American people and others seems to have grown since September 2001. At first, they appeared to be united in loathing terrorism and religious fundamentalism, but somehow that unity seems to have disintegrated. Globalization continues apace, but it is almost as if the United States is no longer identified with it, mentally or emotionally. In the context of our discussion, this amounts to globalization without Americanization.

Globalization and Americanization must be brought back together. Neither globalization without an American input nor Americanization through U.S. unilateralism is a satisfactory solution to the many ills confronting the world today. One hopes that somehow the American people would re-establish their connection to the rest of the world, in particular to the needs and interests of other people, while the rest of the world would reaffirm its faith in what used to be called the American dream but should now be seen as universal visions of freedom and justice.

4 Expansion and Integration: Reflections on the History of America's Approach to Globalization

David Reynolds

THIS CHAPTER EXAMINES some of the ways in which the internal development of the United States influenced the country's approach to globalization. Its focus is on the period before 1945, particularly the nineteenth century. Within this framework, I develop two main arguments. First, the United States was itself a product of an earlier phase of globalization emanating from Europe. Second—and this is my main theme—the way in which the United States engaged in and often shaped the process of modern globalization was rooted in distinctive features of its history.

The United States as a Product of Globalization

In recent decades, the contributions made by Native Americans to the history and culture of the United States have been recovered and celebrated. Nevertheless, most of the country's salient characteristics stem from the European-led era of globalization that spanned the seventeenth, eighteenth, and nineteenth centuries—a complex web of investment and trade, mass migrations and cultural exchange—embracing Europe, Africa, Asia, and the Americas. It is essential to think about the development of the United States within this historical context.

Although there were many trading ventures in the seventeenth century, from an early stage the European presence in North America took the form of colonies of settlement, not clientage. In India, as in much of their accidental empire, the British did not establish direct control but ruled largely via imposed or negotiated alliances with local rulers.[1] In sparsely populated America, however, the native inhabitants were driven west as European settlement spread down the eastern seaboard and into the interior. Local legislatures were established on a broad electoral franchise by men who regarded themselves initially as transplanted Englishmen and then developed their own national identity in opposition to that of the mother country. In this respect, the development of British America was similar to that of later British settler colonies with persecuted indigenous minorities, such as those that became Australia and New Zealand. Yet there was also a major difference. The Americans won total independence from the mother country at a very early date. The Treaty of Paris in 1783 severed all political links with London, whereas the Australian colonies did not become a separate country until 1901. Both Australia and New Zealand relied on Britain for their own defense until World War II; even today they retain the British monarch as head of state.

Political independence did not, however, mean economic independence. In the mid-nineteenth century, Great Britain briefly acted as something like a sole superpower. It produced 40 percent of the world's manufactured goods and imported over a third of the world's trade. Sterling was as good as gold, and the City of London acted as the main fount of international investment. The infant United States remained almost a colony of Britain in economic terms. It had little industry of its own, relying heavily on British-manufactured goods purchased against the sale of primary products, particularly raw cotton. Between 1820 and 1860, nearly half of America's exports went to Britain, which in turn generated 40 percent of American imports. Of the foreign tonnage entering American ports in 1860, 80 percent was British.[2] Transatlantic trade was largely funded by the great London banking houses, such as Barings, which also supplied much of the capital for America's own "internal improvements"—the roads, bridges, canals, and especially the railroads that gradually opened up the West. The Louisiana Purchase of 1803 is widely remembered as one of the moments that made modern America—giving it the potential to stand on its own as a power—and the $11.25 million price tag is rightly seen as an incredible bargain. At the time, however, even that sum was far beyond the means of the new republic, and most of the money was raised by loans from British banks.

Yet the globalization that shaped the United States went far beyond an Anglo American axis. The American colonies were also the product of that central dynamic of the Atlantic economy—the slave trade. The import of African slaves into the United States was officially banned in 1808, but it continued illegally. During the first half of the nineteenth century, the fertility of black slaves, the profitable internal slave trade, and above all the booming world demand for cotton all ensured that slavery continued to prosper in the South long after it had been abolished north of the Mason-Dixon Line. The South's "peculiar institution" became the symbolic focus for rival concepts of national identity and split the Union from 1861 to 1865. Even after secession was defeated and the slaves emancipated, African Americans remained second-class citizens under the network of Jim Crow laws and customs in the South and more insidious forms of residential and economic discrimination elsewhere. Right to the present day, they have proved much less easily integrated into the mainstream of American life than other ethnic groups. In no other "settler colony" has a minority group exerted so powerful and problematic an impact on national history and culture.

In further contrast with Australia and New Zealand, America's voluntary immigrants were far more pluralist. For most of Australian history, immigrants came overwhelmingly from Britain. It was only after World War II that this began to change—less than 40 percent of the two million immigrants arriving between 1947 and 1969 were British; most were from other parts of Europe.[3] From the 1970s, the government abandoned the "White Australia" policy and pioneered the new concept of multiculturalism as it opened the country to people from Asia and the South Pacific. In North America, however, the European presence was remarkably diverse from the earliest stage. France and Spain vied with each other and Britain, leaving their mark on the Mississippi Valley, California, and the Gulf of Mexico in particular. Other national groups, particularly the Irish and Germans, also shaped the colonies long before independence. Even more important was the nineteenth-century Atlantic economy, which opened up America to mass migration via sailboat and steamship—some 25 million people between 1860 and 1914. This, coupled with the high American birth rate, enabled the country to more than triple its population from 31 million to 100 million. These later immigrants came much more from southern and Eastern Europe; whereas English immigrants constituted 12.3 percent of foreigners arriving in the decade of 1881–90, they made up only 4.4 percent in 1901–10.[4] What happened in Australia after World War II therefore occurred in the United States far earlier and on a far larger scale. For most of its history, Australia was too remote geographically and too inhospitable physically. It was deeply influenced by European globalization, whereas the United States was totally transformed.

The Challenges of Expansion and Unification

Although a product of European globalization, the United States went on to generate its own globalizing dynamic. This was rooted in developments of the nineteenth century. When James Madison defended "the experiment of an extended republic" in the fourteenth *Federalist* in 1787, he envisaged a nation that would extend from the Atlantic to the Mississippi. That was roughly 750 miles, less than the 973 miles north-south from the thirty-first parallel to the forty-fifth on which the Treaty of Paris was based. Madison's imagined nation was smaller in area than the loose European confederations of Germany or Poland. His criterion for "the natural limit of a republic" was "that distance from the center, which will barely allow the representatives of the people to meet as often as may be necessary for the administration of public affairs."[5] Most Americans of Madison's generation believed the Rocky Mountains would constitute a "natural" limit; any further expansion beyond them would produce a separate country. "Along the back of this ridge," insisted Senator Thomas Hart Benton of Missouri in 1825, "a Western limit of the republic should be drawn, and the statue of the fabled god, Terminus, should be raised upon its highest peak, never to be thrown down."[6]

By the 1840s, of course, the story was very different. The dramatic acquisition of Texas, Oregon, and California between 1845 and 1848 increased the national domain by 1.2 million square miles—far more than the 800,000 acquired in the Louisiana Purchase—and brought the country's borders to the Pacific.[7] In 1845, the journalist John L. O'Sullivan famously claimed that the United States had a

> manifest destiny to overspread and to possess the whole of the continent which Providence has given us for the development of the great experiment of liberty and federative self-government entrusted to us. It is a right such as that of the tree to the space of air and earth suitable for the full expansion of its principle and destiny of growth—such as that of the stream to the channel required for the still accumulating volume of its flow.[8]

The first sentence is familiar; the second less so but more revealing. O'Sullivan was redefining the doctrine of natural limits to imply that the boundaries of American expansion would be set only according to its capacity to expand.

In part, the spur to westward expansion was the traditional policy of preemption—staking out claims to prevent European empire building, in this case the dispute with Britain about a northern border from Maine to Oregon. The drive west was also a continuation of earlier settler-led, military-backed expansion against weaker continental neighbors, be they native Indian nations or the infant country of Mexico—like the United States a recent product of European decolonization. In addition, new technologies had also expanded geographical horizons since the era of Madison and Benton. Railroad and steamship, telegraph and telephone were the prime agents of globalization in the mid-nineteenth century, and they were also the technologies powering the great waves of transatlantic migration that peopled the modern United States. Within America, they made manifest destiny into practical politics, as O'Sullivan himself noted. "The magnetic telegraph will enable the editors of the *San Francisco Union*, the *Astoria Evening Post*, or the *Nootka Morning News*, to set up in type the first half of the President's Inaugural before the echoes of the latter half shall have died away beneath the lofty porch of the Capitol, as spoken from his lips."[9] The railroad and the telegraph abolished the old sense of geographical limits and made it possible to create a country of more than three million square miles, spreading "from sea to shining sea" in a way that Madison's generation had not seriously imagined.

But could such a sprawling country hold together? European observers around mid-century were very doubtful. The size of the United States, its sectional rivalries, and the weakness of its central government all seemed inimical to unity. Georg Wilhelm Friedrich Hegel, the great German philosopher, spoke of "the North American Federation" as lacking a "real State" and a "real Government."[10] When the South seceded in 1861, many across the Atlantic viewed this as another war of national independence, akin to Italy's recent breakaway from the Austrian Empire. Lincoln's insistence that it was a fight to preserve the Union rather than a campaign to free the slaves strengthened such perceptions. In Britain, William Ewart Gladstone, no friend of slavery, spoke for many of his countrymen in October 1862, after the South's success at Antietam, when he claimed that the leaders of the Confederate States of America had not only made an army and a navy but "what is more than either, they have made a nation." Gladstone welcomed this on the grounds that "it is for the general interests of Nations that no State should swell to the dimensions of a Continent."[11]

In retrospect, the survival of the Union is usually considered by Americans as vindication of Manifest Destiny; those who argued against it—be they Confederates, Copperheads, or British liberals—seem to have been fighting the tide of history. As the war dragged on and the body count mounted, however, there were many in the North who wondered whether a compromise for peace might be better. At times, they included Lincoln himself. In January 1862, with an ineffectual army and near bankrupt government, he had to contemplate "the bare possibility of our being two nations." In August 1864, before the fall of Atlanta, he acknowledged as "exceedingly probable" his defeat in the November election and with it the end of the Union.[12] Lincoln won the election and the war, but the eventual death toll of 620,000—far more than America's dead in both world wars of the twentieth century combined—was a massive price to pay for the survival of the Union. Yet survive it did. The new sense of unity can be glimpsed in Lincoln's growing use of "the nation" rather than "the Union" in war speeches. It can also be seen in what has been called "the transition of the United States to a singular noun"—the United States "is" rather than the United States "are."[13]

Until 1865, the historical development of the United States fit loosely within the general pattern of the Americas during the nineteenth century. Between 1770 and 1820, the whole continent, with the exception of Canada, had broken away from formal European empires. But what followed was an extended postimperial crisis, with independent nations warring over territory and resources. Thus, the American Civil War coincided with the brutal War of the Triple Alliance (Brazil, Argentina, and Uruguay) against Paraguay from 1864 to 1870, during which 310,000 died in combat alone. Extended campaigns were waged against indigenous peoples—the American clearance of the Great Plains Indians was paralleled, for instance, by the Argentinean conquest of Patagonia in the 1870s. These new states were also seeking to establish their economic independence from Europe, on whose Atlantic system they were still dependent. In all these respects, the story of the United States, though spectacular, was not unique. But 1865 marked a watershed. The victory of the Union was also a victory for the system of free farming that had spread across the West and the emerging mercantilist industrialism of the Northeast, whose alliance underpinned the new Republican party. This combination of dynamic agriculture and protected industry was the launching pad for northern development in the last third of the nineteenth century. As Michael Geyer and Charles Bright have argued, this "Northern industrial enclave [was] breaking clear from the hemispheric zone of slave- and plantation-based agricultural and cash-crop production, with its narrow power bases and hierarchical social configurations, in order to forge a more egalitarian and self-consciously national strategy of industrial development in North America." In 1861, the South tried to secede from the Union; in 1865, the United States successfully seceded from the Western Hemisphere's pattern of development and set out on its own path to global power.[14]

Diversity had been embraced, however, not eradicated; ethnicity, race, and sectionalism were still facts of American life. The federal political system—

accepted by most of the Founding Fathers as a compromise between states' rights and the need for a "more perfect union"—remained essential in the postwar era. Despite periodic spasms of centralization during the Civil War, briefly in World War I, and emphatically during the New Deal and World War II, the United States continued to lack what Hegel called a "real State." On the other hand, and perhaps in direct compensation, it developed and sustained an intense sense of nation. If nations are "imagined communities," in the famous phrase of Benedict Anderson, then America is truly a prodigy of imagination. It lacks a shared ethnicity, a compact territory, and a dominant religion—features that are usually the crucibles of national consciousness. "Only in a country where it is so unclear what is American do people worry so much about the threats of things 'un-American,'" historian Michael Kammen has written.[15]

Most nations define themselves in antithesis to "the Other." Eighteenth-century Britishness, for example, was constructed around Francophobia and anti-Catholicism.[16] But self-definition by antithesis has been especially evident in the hyperpluralist United States. For colonial Americans, what mattered was that they were not Indians or blacks (unlike other Europeans in the Americas, British Americans had strict laws against miscegenation). After 1776, independent Americans defined themselves essentially as not British— inhabitants of a new world in opposition to the old with its alien values of monarchy, aristocracy, and empire. Republicans in the 1850s declared themselves "free men" rather than subjects of "the Slave Power," and for much of the nineteenth century antipopery, with its litmus tests of temperance and Sabbatarianism, defined the ethno-cultural battleground of northern politics. In short, antithesis to the Other lies at the heart of American nationalism.[17] Like the size of the country and its essential unity, bipolar Americanism has also influenced the way in which America has engaged with globalization.

Integrating a Continent

During the nineteenth century, Russia, like the United States, was also expanding across its continent. In 1835, Alexis de Tocqueville famously predicted that each of these "two great nations" seemed "called by some secret design of Providence one day to hold in its hands the destinies of half the world." At this stage, before the Mexican War and the struggle for secession, Tocqueville called the inhabitants of the United States "the Anglo-Americans," vying for continental supremacy with the Spanish and the English. Like other European commentators, he doubted that "the accident" of the Union would survive in its existing form.[18] After the Confederacy had been defeated, however, the formidable potential of the United States became evident to most European observers. Michel Chevalier, a French political economist, spoke in 1866 of the "political colossus that has been created on the other side of the Atlantic." He warned of future rivalry, even war, and predicted disaster for the countries of Europe unless they forged a comparable unity.[19]

Nothing of the sort occurred, of course. The first half of the twentieth century saw two suicidal European civil wars; the second half witnessed at best halting progress to European integration and then only in the western part of a divided continent. Further east, the Soviet Union kept Russian imperialism going under Bolshevik leadership after 1917. But the Soviet system was a military–industrial complex based on the repression of civilian freedoms, and its forced integration of Eastern Europe and Central Asia fell apart in 1989–91. Of the three great continental powers existing or imagined in the late nineteenth century—the United States, Russia, and Europe—only the United States has prospered as an integrated economic system.

The precondition for this may be found in article 1, section 8, of the United States Constitution, which forbids any taxes, duties, or preferential tariffs on trade between the states. This constituted a legal framework for the internal market. But the real spur came from the transportation revolutions of the nineteenth century. The opening of the Erie Canal in 1825 reduced the cost of transport between Buffalo and New York City by 85 percent and cut the journey time from twenty-one days to eight. Railroads were even more important. Total mileage rose from 9,000 in 1850 to 53,000 in 1870, 117,000 by 1890, and an astounding 250,000 in 1910. By 1886, all operated to a common gauge—in marked contrast to railroads in Central Europe—and the mergers of the 1880s and 1890s created a continent-wide system of cartels. The railroad, it has been argued, "was in many ways to the United States what the 1992 Single Market program was to the European Union."[20]

At the same time, communications were revolutionized by the telegraph. This, and its successor the telephone, were also run by private corporations, unlike the rest of the world where push-to-talk (PTT) services were operated by government monopolies until the 1980s. Together, the railroad and the telegraph created the transportation and communication networks essential for an integrated market. During the twentieth century, the technologies changed again: air travel supplanted railroads as they had replaced the canals, while telephone, fax, e-mail, and the Internet took over the work of the telegraph. But the effects pointed in the same direction—toward the perfecting of a continent-wide internal market that was unique in the world.

Consider again the potential rivals. Europe developed all the same technologies, usually a little later than the United States, but it was a fractured and fractious continent for most of the twentieth century. Although in 1913 the United States accounted for one-third of the world output of coal and iron, production in Europe as a whole was 30 to 50 percent higher. But this was spread out across a dozen countries, many of them at odds over exactly these natural resources, such as France and Germany over the areas of Alsace and Lorraine. In the United States, by contrast, as one resource region became exhausted, exploitation could move elsewhere within the nation—with copper extraction, for instance, shifting from Michigan to larger and richer reserves in the Rocky Mountains and Southwest between 1890 and 1930. As economic historian Gavin Wright has observed, "A hypothetical United States of Europe would have rivaled America."[21] But European unity remained a dream, and it was not until 1968 that the founding six of the European Economic Community abolished internal tariffs. Full freedom of movement for goods, labor, and capital came only in 1992, and a common currency a decade later.

Russia controlled a continent even larger than the United States, but it was an undeveloped country whose transport networks were primitive by American standards. In 1913, the whole Russian empire boasted only 44,000 miles of railroad track, in various gauges. Moreover, in the autocratic societies of the Tsarist and Soviet era, all communications were rigorously controlled. In 1985, there were some 31 million telephones connected to the Soviet phone network, one-sixth of the U.S. figure even though America had about fourth-fifths of the Soviet population. That same year, the USSR originated 1.8 million international calls, compared with 410 million from the United States.[22]

From America's vast, integrated, and fairly homogeneous market, there emerged appropriate managerial structures. As Alfred D. Chandler Jr. has shown, railroad companies were the precursors of the modern American firm, run by professional managers on sophisticated statistical and accounting practices. They also stimulated the growth of large-scale investment banking and big construction companies. Managerial capitalism was pioneered in the United States; elsewhere, the norm remained family firms of varying size. The size and relative homogeneity of the mass market also encouraged techniques of mass distribution, such as chain stores and mail-order houses, and of methods of mass production that became world famous, such as Fordism. Even more important was the integration of all phases of production and distribution in a single form, as demonstrated by James Buchanan Duke in cigarettes or H. J. Heinz in processed food. Economies of scale and speed performed by integrated managerial corporations were America's unique contribution to the development of international capitalism.[23]

Accustomed to exploiting a vast internal market, the United States was thus well placed to exploit the foreign opportunities that opened up in the early twentieth century. The movie business provides a good example. On the eve of World War I, the U.S. film industry was just emerging from what one might call the early railroad stage, with a dozen well-established producers and scores of small operators. At this date, the majority of movies were produced in France: the Pathé Frères company alone released more films than the major American companies combined. In 1914, however, Paramount Pictures became the first nationwide distributor. From that platform, it developed as a producer and exhibitor as well, integrating studios and cinemas into its business empire. Fox, Loews, and a few others followed suit. By the late 1920s, "the Big Five" formed a mature oligopoly that not only dominated the American market but also supplied at least 80 percent of the motion pictures exhibited abroad. During the Depression and World War II, European and Asian markets collapsed, but the American giants turned to Latin America. After 1945, European governments imposed restrictions on American films, either for cultural reasons or to protect scarce foreign exchange. To get around these barriers, the American companies moved production abroad. Whereas in 1939 about one-third of the revenue of U.S. film companies came from abroad, the proportion was over half by the 1960s. Like the railroads in the nineteenth century, the movie industry in the twentieth had an impact far beyond its immediate economic domain. "What the people of the world see their screen heroes wear, and eat, and use, they want for themselves," claimed a 1927 prospectus for investors in the film industry. Instead of the old cliché "trade follows the flag," it now seemed that "trade follows the film." In interwar Britain and later in postwar France, Hollywood was widely feared as an instrument of cultural Americanization.[24]

The rise to globalism of the American movie industry is a tribute in part to the business practices described by Chandler. But it must also be understood against the patterns of European globalization emphasized earlier. World War I was an economic watershed. Not only did Europe's business and trade collapse, never fully to recover, its demand for wartime supplies and finance helped turn the American economy outward. The war allowed American business to increase its penetration of Asia and Latin America. Allied demand for war loans turned the United States from a net-debtor into a net-creditor nation and also fostered new interest and expertise in foreign investment in houses such as J. P. Morgan and National City Bank. By 1931, America had displaced Britain as the world's largest foreign investor.[25] Thus, the contraction of Europe as a consequence of war facilitated America's expansion. At the same time, the United States often moved along grooves already carved by the early phase of British-led European globalization. Again, the movie industry is a prime example. America's displacement of France in the decade or so after 1914 was the result not merely of business practices but also of the dramatic mid-1920s eclipse of the silent films. Once movies became "talkies," they were no longer universal. Language mattered, and the language of America was the one that Britain had already made into an international lingua franca. French talkies still had a big global market, but it was circumscribed by the bounds of Francophonia, whereas U.S. filmmakers built on earlier British cultural penetration of Asia, Africa, and Latin America. "The film is to America what the flag was once to Britain," asserted one British newspaper in 1923. "By its means Uncle Sam may hope someday, if he be not checked in time, to Americanize the world."[26]

War-making and "Self-Defensive Expansionism"

Despite the dogmas of free enterprise capitalism, the expansion of American business cannot be understood without reference to the visible hand of Uncle Sam. Again, this has historical roots. Take the case of westward expansion, which Thomas Jefferson foresaw as creating a great "empire of liberty." Popularly, the opening and settlement of the West is celebrated as a saga of rugged individualism—Lewis and Clark, Daniel Boone, the Mormons, the Forty-Niners, and the cowboys. Yet the role of the federal government was of decisive importance. The long battle over public land policy culminated in the Preemption Act of 1841 and the Homestead Act of 1862, under which Washington subsidized the settlement of the West. Its cultivation was also bankrolled by Uncle Sam. Without the massive dam projects on the Columbia and Colorado Rivers in the 1930s, the postwar demographic and economic growth of California and the Pacific Northwest would have been impossible. Federal defense spending in World War II and the Cold War sustained the economies of southern California, the Bay Area, and Puget Sound. The "Atomic West" brought jobs and prosperity to interior communities from Albuquerque, New Mexico, to Hanford, Washington. Even today, nearly half the area of the eleven westernmost states is owned by the federal government—86 percent in the case of Nevada.[27] Large areas are national parks; even larger areas are retained for weapons testing.

The role of the military in the West opens up a larger theme. For much of U.S. history, national ideology celebrated emancipation from the war-driven imperialism of Europe. The polarity of the old world and the new was ingrained in the national self-image. "I would not give the polite, self-denying, feeling, hospitable, goodhumoured people of this country and their amiability in every point of view," wrote Thomas Jefferson from Virginia to Abigail Adams in London in 1785, "for ten such races of rich, proud, hectoring, swearing, squibbling, carnivorous animals as those among whom you are."[28] Yet as the twentieth century passes into history, so the myth of American innocence seems harder to sustain. This was indeed a country made by war. "Since 1775 no nation on earth has had as much experience of war as the United States: nine major wars in nine generations," insisted Geoffrey Perret after Vietnam. "America's wars have been like the rungs on a ladder by which it rose to greatness."[29] The West was won by war, notably against the Mexicans and the Indian nations; the South was coerced back into the Union by a war of attrition that devastated much of Virginia and Georgia. The Mexican and Indian wars were relatively low-tech affairs, but they established the principle of superior firepower on which Grant's bloody victories of 1864–65 were won. In the twentieth century, America harnessed industrialism to war-making with spectacular effect. It is the only country to have used nuclear weapons in warfare, causing an estimated 127,000 deaths in August 1945. In addition, U.S. conventional bombing killed more than 900,000 Japanese civilians in the last five months of the Pacific War. Perhaps one million North Koreans died as a result of American action in 1950–53, and about a third of a million Vietnamese during the Vietnam War, during which the United States dropped almost three times the bomb tonnage it used in the whole of World War II.[30] All these conflicts can and have been defended as just wars, of course, but this does not undercut the factual point. Measured by deaths and damage caused, the United States has been historically the most potent user of weapons of mass destruction.

At the heart of American war-making has been an expansive doctrine of security. George Washington's dictum that "offensive operations often times is the surest, if not the only (in some cases) means of defence" became a refrain of American history. Washington was speaking in 1799 of the Louisiana problem, but the same idea underpins the Monroe Doctrine of 1823 and its successive embellishments. Note that Monroe did not merely stigmatize European colonialism but insisted that "we should consider any attempt on their part to extend their system to any portion of this hemisphere as dangerous to our peace and safety." The word "system" connoted political values and trading networks, not just European territorial expansion. As Senator Lewis Cass said in 1853, "We do not intend . . . to have this hemisphere ruled by maxims suited neither to its position nor to its interests." In the hands of Teddy Roosevelt and Woodrow Wilson, this sweeping definition of security prompted intervention in Central America; it also justified the annexation of Cuba and a growing interest in the Caribbean islands under Danish and British control. All were phases of this history of "self-defensive expansionism," in the words of historian Albert K. Weinberg.[31]

When Weinberg published his classic study of Manifest Destiny in 1935, he concluded that "American history since McKinley's time has been characterized by a rather steady decline of the expansionist temper." The imperialist flurry of the Spanish-American War seemed an aberration; the Philippines, its main legacy, were now being prepared for self-government. So Weinberg spoke of "the virtual disappearance" of this "long dominant force of American life."[32] Within less than a decade, however, the policy of preemptive expansionism was resumed. In 1940–41, Franklin Roosevelt insisted that America's "front line" was now in Europe; he argued that the new air age rendered concepts of hemisphere defense based on classic sea power totally out of date. To help arouse his countrymen, he talked about the United States being in a "world war" long before Pearl Harbor—as early as March 1941, in fact. And in a fireside chat in February 1942, Roosevelt attacked the "isolationists" who, he said, "wanted the American eagle to imitate the tactics of an ostrich by burying its head in the sand to avoid danger." No, said the president, "we prefer to retain the eagle as it is—flying high and striking hard."[33] But to do that in an air-age world war required safe perches around the globe. As early as 1943, the joint chiefs of staff began drawing up plans for a grid of air bases from the Philippines to the Azores to extend America's defense perimeter across most of the Pacific and the Atlantic.[34]

The newly fashionable concept of "national security" was entrenched by the Cold War. This justified prolonged military occupations of Germany and

Japan, an unprecedented peacetime military commitment to Western Europe, and a network of bases that girdled the globe. NSC 68, that classic if by no means uncontested clarion call by hawks in April 1950, treated the Cold War as a zero-sum game. Echoing Lincoln's great "House Divided" speech of 1860— itself a justification of self-defensive expansionism—NSC 68 depicted "a basic conflict between the idea of freedom under a government of laws, and the idea of slavery under the grim oligarchy of the Kremlin. . . . The implacable purpose of the slave state to eliminate the challenge of freedom has placed the two great powers at opposite poles."[35] The Cold War fused the bipolar concept of American nationalism and the self-defensive doctrine of American expansionism. But, as I have emphasized, both of these preceded the Cold War. They would also survive it, as is clear from President George W. Bush's *National Security Strategy of the United States of America* of September 2002.

Expansion and Integration

The late twentieth century did not mark the end of history or the start of globalization. The globalization promoted by the United States in recent decades is only one phase in a much longer process. Yet this phase is historically distinct. I have tried to unearth four important roots. First, American-led globalization was shaped by the British-led European globalization that preceded it—both the expansion of Europe in the eighteenth and nineteenth centuries, which decisively shaped America, and the contraction of Europe during its war-torn twentieth century, which gave the United States its reason and opportunity to expand. Second, its platform for globalization was a country that survived a potentially suicidal civil war and expanded uniquely to embrace a whole continent of diverse sectional and ethnic groups. This process generated the fierce bipolar nationalism with which the United States has habitually confronted the outside world. Third, that continent was integrated during the late nineteenth century into an unprecedented successful and dynamic economic system, which then served as the launching pad for twentieth-century expansion overseas. Finally, that system was guided and promoted by a federal government for whom war was a familiar instrument of state-building and "security" a constant spur to expansion.

It might be felt that this account takes globalization too much as a process of unilateral expansion rather than global interaction but, in my judgment, the American role in globalization has involved both tendencies. The United States offered a model of connectedness that has been profoundly attractive and influential—namely an extension of the economic integration by which it developed its own continent. But it offered and promoted this in an era when the world was riven by hot wars (1914–18 and 1937–45) or by the Cold War and also seduced by alien ideologies (notably communism and, more briefly, fascism). This conflicted state of the world accentuated the "us versus them" mentality rooted in America's national past and encouraged its propensity to use decisive military power, both tendencies justified by a concept of self-defensive expansion. Although integration was putatively global, in practice—given the circumstances of the Cold War world—it became regional in extent.[36] Yet the globalizing tendency always remained, and this was based on America's distinct historical model of expansion by integration.

American Exceptionalism and Uneven Global Integration: Resistance to the Global Society

Ian Tyrrell

THEORISTS DATE NEW GLOBALIZATION from the 1960s to the 1970s,[1] and it is generally agreed that the United States today forms the key actor within this new international system. As the sole hegemonic power of the early twenty-first century, the United States is well known to be a sometimes reluctant participant within the international order of which it is, paradoxically, the chief author and agent. This paradox can be explained by a tandem set of influences. One is the ideological inheritance of American history—the cluster of values that the majority of Americans share—that make up American traditions. The other is the material structure of American politics—government, demography, markets, and natural resources—which has often pulled in different directions from the economic forces of globalization.

This chapter will explore key variables that have inhibited or conditioned U.S. involvement in the international system. The ideological inheritance will be considered first in the form of exceptionalism, but it will be argued that exceptionalism has varied in its impact over time and that it operates within the confines of political and legal institutions that shape the practice of American interactions with global systems. It must also be emphasized that at no time have these pressures toward disengagement from the world succeeded in overriding American connections to evolving patterns of globalization. Those connections have, however, been uneven, productive of a lopsided relationship, and characterized by a lack of synchronization between economic and political objectives.

How may we understand these anomalies of America's global connectedness? C. A. Bayly and the contributors to A. G. Hopkins's *Globalization in World*

History provide some clues through their perspectives on the longer history of globalization. Their work warns us against seeing globalization as either an entirely new process or as one in which there is one-way traffic toward integration. Their accounts of past histories of globalization raise questions as to whether America's involvement with the rest of the world was a purely unilinear process and whether the state structures forged in the period from 1776 to 1920 and attitudes of exceptionalism inherited from the seventeenth and eighteenth centuries made U.S. involvement distinctive, in perhaps yet another endorsement of American exceptionalism. Only the comparative study of the integration of other areas into the world economy and polity could throw further light upon that subject; this is beyond the scope of the present chapter. However, the globalization process might be seen as involving the local production of modernity, a process in which the United States has taken part. Arjun Appadurai's *Modernity at Large: Cultural Dimensions of Globalization* (1996) is useful here in arguing, as Bayly puts it, that global and local forces "cannibalised" each other, accentuating "the appearance of difference" but expressing it in "similar ways."[2]

The idea of American difference has itself taken root in the period of global imperial expansion since the fifteenth century. American exceptionalism has been discussed extensively in the literature of American and comparative history, but its importance in structuring American global and other transnational connections has been only infrequently studied.[3] The idea of the United States as a unique and indeed superior civilization outside the normal historically determined path of human history lies at the heart of American exceptionalism. Originally formulated as a coherent concept in regard to class analysis by Werner Sombart and other Marxist-influenced theorists who concluded that the United States was an exception to Marxist class patterns, the idea has had wide purchase to describe a range of potential or actual differences between the social, cultural, and political order of the United States and that of other modern nations, for example, in the areas of violence or gender relations.[4] Paradoxically, though American exceptionalism separates the United States from other nations, in political rhetoric American ideals that are rooted in American exceptionalism, such as freedom, liberty, and democracy, can be applied as a model for other societies. Americans and American governments have frequently sought to effect such a global transformation. In this formulation, the United States provides an example. It leads, with other nations seeking always to emulate American achievements; they attempt to catch up but never quite make it, because the United States continues to forge ahead.

The United States has not been the only nation claiming exceptional status. Exceptionalism has been part of modernity's proliferation of distinctiveness within the construction of comparable nation-state structures and nationalist beliefs across the developing world in the nineteenth century.[5] This fact makes it desirable to treat exceptionalism as an intellectual process rather than as a description of historical reality. Though American exceptionalism is quite an ahistorical notion—rooted in the departure of the United States from the accepted laws of historical change—the phenomenon itself is indisputably historical.[6] There is no doubting the existence through great swaths of American history of such an ideology of exceptionalism, but its shape has not been constant and it has not been purely and simply an interpretation of historical reality. Rather, the notion has been the product of intellectual inheritance and of a particular conjuncture of conditions.

Belief in exceptionalism has waxed and waned. It was originally a European concept in which Europeans compared the New World with old Europe. This duality was based on the Eurocentric notion that Europe set the norm from which other places diverged. The European origins of American exceptionalism also included, of course, the activities and perceptions of Europeans who settled in the American colonies and became what are now known as Euro-Americans. At first, Europeans treated the whole of "the Americas" as exceptional. They associated the concept with the wealth of nature on both continents (and the strangeness of its indigenous peoples and their customs). The prosperity that flowed materially from nature's bounty in the colonial period was seen as exceptional vis-à-vis Europe but still shared across the hemisphere to a degree. Indeed, both utopian and dystopian fantasies were projected equally upon the Americas, both north and south.[7]

For North America, however, a second theme beyond mere abundance had already begun to shape the distinctive intellectual heritage of the United States. Attendant upon English settlement in the seventeenth and eighteenth centuries, the nascent sense of exceptionalism narrowed to the British possessions. The Puritan inheritance, with its theme of God's divine mission in the wilderness realized through the settlement of New England, laid the foundation for distinguishing between the indisputable abundance of "the Americas" as a whole and the exceptionalism of the English North American colonies.[8] The British colonists also brought political as well as religious traditions of "freedom." They brought their British liberties and parliamentary traditions; they saw their Protestant civilization as a radical break from Rome, an expression of human liberty, and thus an exception. This way of thinking about the achievements of themselves and others ruled the Spanish and French settlements out of the inheritance of exceptionalism. In fact, the Spanish—because of their devastating impacts upon Amerindian peoples whom they conquered, suppressed, and infected with diseases—were dubbed the "Black Legend."[9] Though North Americans also exterminated Native Americans, they rarely enslaved them, and the demographic collapse was extended over a much longer time period. The considerable ills wrought by Anglo Americans upon the indigenous people were thought both unintentional in many instances and justified in the interests of spreading Protestantism.

To this already heady mix was added, in the 1776–89 period, momentous events that set the United States apart from both Europe and Latin America in the pioneering of political liberty through the form of a functioning republican government. The special character of the United States as uniquely based on democratic ideals and personal liberty was thereby linked to the formation of a new nation-state.[10] Sometimes this special character is inferred from the nature of American political documents founded at that time—the Declaration of Independence and the Constitution. The American Revolution and its aftermath freed the United States from British control, and with that decisive break the application of exceptionalism became narrowed not merely to Protestant, British North America, but specifically to the United States. Yet the new nation remained closely linked to the older ideas of material prosperity, abundance, and Protestant freedoms.

In the nineteenth century a frontier version of the theory was tied to ideas of social mobility, in which a safety valve of "free" land available in the American West provided for the hardworking and opportunistic. Thus, political distinctiveness continued to be underpinned by material differences brought about by the wealth and resources of the United States.[11] In the twentieth century, the outbreak of class revolutions in Europe in 1917 and the experience of Nazi and Soviet totalitarianism reinforced this sense of exceptionalism. The United States avoided these traumatic experiences, and the contrast fueled concepts of U.S. exemption from class analysis. The image and reality of European social turmoil received further backing from the impact of World War II itself. With the United States emerging into world power, school and college history textbooks and curricula began to emphasize more than in the past the importance of studying U.S. history and civilization.[12] Conversely, world history and European history suffered in the schools' curricula. Americans argu-ably became more ignorant of foreign places too, as geography as a discipline contracted and became focused on instrumental goals.[13] The post–World War II revolutions of globalization and attendant industrialization fueled so-cial disruption, and the collapse of European empires increased the U.S. sense of intellectual and ideological distinctiveness as an especially favored place. In the work of some post–World War II political scientists and historians later described as consensus scholars, the United States appeared as a middle-class society with a resilient and distinctive liberal ideology.[14]

Many aspects of American history are left out or distorted in these nar-ratives associated with exceptionalism. This observation is, in the light of the new social history of the 1970s and 1980s, commonplace of historiography, particularly with regard to the expropriation of Native Americans and the contribution of other ethnic groups that preceded the Anglo Americans, such as Hispanics. Yet American exceptionalism was not about historical reality but about how historical events and traditions were represented in popular culture, intellectual discourse, and political practice. Whatever the hotly con-tested status of American exceptionalism within the academy, politicians con-tinued to ply the notion, and it formed the rationale for highly influential political actions. This was especially evident in such ritualistic occasions as State of the Union and Fourth of July addresses where the idea of the United States as a special place has won repeated endorsement. On Independence Day, 2004, George W. Bush proclaimed, "We remember names like Washington, Adams, Jefferson, and Franklin—and we honor their courage and vision. We are grateful that our Founders pledged their lives, their fortunes, and their sacred honor to create an independent America. And we are thankful that this Nation under God is still free, independent, and the best hope of mankind. America is a place of freedom and opportunity. . . . May God continue to bless the United States of America."[15] Presidents have also used American excep-tionalism to explain and justify American foreign policies. In his 2004 State of the Union address, Bush announced, "America is a nation with a mission, and that mission comes from our most basic beliefs. We have no desire to domi-nate, no ambitions of empire. Our aim is a democratic peace—a peace founded upon the dignity and rights of every man and woman. America acts in this cause with friends and allies at our side, yet we understand our special calling: This great republic will lead the cause of freedom."[16] Despite the apparently dramatic shift in post-9/11 American foreign policy under George W. Bush, the rhetoric was little different from that of earlier presidents and Fourth of July orators who reinforced in similar ways this sense of national exceptionalism.[17]

Along with the tradition of exceptionalism went an ideological anticolonialism that discouraged direct engagement with the world politically insofar as that process involved implication in the dealings of European empires. The Washingtonian injunction (1797) against entangling alliances was directed at this fear of imperial entanglement. As David Reynolds has observed, the United States developed an "intense anti-imperial ideology."[18] Americans generally do not think that their country is an empire today or that it has been in the past. The United States has been formally anticolonial. This stance was encapsulated in Donald Rumsfeld's statement in reference to Iraq in 2003 that Americans "don't do empire."[19] Other countries have empires, not the United States. In practical political terms, there was haste on the part of the American military conquerors and their allies in the second Iraq War to hand sovereignty back to an indigenous though necessarily interim Iraqi government by June 30, 2004. This anticolonialism was a strong tradition in Cold War America as well, with Ronald Reagan referring in a celebrated address to the Soviet Union as the "evil empire" in 1982.[20]

The deeper origins of this anticolonial tradition can be traced to the American revolt against empire in the form of British rule in 1776 (no taxation without representation). The United States also sided rhetorically early on with revolutions against imperial rule across the Western Hemisphere. The Monroe Doctrine (1823) was designed to keep European empires from meddling in the affairs of the Western Hemisphere. The acquisition of the Philippines in 1898 and the bloody insurrectionary war that followed called this anticolonial tradition into question. Americans at first bitterly divided themselves and then sought to overcome these divisions by working to distinguish U.S. colonialism from European. They soon reemphasized that even within the experience of empire, the American version would be benevolent, enlightened, and temporary.[21] The decision in 1935 to give the Philippines its independence ten years hence was superseded by events in the form of the Japanese invasion of 1941. Nevertheless, Philippine independence enabled the United States to treat the cases of territorial empire acquired from the Spanish-American War as the "great aberration"—the exception to American exceptionalism in the matter of empire.[22]

However compromised from 1898 until 1946, this tradition of anticolonialism served the United States well in the twentieth century. Professed opposition to European empires and faith in self-determination combated the anti-imperialism of the communist revolutions after 1917, from the time of Woodrow Wilson, who advocated the substitution of League of Nations mandates for the colonial regimes of Germany and the Ottoman Empire. Anti-colonialism has allowed the United States to undermine other empires, as with Franklin D. Roosevelt's wartime opposition to European plans for retention of imperial domains after World War II, especially the French. Similarly, the United States failed to support Britain and France in the Suez conflict of 1956.[23] Many historians have noted that the United States preferred the informal "empire" of trade and investment to formal colonies and acquired the latter only when needed to help enforce the former.[24] No country possessed greater influence after World War II, yet America's own informal empire avoided violating its sense of anticolonialism by seeking to be invited to help other nations in a system described by Geir Lundestad as "empire by invitation."[25]

One key tenet of exceptionalism underpinning the American sense of itself as an anticolonial nation—in but not of the world—was Protestant evangelicalism. The Protestant sense of mission has had enormous influence in structuring American perceptions of the world at large and in shaping the efforts both to transform the world and yet remain distinct from it. Many American evangelicals shared a widespread belief that the United States was part of a providential plan to prepare for the coming of Christ. These ideas could be easily seen in the social and political thought of such prominent early–nineteenth-century American clergy as Lyman Beecher and his equally well-known daughter Catherine, author of *A Treatise on Domestic Economy* (1841).[26] Both stressed the moral uniqueness of the American people: "The democratic institutions of this Country are in reality no other than the principles of Christianity carried into operation," stated the daughter. The American republic was the means by which "the Messiah of the nations" would reform the Earth and establish his earthly kingdom. Though the American Board of Commissioners for Foreign Missions began operation in 1810, the Christian millennialism behind it did not, however, inspire dynamically extensive overseas missionary work until the 1880s. The late nineteenth century saw a massive missionary effort to mobilize Americans to save the rest of the world, especially through the overseas efforts of the YMCA, the YWCA, and the Student Volunteer Movement. The last of these, under the leadership of John Mott from 1885, inspired thousands of young college men and women to join the ministry and seek service in such mission fields as China and India.[27]

These efforts would, it was fervently hoped, improve the world and help to bring about the Second Coming. Such moral campaigning was not closely tied to American power in any formal sense; it was not necessarily supportive of American intervention abroad militarily or politically. But religious millenarian sentiment did divide the world into camps of good versus evil. "Evil," for some Americans, already included Islam in the nineteenth century.[28] Rooted in American individualism, the individual conscience of evangelical revivalism, and attitudes toward the bourgeois nuclear family, American Protestant religiosity displayed antipathy toward Islam as one of a number of collectivist religions from the early nineteenth century. Informed by orientalism, American Protestants directly linked Islam to the level of "barbarism" in the stages of civilization idea derived from Enlightenment thinking.[29] Humanitarian reformers also found their fears of Muslim barbarism confirmed by the late–nineteenth-century atrocities committed against the Armenian people by the Ottomans in 1895. Humanitarians such as Frances Willard strove to help these people and others thought to be in need of uplifting through international reform and relief efforts. But American Protestants also found much to complain about in Orthodox Christianity and Catholicism as practiced abroad. Only the Protestant evangelical faith secured the right of individual conscience, the status of women, and other benchmarks of a "civilized" society.[30]

This commonplace orientalist discourse dealt not only with distant threats but also with those within the United States. During the 1830s, anti-Catholicism and anti-Masonry became the first two in a long series of movements against un-American activities, in which fear of foreign subversion and allegiance to a foreign power lay behind attempts to expose antievangelical influences. Political historians have shown, for the nineteenth century, just how powerful and persistent in mobilizing voters these identifications with ethnocultural values could be.[31] But a closer parallel with the Protestant opposition to foreign and barbaric religions came from home-grown Mormonism. This faith evoked a powerful source of intolerance within the wider American community not settled until the admission of Utah as a state in 1896. Mormonism provided for nineteenth-century Americans a prototype of unorthodox familial relations through the practice of polygamy. Mormonism became known in the second half of the nineteenth century as the "Islam of America."[32]

From the early nineteenth century, evangelical Protestantism sought not only to make the world over in the image of the United States; it also sought to inoculate the United States from foreign influences by shaping the moral structure of the state through reform as a substitute for church-state links dissolved after the Revolution. The "Benevolent Empire" of moral reform societies emerged in response. After the Civil War, this activity took various forms, including lobbying the state for Christian reform legislation.[33] National prohibition achieved in 1919 was in part a product of this quest to create a moral state. In the wake of the failure of national prohibition and the embarrassments of fundamentalist evolutionism in the Scopes Trial (1925) and the revived Ku Klux Klan, however, popular religious Protestant influence on politics lessened for a time after 1929. The modern descendants of nineteenth-century evangelicalism—the fundamentalist faiths—moved to the margin of American political influence. Modernism and liberalism, as well as a variety of non-Protestant faiths, grew in strength.[34] Yet by the 1960s, a countervailing movement had begun. It demonstrated the enduring significance of religion in the values that have complicated and compromised the processes of international engagement and global integration. Alarm over the election of the Catholic John Kennedy as president in 1960 again roused, along with the Cold War fear of communism, the desire of evangelicals to exert power within and upon the state. Yet not until after the moral crisis of Watergate did evangelicals have much visible success in influencing presidential administrations. Jimmy Carter (1977–81) was himself an evangelical of undoubted faith, but overt political influence came after 1980 with the Moral Majority of the Reagan years and the Christian Coalition of the 1990s. This resurgent influence should not be exaggerated, at least until the time of President George W. Bush's administration. The organized Christian forces of the evangelists still remained largely as a political lobby group given concessions and symbolic victories, without having real power within presidential administrations. However, these victories have had international repercussions. For example, the Reagan administration gave symbolic support to antiabortion forces by opposing international efforts for population control in the mid-1980s. The denial of funds to sustain family planning efforts abroad went directly against world population control and United Nations policies.[35]

Exceptionalism was not simply a product of this set of inherited ideas, however. It has been greatly augmented by the growth of a patriotism centered on the nation-state in the twentieth century. American allegiances were diverse and fragmented in the nineteenth century. The United States had a federalized state structure inherited, as every college history textbook notes, from fear of centralized power. In the early years of the Republic, "a weak but popular national state loosely connected a fragmented, ethnically heterogeneous society," John Higham noted. "Cultural nationalism, in the sense of a deep popular consciousness of being a single people, hardly existed."[36] The weak state was one of the chief factors facilitating the nation's growing international connections. It allowed foreign influences in as part of global integration, but the very weakness of the state and the threats to social cohesion posed by states' rights and by cultural and religious conflict connected to the extensive foreign penetration also prompted attempts to control these influences by projecting nationalism and patriotism. Antiforeign and anti-Catholic sentiment surfaced virulently in the Know-Nothing movement of the 1850s, but this movement did not or could not stop foreign immigration to the United States or shape its composition, because the demand for labor was so strong.[37] Rather, nativism sought to control the assimilation of these strangers into American citizenship and to restrict their contribution to the American political process. These nativist convulsions had impacts on the American state, mainly by contributing to the collapse of the Second Party System and thus to the coming of the Civil War.[38] But the Know-Nothings proved an ephemeral political movement; they did not contribute to the rebuilding of the state. Only with post–Civil War nativism did the symbols of patriotism become located in a stronger nation-state.[39]

The lasting change in regard to patriotism and the nation-state came in the 1880s and 1890s in response to massive European immigration—which brought much larger numbers of Catholics, Jews, and even socialists and anarchists to American shores—and in response to increased awareness of external security challenges faced from the time of World War I. Modern American nationalism was a creation of this dual challenge to security and led to a proliferation of coherent and powerful symbols focusing on the nation-state.[40] Thus, Baptist clergyman Francis Bellamy wrote the Pledge of Allegiance in 1892 for the Columbian Quincentennial and, in the midst of labor, radical, and anti-immigrant turmoil in that decade, it quickly spread in use for students across the nation's schools. In 1923–24, this ritual took a more statist form of a pledge to "the flag of the United States of America" rather than "my flag" after lobbying from the National Flag Conference, in which the American Legion and the Daughters of the American Revolution were prominent. With the addition of "under God" in 1954, the modern pledge—conceived as both oath and quasi-prayer—was complete.[41] Other popular rituals constructed in the tumultuous period of the late–nineteenth-century period included the Katharine Lee Bates patriotic hymn "America the Beautiful" (1893). The monuments of the American nation-state and the public celebrations surrounding their commemoration similarly proliferated with the commencement of the Arlington National Cemetery Memorial after 1910. Dedicated in 1920 with the interment of the Unknown Soldier, this commemorative structure unified the nation around wars that Americans had fought.[42] Self-consciously titled "national parks" also expanded in number markedly in the Progressive Era from small beginnings made between 1872 and the 1890s. Roderick Nash has pointed out that concern with the preservation of wilderness in the United States closely reflected feelings of anxiety that the primitive struggle with nature was over and of fears that European immigrants would lack American pioneering values or any understanding of the American heritage tied up with the frontier.[43]

Not only were the symbols and ceremonies of the nation-state effective in providing material reinforcement for ideas of exceptionalism after 1890; other circumstances contributed, too. One has been the development of a huge internal market, which provided the economies of scale that underpinned specialization in American industry and spurred the innovations of mass production. Immigration and high birth rates contributed to an extraordinarily high population growth rate that powered internal economic development in the first sixty years of the nineteenth century, with decadal growth never dropping below 33 percent. After the Civil War, the absolute increases were still impressive. Population went from 31 million in 1860 to 76 million by 1900 and to 105 million by 1920, though decadal growth dropped to 20 percent by the end of the century and continued to fall thereafter.[44] The potential of this internal market was also bolstered by relatively high wages due partly to the nineteenth-century "safety valve." A large part of the northeastern rural population went west to urban, mining, and rural frontiers rather than become crowded as a surplus labor supply in older eastern cities.[45] Adding to the pressure on labor prices and the incentive to innovate were bottlenecks in areas of mechanization of industry together with the protective activities of craft unions. Though skilled labor's position was continually eroded by technological change, opportunities for material prosperity through realistic patterns of incremental social mobility for workers have been repeatedly emphasized by historians.[46] This is not to deny that prosperity and population growth applied only to certain areas and sectors. There was much poverty and many regional disparities, with large areas of the rural south and other agricultural areas losing people to the North and to cities everywhere from the 1890s onward.[47]

Historians have often located exceptionalism in another set of material realities as well: those of abundant natural resources. Conditions of abundance were closely associated with the expansion of the American frontier, which proceeded apace after the Revolutionary War but especially after the end of the War of 1812. The frontier created a sense of "free security," of leaving Europe behind, of internal expansion. The abundance of land and its attendant resources partly explains how and why the United States could be self-sufficient in some respects—and seemingly not in need of close contact with the rest of the world. The United States could supply most of its own foodstuffs and energy requirements until after World War II. Indeed, the United States was a major exporter of wheat, cotton, and corn, providing Europe with vital grain supplies in the nineteenth century through the end of World War I. Despite the "closing" of the frontier in 1890, the mentality of abundance persisted; it was transferred partly into the consumer abundance that mass assembly-line production of the 1920s made possible. The pinnacle of the frontier culture of abundance's mutation was captured for the 1950s by David Potter in his felicitous phrase, "people of plenty."[48]

The experience of abundance created uneven integration into global political and economic activities. As early as the late nineteenth century, a number of vital commodities in the manufacturing economy, for example, rubber and industrial diamonds, and other items in the consumer economy, such as coffee, needed to be imported.[49] The frontier of resource abundance was always a relative and changing one and tended to diminish over time. Economic integration increased from the 1950s still further due to U.S. dependence on foreign sources of key metals such as titanium needed in strategic and defense industries.[50]

One nineteenth-century effect of the abundance of land and other resources with enormous consequences for the period of new globalization since the 1970s was a wasteful use of energy. This was closely tied to "frontier" conditions. Not only did the United States hold ample supplies of raw materials for industry within its vast national borders, these were effectively exploited for industrialization from the 1870s to the 1920s, in part due to labor scarcity and substitution of intensive resource use and capital for labor.[51] As a result, a labor-energy trade-off occurred due to low labor-to-land ratios. This process and its attendant environmental problems were particularly noticeable in agriculture. Wastefulness had its origins in the treatment of forests and other natural resources in a process that bred a culture of abundance. By the late nineteenth century, the image of scarcity loomed, prompting regulation of the use of resources. The Progressive Era conservation movement was in part an attempt to use European-style regulation of natural resources to promote national self-sufficiency.[52] Yet the exploitation of such resources shifted increasingly overseas, thus reinforcing U.S. global interdependence in the twentieth century.[53] The transition from public to private transport through the expansion of the automobile industry fueled, along with the growth of other industry, a rapid expansion from the 1920s in the use of petroleum products. This was accompanied by growing dependence on world energy supplies. The United States consumed 45 to 50 percent of the world's energy by 1945 for a population that made up approximately 5 percent of the world's total. Though historically almost self-sufficient in petroleum products, the United States had become by the 1970s vulnerable to the Middle Eastern oil supply, with imports providing 46 percent of the petroleum consumed in 1977. While this figure had dropped to 27 percent in 1985, imports again accounted for almost half of the U.S. oil use by the mid-1990s.[54] World economic development has since spread the percentage burden of culpability with regard to fossil fuel consumption more evenly on a global level, but American consumption continues to grow in absolute terms, and the nation still ranks as the world's most prodigious user and chief polluter. In 1995, the United States still used 25 percent of the world's energy with only 5 percent of the world population.[55]

In these ways, traditions of abundance associated with the frontier experience produced strong contradictions. The United States developed a high-energy-consuming culture. The nation's economic abundance rooted in its tradition of resource richness fueled economic growth and consumerism; it thus reversed the position of resource independence of the nineteenth century and created increasing dependence on world markets. Yet this very pattern of global interdependence since the 1960s has made the United States unwilling as the greatest fossil fuel user to disrupt the American economy to support attempts at limiting planetary climate change through countermeasures. While economic factors such as resource needs increasingly encouraged highly contested forms of international interdependence, political structures continued to create different priorities, emphasizing distinctiveness. These political structures in the American case revolved around federalism. As already indicated, the weak state of federalism and the states' rights tradition at first encouraged foreign influences in the nineteenth century because there was no strong central authority to regulate patterns of integration into the global economy. National citizenship—until the passage of the Fourteenth Amendment in 1868—derived from state citizenship, immigration controls were completely ineffective prior to the 1880s, and state passports were valid until 1856.[56] From the creation of the republic to 1865, the centrifugal forces were immense. A series of rebellions or threatened revolts between the Whiskey Rebellion of the 1790s and the nullification controversy of 1829–32 in South Carolina showed that local and state objections to central power were substantial and raised the possibility of foreign intervention. The perils of a breakaway were illustrated with devastating consequences in the Civil War. Though the outcome of this fratricidal conflict put an end to secession, the state remained weak relative to most European countries until the 1930s. Thereafter, a strongly Keynesian state did develop, especially after 1941, but it was based on military expenditure as much as genuine commitment to Keynesian economics.[57]

Though the federal state has often been seen as distinctively American, a growing number of modern nations have adopted a federal system, for example, Nigeria, Germany, and Australia. A division of powers between state and federal governments has not only been less distinctive than sometimes suggested but also less important when divorced from the structures and the procedures of the political system of the federal government itself and the Constitution. A more important factor in promoting difference was the conflict between the executive and legislative branches. The critical impact of this separation of powers was famously highlighted in the reception of the Treaty of Versailles, where President Wilson could not carry the country with him in the ratification of the League of Nations by the Senate. Though complicated by Wilson's maladroit handling of the situation, the ability of the president to conduct foreign affairs was compromised also by the jealousy of the elected representatives on the question of treaty powers. Presidential powers, or at least the capacity to exercise that power through an "imperial presidency," have clearly grown in the period since the 1930s. Yet presidents seeking to enact international treaties rely on support for their efforts within the legislative branch of government to a greater extent than the executive must in many comparable countries. Even with presidential agreement, a Kyoto-style environmental agreement would be extremely hard to get through the Senate. President Clinton did not try on this matter, and with regard to the United Nations Convention on Biological Diversity, he met defeat in the Senate in 1995.[58] This pattern of resistance to international treaties has become pronounced since the 1980s, just as the number of potential international agreements under the United Nations has increased. As in the case of the criminal court, sovereignty is a key issue, but Senate resistance to treaty ratification during the 1990s represented more than ideological forces derived ultimately from American exceptionalism. The resistance also reflected economic interests that continued to exert influence through the system of representation in the Senate, which favors regional pressures from particular farm or industrial lobbies, and through the election of the U.S. president via the electoral college system. This mode of election, too, encourages concessions to regional interests during presidential campaigns.

The impact upon international cooperation of regional and special economic interests exerted through the political system is not new. It has best been shown through the course of American history with regard to tariffs. Despite its integration in the globalizing world through capital flows and migration, parochial protectionist interests conflicted with this integrationist pattern and worked against ideas of free trade in politics and the open door time and time again. One of the consequences of the large, increasingly well-integrated internal market in the nineteenth century was the encouragement of tariff protection. The principle of tariffs had been established at the founding of the American republic by the first secretary of the treasury, Alexander Hamilton. At first, tariffs benefited mainly northeastern industry, and southerners tended to oppose them. Thus, the years of Democratic ascendancy from the late 1820s to the Civil War tended to be marked by tariff reductions. However, special political interests such as the Pennsylvania iron industry were able to extract high tariffs from Democrats as well as from Whig presidents and legislators.[59]

The Civil War ushered in a period lasting until World War II when high tariffs generally prevailed. These were mostly the years of the so-called Republican ascendancy in federal politics. The chief alternative source of federal government revenue was land sales—a diminishing possibility over time as the best arable land had already been taken up by the time of the Civil War. After the Civil War, tariffs generated about half of government revenues. Though tariffs were most closely identified with "infant" manufacturing industries, in fact sectional interests in agriculture also assiduously sought protection, for example, hemp, wool, rice, and sugar in the early nineteenth century. After the Civil War, tariffs provided even broader agricultural as well as industrial subsidies. For example, the Republican administration after 1896 introduced tariffs on such items as wool and hides for regional political reasons to placate western ranchers even though few people benefited directly. (The party was thought to be hostile to the West because of its opposition to the Democrats' monetary policy of free silver under the leadership of William Jennings Bryan.) The tariff policy on wool, for example, stymied trade, hurting the export industries of Australia and also making shoes and woolen goods more expensive in the United States. In the twentieth century, tariff protection remained tied to politics and specifically to the special interests that regional diversity and federalism allow to flourish. As economist Douglas A. Irwin has noted, "The institutional structure of Congressional decision-making was biased in favor of protection-seeking interests, thus resulting in relatively high tariffs."[60]

Tariff policy demonstrated the contradictory nature of American foreign economic policy. While American historians have argued that policymakers sought the open door from the 1890s,[61] this policy prescription had to contend with parochial and sectional interests. True, the use of reciprocity treaties partly offset this protectionist regime. Tariff reductions could thereby be used to promote American exports and the open door. Yet this process cannot explain the persistent political obstacles to free trade that pro-tariff interests represented and cannot deny the reality of their effects nor the asymmetric way in which trade policy functioned to promote internal economic growth at the expense of multilateral foreign trade.[62] These contingencies meant that, in reality, the United States sought to export as much as possible and import as little as possible. This was the practical impact of the McKinley Tariff of 1890 and the Dingley Tariff of 1897, but the heavily protectionist Fordney–McCumber Tariff of 1922, the Smoot–Hawley Tariff of 1930, and the McNary–Haugen farm bills of the 1920s carried the principle to new heights (or depths). The last sought to soak up the agricultural surplus and subsidize its dumping upon foreign markets. Such a bold initiative, though unsuccessful in the 1920s, illustrated the contradictory drives in American political economy, with higher price supports in the United States and dumping abroad designed to advance farmers' welfare on both fronts—at the expense of foreign farmers and domestic consumers of food.[63]

Tariffs were often ineffective as an agent of economic development, to be sure. Modern economists show that their impact on economic growth was marginal, particularly in the long term, but they did boost specific industries, influence the timing of growth, distort the domestic economy, and cause international friction. Thus, for example, the highly inefficient and uncompetitive sheep industry was repeatedly subsidized.

The catastrophes of the Great Depression of the 1930s and World War II strengthened the hand of free trade advocates in the United States, as it was widely conceded that global protection and autarky had contributed to the Depression and the rise of Hitler. The introduction in 1947 of the General Agreement on Tariffs and Trade (GATT) began a long series of initiatives, culminating in 1995 in the formation of the World Trade Organization (WTO), that have brought a stronger synchronization of American economic trade policies with internal economic policy. Yet sectional interests continued to command support in Congress, via the continuation of various farm subsidy programs (first introduced under the New Deal) and through import quotas set on sensitive farm products.[64] These included, in the era of new globalization, restrictions on sugar, lamb, and beef. Tariffs on steel imports were also introduced by the Bush administration in 2002 in direct conflict with the WTO, and even the series of bilateral free trade agreements pursued by the Bush administration since 2001 have contained exemptions that favor American production. The struggle between advocates of open international trade and those of protectionism within the American government—and among labor unions, farmers, and political parties—provides one of the clearest indications of the complications for U.S. international engagement in the era of new globalization. Yet the forces of global integration have gradually gained the upper hand since the 1950s. As Irwin has argued, "The importance of the GATT and the agreements it has fostered cannot be measured in terms of reducing U.S. tariffs, perhaps, but in strengthening the vested interests that have a stake in perpetuating open trade policies. The GATT has provided an institutional means of giving stability and credibility to such policies by making their reversal more costly."[65]

Political structures of federalism and the division of powers; the consolidation of the nation-state around a superpatriotic ideology; and the material force of internal markets, population, and resources together created the underpinning for the aberrant position of the United States within the globalizing world. This has produced a reciprocal relationship with global processes in trade and politics that is unequal and uneven. Integration has not been an inevitable or smooth process. This lopsided globalization in no way denies the long history of connections with wider structures and processes. Yet it does point to the problematic feature of those patterns of integration, patterns that policymakers have to deal with in the opening years of the twenty-first century.

6 Crisscrossing the Gods: Globalization and American Religion

N. J. Demerath III

OVER THE LAST DECADE AND A HALF, I have been involved in a multicomparative, cross-cultural examination of "world religions and worldly politics" in some fourteen countries other than my own around the globe.[1] Throughout the project, I have felt like a pilgrim wandering in search of an answer to the worldwide scourge of religious violence. But I was also a pilgrim in another sense. My travels led to an informal global inventory of national similarities and differences, and I became an unwitting enlistee in the great international army of researchers examining evidence of "globalization." Here I want to share some observations on the latter issue, focusing especially on American religion in the past and present global context and viewing it from the outside-in as well as from the inside-out. I shall begin and end with some conceptual and cautionary comments on globalization overall and its relation to religion. In the interim, I shall devote the bulk of the chapter to the United States and its various religious imports and exports.

The Culture of Globalization and the Globalization of Culture

In recent years, few terms have enjoyed a quicker transition from social science jargon to popular cliché than "globalization." During the same period, few terms have spawned such sprawling, sometimes facile, multidisciplinary literature as has developed over globalization's causes, consequences, and problematic reality. Although the error of underestimating globalization is neither rare nor trivial, the mistake of overestimating it is becoming more common and more lethal. A "culture of globalization" has emerged that sometimes hypes, caricatures, and distorts the "globalization of culture." This has given a new and perverse meaning to the mantra "Think globally but act locally."

It is true that virtually no society has been impenetrable to such global incursions as the Avon representatives now plying the waters of Brazil's Amazon River in dugout canoes, India's new McDonald's franchises selling "Maharajah Macs" made with mutton so as to offend neither Hindus with beef nor Muslims with pork, or the Western weddings and wedding dresses now so popular in Japan. There is no question that areas once isolated are now linked, and linked to a wider transnational community in the bargain. The rural hut with a television antenna and satellite access to the Internet looms as a twenty-first century icon. While visiting a remote fishing village 200 miles off the coast of Papua New Guinea, I was struck by three "modern" artifacts: the two-cycle outboard engine, churches brought by Western missionaries, and World Cup soccer, all of which came in the wake of the World War II U.S. fleet, whose anchoring offshore and subsequent off-loading led to the famous "cargo cults," vestiges of which remain.

Globalization has taken on a variety of valences. Some enthusiasts project nothing less than a single global society—if not in my lifetime, perhaps yours. Other global prophets are less utopian than dystopian,[2] stressing the negative rather than the positive. Globalization can be seen as something old as well as new, though sometimes the old is saved by the new as, for example, tourism can produce a recrudescence of traditional arts as marketable commodities. Then again, one person's promising new global reach can be another person's old-fashioned Western imperialism. But globalization is easily exaggerated in all directions. Although there are few outposts untouched by outside global influences, it is one thing for a cultural import to touch and exploit but quite another for it to be embraced and absorbed. Moreover, most local residents have a badly undersampled exposure to what other cultures comprise. We tend to extrapolate from a few globalized fragments that can be woefully misleading. The contemporary United States is no more faithfully depicted by its widely exported soap operas than is, say, Brazil by its "Carnival," or India by its "Bollywood" movies. To skeptics, globalization is more a surface veneer that reaches only a growing international elite rather than producing a deeply penetrating change in what the anthropologist Clifford Geertz calls any society's "thick culture."[3]

Some will protest that the above examples are superficial. For them, real globalization involves the basic cake of economics, technology, and power, not the cultural whip cream on top. This cues the critical distinction between *structural globalization* and *cultural globalization*.[4] Structure involves industrial development, the spread of the Internet, political realities, and organizational infrastructure; culture entails those symbols and practices that make sense of the foregoing by interpreting both "what is" and "what ought to be" at any given time. Although neither form of globalization is as totally engulfing as popular mythology would have it, the received wisdom is that structural change tends to both precede and exceed cultural change, and structural globalization provides the highway on which cultural globalization travels.

An American sociologist of the mid-twentieth century, W. F. Ogburn, coined the phrase "culture lag" for instances in which culture changes more slowly than structure and tensions result from their lack of synchronicity.[5] Culture lag and its problems are common when we are slow in adjusting to new technology—for instance, the Internet or the condom. But there are also cases of "structural lag" in which structure changes more slowly than culture, resulting in tensions of a different sort. For example, new environmental expectations may run afoul of old industries, and new hopes of ending ethnic, class, and gender differences are often stymied by institutionalized patterns of discrimination. In fact, one of the leading sources of frustration and conflict in the world today is the spread of cultural ends unaccompanied by the structural "means" necessary to achieve them. This structural lag syndrome and its resulting "relative deprivation" can be seen throughout the Third World with respect to everything from consumer goods to democracy.

Meanwhile, a related issue concerns the distinction between globalization that occurs through *structural determinism* versus globalization that occurs through *cultural diffusion*. The distinction turns on whether cultural convergence is the result of similar cultural responses to increasingly shared structural characteristics or whether cultural convergence results from a direct diffusion of culture that is independent of structure. The first scenario suggests that as older forms of industrialization and more recent technological developments spread, they carry their own cultures with them. This is close to what Karl Marx had in mind when he predicted that even "barbarian nations" would be sucked into "civilization."[6] It is also a premise behind the no-longer-fashionable school of "modernization theory."[7] On the other hand, the latter image of a global, free-floating, cultural diffusion may seem to be one more factor underlying prophecies of a global postmodernism. As cultural clouds descend unevenly and unwarrantedly on innocent societies unprepared for them, one can imagine the bricolage, confusion, and anomie that may follow.

But, of course, these scenarios are also exaggerations. Neither culture nor structure travels wholly without the other. Moreover, globalization generally honors a corollary to the "think globally but act locally" axiom—namely, "import globally but implement locally." Every structural or cultural element that finds its way into a country from the outside has to find its place among locally preexisting patterns. This often leads to cross-national distortions and frustrations. For example, questions of authenticity abound concerning the so-called Mexican, Italian, and Chinese food advertised as such in U.S. restaurants. The concept of bureaucracy has lost a good deal in translation in its global travels from Germany. Even the notion of democracy has vastly different meanings and implications in different settings. And the reason I studied fourteen nations in my research on world religion was to put more emphasis on a faith's contextual variations than its canonical traditions. As but one case in point, there are important differences between Islam in Egypt, Turkey, Pakistan, and Indonesia, let alone Israel and India.

Globalization and Religions

As a student of culture and religion, I have sometimes felt marginal both to my own discipline of sociology and to considerations of globalization. Until recently, structural factors and analyses have dominated both discourses. But now each has evidenced "a cultural turn,"[8] and where culture goes, religion is almost sure to follow as one of its most critical components. Perhaps encouraged by the realization that two of the field's pioneers, Max Weber and Émile Durkheim, took religion seriously but not personally—each was, in Weber's phrase, "religiously unmusical"[9]—social scientists have begun to pay more attention to religion, though many still seem to avoid it like a virus that can be caught on analytic contact.

Certainly developments over the last quarter century confirm religion's importance in even nonreligious terms. In 1979 alone, there was a surge in Catholic liberation theology in Latin America, partly in response to the global spread of Pentecostal Protestantism but with major class and political ramifications. The year also witnessed the Polish–Catholic partnership with Solidarity that brought down the communist regime a decade later, the Camp David peace accords that produced at least a pause in the armed hostility between Jews and Muslims in Israel, and the establishment of Ayatollah Khomeini's Iranian republic after 66 U.S. citizens had been taken hostage. These and many subsequent events suggest the error of any global reckoning that lacks religious soundings.

But as these examples also imply, it may be easier to portray religion as a brake on globalization than as a lubricant. Religion may even seem the last refuge of the antiglobal scoundrel. It is true that virtually every religion holds out fervent hopes for a march to world peace and unity, but it is also true that virtually every religion imagines itself at the head of the procession. Of course, in the absence of any globalization, regional religions may be separate and autonomous from one another, thus ensuring no interreligious conflict—a condition that was at least approximated in some areas of the world until the end of the eighteenth century. However, insofar as partial globalization brings formerly distant religions into contact without providing for their integration, this may actually spur religious conflict. Both the Crusades of the twelfth century and the current war over terrorism illustrate the consequences. But what are the possibilities of a more complete globalization? Let me assess three ways in which religion might contribute to such globalization: first, a world civil religion; second, one religion emerging triumphant; and third, increasing secularization.

A Global Civil Religion?

"Civil religions" sacralize the state by invoking the society's dominant religions or other sacred systems. Working in the tradition of the eighteenth-century Enlightenment philosopher Jean-Jacques Rousseau and the early–twentieth-century sociologist Durkheim, Robert Bellah[10] provided the classic account of U.S. civil religion as celebrated, for example, by largely Christian, nondenominational prayers on Thanksgiving, the Fourth of July, and the start of daily business in Congress and all of the fifty state legislatures. Virtually every other nation has a similar version, though it may take a more secular form as in the cases of, say, China, the former USSR, and Turkey; it may be more imposed from the top than something that seeped up from the bottom; and it may sanctify process instead of outcomes as part of what I have called a "religion of the civil" as opposed to a civil religion. One can also detect regional civil religions in, for instance, the claim of many that Christianity is the uniting force behind Europe and the efforts of others to let out more notches in the Koran belt extending from Africa across the Middle East to Southeast Asia. Surely the notion of a global civil religion has had its advocates from the early days of the World Federalists to current supporters of a bolstered United Nations.

But civil religions can also sacralize aspirations to statehood in the form of tribal nationalism. They can produce cultural upheaval by legitimizing new civil states, regardless of whether they have reasonable chances of sur-

vival as autonomous economic units. As examples, religion is deeply implicated in efforts on behalf of (Catholic) Northern Ireland's independence from
(Protestant) Britain, (Muslim) Palestine's independence from (Jewish) Israel
(and vice versa), (Muslim) Kashmir's independence from (Hindu) India, and
(Christian) East Timor's independence from (Muslim) Indonesia. These conflicts illustrate how Samuel Huntington's vision of a "clash between civilizations"[11] can be translated into civil religious terms. They also give an indication of the increasing proportion of world conflict that is occurring *within*
once-established nations rather than *between* them.

As all of this suggests, the chances of a single global civil religion or even an
ecumenical concordat among civil religions are not high. This is in large part
due to religion's efforts to capture state power. Like the image of the "moth and
the flame," religious moths are attracted to the political flame, and vice versa.
In each case, the light and heat that are sought may become all-consuming. Because even members of the same religion are sometimes divided within nations,
it is difficult—though not impossible—for religion to become united across nations. A common external foe can do wonders in healing internal strife.

A Single Triumphant Religious Tradition?

If the chances are not good for a single global civil religion, it is hardly surprising that the chances are even poorer for a single religious tradition to achieve
global dominance. Over the past fifty years, the two religions that have had
the highest rates of world expansion are Islam and Christianity, especially the
latter's Catholic and Pentecostal Protestant wings, as we shall see later. Islam's
greatest increases have occurred in Africa, where its ethic of personal and social discipline is in fierce competition for converts with the Christians. Meanwhile, Protestants have made major gains in Latin America, where they have
proselytized at the expense of an impersonal, hierarchical, and patriarchal
Catholicism. Islam and Christianity have each recruited successfully among
both lower and middle classes. But each has a tendency to make enemies in
the very process of attracting converts. Although Islam and Christianity are
different branches of the same Abrahamic tree, they are far more likely to treat
each other as satanic opponents rather than saintly allies. Hence, each has a
ceiling on its world growth: a stained glass ceiling in the case of the Christians
and a mosaic tile ceiling in the case of the Muslims.

Nor are other world religions likely candidates for attaining global religious dominance. Hinduism has never traveled well or become a religious force

outside of India, Nepal, and Bali, Indonesia. World religions such as Judaism, Jainism, and Sikhism are limited by their geography and by their very small current numbers. I will have more to say shortly about Buddhism's liabilities for growth. Meanwhile, it should be clear enough that the prospect of global unification under any one religious banner is the stuff of miracles.

Global Secularization?

However paradoxically, the greatest service religion could render globalization is to participate in its own secularization. Because religion, like culture overall, has been more divisive than unifying on the world scene, globalization depends first and foremost on its declining rather than increasing salience. This is especially true of those religious elements that lead to aggressive particularism as opposed to more tolerant universalism—elements such as an unchanging and uncompromising doctrine, a rigid morality, and a penchant for political mobilization. This is where secularization comes in for religion and any other form of sacred culture.[12]

It may seem a fool's errand to search out religions most likely to support secularization. But although every religion is constantly experiencing it to some degree, two traditions deserve special mention. The first is America's own Liberal or "Mainline" Protestantism—a tradition that includes denominations such as Congregationalists, Episcopalians or Anglicans, some Lutherans, Methodists, Northern Baptists, Presbyterians, and Unitarians. But in contrast to growing Catholicism and the more conservative evangelical Protestant denominations, these liberal groups' numbers have been declining. I have argued elsewhere[13] that they have won a major cultural victory in implanting liberalism in the United States as a whole, but the victory has come at the cost of their own organizational weakness. Values such as freedom, individualism, tolerance, democracy, and intellectual inquiry have become centerpieces of American culture, but they can be anathema to the sort of faith and commitment required by any organization, especially those that are religious. Still, the tendencies toward secularization within the once-great Liberal Protestantism establishment helped the United States to cohere despite its religious diversity. Global coherence would require a parallel development on a far larger scale, perhaps with leadership from the East as well as the West.

No Eastern religion has won greater respect in the West than Buddhism—at least in the abstract and among thinking seekers—in part because of its receptiveness to secularization. As a faith centered more on spiritual self-discipline than divine religious authority, it adapts relatively easily to new settings with a minimum of alien cultural baggage. Buddhism's commitment to the reasonable "middle way" might be seen as both a blessing and a curse. On the one hand, it is responsible for a good deal of Buddhism's recent appeal to those Westerners retreating from the mystifications of Christianity but seeking a spiritual dimension that will lift them out of an all-too-materialistic lifestyle. On the other hand, members of more other-worldly religions might wonder where the magic lies in Buddhism. As reasonable as it might seem to anoint Buddhism as a force for global secularization, the fact is that it has not fared well in the competition for numbers and nations since roughly the thirteenth century.

There is one final point to be made about secularization. Paradoxically, secularization cannot be understood except in dialectical tandem and oscillation with "sacralization." Just as old forms of the sacred die out, new forms of the sacred are continually born. Again, this is true not only of religion but of all aspects of culture where the sacred takes many other forms. But if this is good news for those in the religion business, it is bad news for those with high hopes for globalization. In the final analysis, it is those sacred aspects of culture that produce both our cohesion and our conflicts. It appears that we are once again back to a world that is multicentered, if not wholly decentered.

Religion remains a potent force all over the world today, and yet even its most localized varieties operate with a broader sense of their global context.[14] For instance, during my visit to the aforementioned fishing village in Papua New Guinea, the leader of its indigenous religion called Wind Nation asked me to set up an appointment for him "with President Clinton, because the two of us can combine our religions to save the world." When I pointed out that this would be difficult in light of the American custom of separating religion from the state, he thought for a moment and then replied, "That is a good idea. Cancel the appointment."

The United States as Global Religious Consumer

Because globalization is so often portrayed as a triumph of U.S. dominance, it is easy to suppose that we have always been primarily a world exporter rather than a world importer. But if there is any aspect of our national life that belies this notion, it is religion. Although we shall see later that the country has a long history of sending our religious ideas and institutions abroad, our record of religious imports provides a more balanced record of exchange. Native Americans aside (where they have been mostly pushed), every schoolchild knows we are a nation of immigrants. Moreover, religion is arguably the single most enduring piece of cultural baggage accompanying each newly arriving group. This is not the place for a full-fledged history of the religious aspects of American immigration, nor am I the person to provide it.[15] However, I do want to comment briefly on several principal immigrant episodes that have shaped our religious past, present, and future.

The colonists who came to this country in the early seventeenth century have been variously described, in part because they did in fact vary. But here, "what every schoolchild knows" may be a bit off the mark. The hagiographic account is of a put-upon band fleeing persecution in search of religious freedom. In fact, the opposition they experienced occurred mostly because English authorities resisted Puritan attempts to establish theocracies there. Finding no such opposition here, they quickly transformed the Massachusetts Bay Colony's "city on a hill" into a rigid religious establishment—the very thing their heirs would so inexplicably yet brilliantly prohibit some six generations later in the first clause of the first line of the First Amendment to the U.S. Constitution: "Congress shall enact no law respecting an establishment of religion, nor prohibiting the free exercise thereof."

If anything, the words and their setting were meant more symbolically than legally. While the fledgling U.S. government was able to avoid falling into religious hands, this was not true of state governments at the time of the founding—for example, the Congregationalist New England states, Dutch Reformed New York, Presbyterian New Jersey, Episcopalian Virginia, or the Methodist South. By the time of the nation's founding, the country was already riven by regional and denominational differences.[16] Because of the patchwork quality of the U.S. population and the continuing stream of new arrivals, the country lacked the kind of consensual and deeply rooted traditional culture that characterized such countries as England, France, Russia, China, or Japan. It is true that Christianity was a common element and a major common denominator of the nation's sense of itself and its patriotic civil religion. But gradually the nation found a cultural core in the Constitution itself and its Bill of Rights. As a system of procedural means rather than absolute ends, the result was well suited for accommodating heterogeneity. It offered a level playing field to all comers and became an important element in what William Hutchison has chronicled as the gradual and contentious shift from conflicted diversity to proud pluralism.[17]

At least this was true in theory and in principle—both of which sometimes crumbled in practice. Clearly, the most glaring exception involved those involuntary "immigrants" who, over more than a century, brought one of the country's most distinctive cultural heritages and its most protracted social problem.[18] Of course, the legacy of slavery is shameful. But it is also rich. African American churches have been a source of both inspiration and innovation for the country's broader culture. Their influence was felt not just by white religion as an early form of Holiness Pentecostalism. As we all know, black church music also affected white secular music through blues and jazz, and the style of the black pulpit and its politics continues to resonate among America's social movements and on its campaign trails.

Still, the African American experience is not widely heralded as a triumphal case of globalization. It represents the underbelly of the globalization process and a part of the narrative that is rarely told and never celebrated. And yet the experience of the "black churches" shares an important characteristic with many other globalizing forces that reached the United States: they all have tended to start at the bottom of the social ladder and only gradually work their way upward. This has certainly been true of the African American religious history following its beginnings in slavery. There are now seven well-institutionalized denominations that together account for some 80 percent of the African American religious community. Of these, the National Baptist Convention, USA, is the largest, and the African Methodist Episcopal Church ranks highest in socioeconomic status. But myriad storefront sects have just begun their climb.[19]

This rags-to-(very problematic)-riches saga also characterized the country's greatest immigration tsunami. From 1830 to 1930 (and especially from 1880 to 1910), some 38 million largely German, Italian, Irish, Polish, and French-Canadian immigrants arrived to swell the ranks primarily of Catholics but also of Lutherans and the country's very small percentage of Jews. Again, the national story here is too familiar to require retelling. However, it may be worth reporting on a small corner of it as experienced in Springfield, Massachusetts, a city where a colleague and I examined changing church-state relations over the nineteenth and twentieth centuries.[20]

Springfield was a major East Coast center for Irish settlement, and as the Irish experienced far fewer language problems than members of other newly arrived ethnic groups, they quickly jumped ahead of the city's Italians and French-Canadians in the march to mobility. Although it is now scarcely known within the city, Springfield's first Catholic mayor was a man named William Hayes who passed as a Congregationalist and was elected in 1900–01. But real mobility for Catholics occurred in three stages over multiple generations. Although national census data concerning religion were by then precluded by the separation of church and state, it was clear that Catholics had achieved a *demographic* plurality, if not majority, by 1920. It took another thirty years to transform this plurality into a governing *political* coalition, but by 1950, Catholics could claim not only the mayor's office but also control of the city council and the all-important school committee. Finally, it was not until the 1980s and after another generation that Catholics achieved *economic* parity in the city's company boardrooms and CEO positions.

One might think that Springfield's Catholics were now poised to turn the tables on the Congregationalists who had ruled their lives for a century and more. But ironically enough, Catholics achieved religious power only when it was no longer fashionable to have religious power. Rather than globalize Springfield, the Catholics were localized by Springfield. The church turned away from the old Catholic model of a hierarchical church ruling jointly with its parishioners in positions of political power. Many middle-class Catholics had become surprisingly "Protestantized," and the power of diocesan authority had atrophied. As one bishop told us wistfully, "In the past, it was 'Yes, Bishop.' Now it's 'Why, Bishop?'"

For many, this might seem the end of the tale of global religious importation through immigration. But still another chapter has been underway and gathering momentum since 1965, when the U.S. Immigration and Nationality Act greatly liberalized entry requirements after four decades of draconian quotas. By 1980, Pete Seeger had set prophetic new lyrics to the tune of "Gimme that Old Time Religion":

> We will pray with Aphrodite; we will pray with Aphrodite
> > she wears that see-through nightie, and it's good enough for me.
> We will pray with Zarathrusta; we'll pray just like we useter
> > I'm a Zarathrusta booster, and it's good enough for me.
> We will pray with those old Druids; they drink fermented fluids
> > Waltzing naked through the woo-ids, and it's good enough for me.
> I'll arise at early morning, when my Lord gives me the warning
> > That the solar age is dawning, and that's good enough for me.[21]

Seeger had the right idea, if some of the wrong particulars. The actual numbers of the post-1965 immigrants are similar to the numbers that arrived between 1830 and 1930—between 30 and 40 million. Although the earlier

wave accounted for a much larger proportion of the then-smaller U.S. population, the latter's global reach and mix have been incomparably greater. According to historian Rudolph Vecoli, "While almost 90% of immigrants from
1840–1960 were from Europe, only 10% from 1960 on."[22] Sociologists Fenggang Yang and Helen Rose Ebaugh describe a current Southwestern Assembly
of God church in Houston, Texas, "whose membership includes people from
48 nationalities speaking 59 different languages."[23] And five years ago, Stephen Warner and Judith Wittner described the results of a systematic effort to
estimate the number of new immigrant religious services even when they are
tucked away in the nooks and crannies of generally urban America:

> Today there are some 3,500 Catholic parishes where mass is celebrated in Span-
> ish and 7,000 Hispanic/Latino Protestant congregations, most of them Pente-
> costal or evangelical in theology. By actual count in 1988, there were 2,017
> Korean immigrant churches, and in 1994 there were an estimated 700 Chi-
> nese Protestant churches in the United States. Two different research projects
> counted between 1,000 and 2,000 mosques and other Islamic centers in the
> early 1990s, and at the same time Buddhist temples and meditation centers
> (many of the latter having white American constituencies) numbered between
> 1,500 and 2,000. Hindus could worship in some 400 temples.[24]

Such numbers are not easy to come by, and others are in dispute. For example, Diana Eck's recent celebration of "a new religious America" includes
what has become a canard that "there are more Muslim Americans than Episcopalians, more Muslims than members of the Presbyterian Church U.S.A.,
and as many Muslims as there are Jews."[25] But estimates of Muslim numbers
vary widely, depending largely on whether one joins Eck in including the long-
standing American "Black Muslims," who some assign approximately three
million in their own right.

However unimaginable it may seem to most Americans, there are now
missionaries arriving from other shores to save our souls. As we shall see later,
this is likely to reach a crescendo as Americans continue to occupy the global
religious left flank in, for example, formally approving a gay Episcopal bishop
and informally supporting female ordination and an end to required celibacy
for Catholic priests. Protests have come from conservative officials around
the globe, including Nigerian Anglicans and Vatican Catholics. And beyond
the global politics of the established churches, myriad cults or "new religious
movements" have come to the United States from afar in order to bring their

distinctive messages and benefit from our rich recruitment possibilities.[26] Examples include Reverend Moon's Unification Church from Korea, the International Society for Krishna Consciousness (ISKCON) from India, the lay Buddhist group Soka Gakkai from Japan, and the Bahá'ís from Iran. All of these groups and many more have developed networks that are self-consciously cosmopolitan as complements to their missions of reducing world conflict. But they are part of a large number of missionary agencies crisscrossing the world in order to save it.

As we are about to see, the impulse has hardly been foreign to U.S. religion. But such movements are inevitably caught up in some of the local-versus-global tensions captured by the awkward term "glocalization."[27] The issue of who is influencing whom and whether the prevailing influence is global or local first arose in the description of late–nineteenth- and early–twentieth-century Catholics in Springfield. Yang and Ebaugh raise it with reference to the arrival of more recent religious communities. They report that the overwhelming majority of immigrant religious groups are here to serve their own people. However, because most immigrants to the United States enter toward the bottom of the socioeconomic ladder, their relations to the host culture are more influenced than influential as they move upward. Perhaps no cliché of American history is more misleading than that of the melting pot. In addition to those who have come as Christians or converted to Christianity, others have adapted their faiths to such Christian religious practices as the congregational form, a stress on theological ecumenism, and reaching out to people in other traditions—all as a way of enhancing their acculturation and success by deferring to the dominant host culture of the world's most dominant host nation. In fact, not all scholars agree with the subtitle of Eck's book noted above: "How a Christian Country Has Become the World's Most Religiously Diverse Nation." While Eck is undoubtedly right about the profusion of world religions newly represented by temples and shrines across the country, many of these are tiny groups, and the number of represented faiths should not be confused with the numbers of represented followers. Indeed, Philip Jenkins argues that a more accurate summary might be,

> How Mass Immigration Ensured that a Christian Country Has Become an Even More Christian Country. For better or worse, in numerical terms at least, the United States is substantially a Christian country now, and Christian predominance is likely to be still more marked in decades to come. Out of all the

leading Christian nations of the past two-hundred years, the United States will be the last to occupy this role in the twenty-first century.[28]

Finally, much has been made of the U.S. tendency to valorize its diversity under the self-congratulatory banner of tolerant pluralism.[29] But there are notable exceptions. Recent evidence suggests that American Christians have tended to qualify their acceptance of non-Christian Americans. It is true that, according to a 2003 survey conducted by Robert Wuthnow,[30] sheer contact with persons of other faith traditions is now surprisingly widespread (48 percent with Muslims, 35 percent with Hindus, 34 percent with Buddhists), and close to 10 percent have attended services in Muslim mosques, Hindu temples, and Buddhist centers. However, the evidence of internal globalization takes a chilling negative turn when one considers religious hate crimes or when survey respondents are asked whether members of these traditions are fanatics or should be allowed to conduct worship services here in the United States. Here is Wuthnow's own summary:

> By the end of 2001 . . . the number of religiously motivated hate crimes had risen to 1,828, an increase of 32% (since an FBI report of 1998), and 26% of these incidents were now against Muslims. . . . These figures probably under-report such incidents. Surveys at least report considerable misgivings about religious differences. In the Religion and Diversity Survey . . . 47% of the public said the word "fanatical" applied to the Muslim religion and 40% said the word "violent" did. Nearly a quarter (23%) said that they favored making it illegal for Muslim groups to meet in the U.S. for worship. Perceptions of Hindus and Buddhists were more favorable (only 25% and 23% regarded the two, respectively, as fanatical); still one person in five favored making it illegal for these groups to meet.[31]

These results no doubt partly reflect the aftermath of 9/11, though it is easy to overstate the extent to which the al-Qaeda attack and the war on terrorism represent a dominantly religious clash as opposed to a political-economic-cultural-religious conflict. Clearly, globalization takes on different meanings when it moves beyond distant and incidental acquaintance. This is true not only of America's globalization at home but also of its attempts to globalize abroad.

Taking U.S. Religion on the Road

One image of U.S. religious globalization abroad that comes quickly to mind is that of kindly and capable missionaries manning small chapels, schools, and hospitals in obscure outposts from "darkest Africa" and "poverty-ridden India" to "ancient China." Hollywood has taught us all to breathe a sigh of relief when a lost Western explorer or downed airman stumbles into their clearings. This "foreign mission enterprise" began in the early nineteenth century and, by the early twentieth century, it had become a growth industry. Overall, it has sent close to a million representatives and their families into the cultural fray—including not a few children whose sense of mission ultimately led them into the social sciences, often as "area experts" in the countries and languages they had experienced at an early age.

The dual injunction to Christianize and to civilize the world was redundant for many. Mostly well educated by the standards of the day, these missionaries saw themselves as beacons in the wilderness with radiating influence. Indeed, if the carriers of our global cultural *imports* have tended to enter the United States toward the bottom of the status ladder and work their way up, the *exporting* missionaries illustrated a quite different pattern as elite visitors whose social and cultural resources often helped in getting their messages out and having them filter down.

But, of course, troubles and self-doubt were lying in wait. Outright hostility was not uncommon, as this is hardly the only globalizing venture that has produced an entrenched localism in response.[32] The term "rice Christian" became shorthand for those "parishioners" who attended services only when handouts of rice or other valuable commodities were in store. Not a few missionaries—and later Peace Corps volunteers—experienced a smiling but stubborn disinterest on the part of those shown new ways, whether this involved leaving a little-used new water pump to rust or reverting to picking small "cucumbers" after being shown that waiting a bit longer yielded large watermelons. More important, simply determining one's basic priorities was a "no-win situation."[33] Cleaving to the religious message left one feeling insensitive to the local culture and its material problems. But reversing the two left many vulnerable to charges of "going native." Through it all, the scent of a chauvinistic imperialism was in the air for those inclined to sniff.[34]

Today it is almost *de rigueur* for sophisticated "cultural relativists" to scoff at such mainline mission efforts, however well intended. But there are several reasons to pause before coming down too hard. The well-known scholar of African religion, Lamin Sanneh,[35] points out that mission schools often had the latent, if not always manifest, effect of breaking the hold of tribal customs and preparing students for changes that lay inevitably ahead—changes involving new forms of education, commerce, and perhaps above all, nationalism.

While Sanneh was himself a product of such schools and may be suspected of refraining from biting the hand that fed him, the point is not his alone.

Although I know of no rigorous evaluation of the mainline missions in religious or any other terms comparable to, say, Niall Ferguson's recent assessment of the British Raj in India,[36] it is clear that several faith communities are beginning to reap a bitter harvest from their successful planting. As noted earlier, both the Catholic Vatican and the Anglican Communion in Canterbury are now nervously eyeing a problem that may lie ahead for some American denominations. Third World Catholic cardinals and Anglican bishops tend to be far more conservative than their Western colleagues, and they may soon be sufficiently numerous to cast the critical votes in any balloting.

Meanwhile, traditional missionary efforts have undergone considerable change. Lone representatives of a local U.S. church, diocese, or foreign mission board are now rare; professionalized agencies engaged in refugee and relief work have become more common. American organizations such as Catholic Relief Services, Church World Service of the National Council of Churches, and the more evangelical World Vision have all become major players internationally. Bruce Nichols[37] has detailed their operations in Thailand, Sudan, and Honduras while noting that many pose a problem of church-state separation that has long been kept beneath the surface. Most of these agencies receive major funding from the U.S. State Department and the U.S. Agency for International Development, which have virtually no alternative vehicles of aid distribution. While the U.S. courts have long approved the disbursement of government funds to religious groups for purely secular purposes, there is widespread private acknowledgment that considerable proselytizing may occur as part of the various operations involved, especially among evangelicals. Of course, this is hardly the only case in which potential First Amendment problems are brushed aside with a wink and a nudge. Another may be emerging from the shadows soon, as I shall show momentarily.

So far I have focused on the missionary ventures of the large, mainline Protestant denominations and the Catholics. But another major change occurring involves the exploding numbers and often explosive results of the American evangelicals and our own "new religious movements." Steve Brouwer, Paul Gifford, and Susan Rose describe the shift this way:

> As the twentieth century progressed, the changing focus of missions was accompanied by a great shift in the origins of Protestant missionary fervor. A

century ago, most missionaries, whether they were conservative or biblically literalist or more liberal in outlook, were sent abroad by the old mainline denominations. By 1953, two new strains of twentieth-century Protestantism . . . had helped to even the score: the National Council of Churches sent out 9,844 full-time personnel to other countries, while 9,296 people were dispatched from more conservative evangelical sending agencies, which included both old-style fundamentalists and Pentecostals. By 1985, the National Council of Churches' number had fallen dramatically, to 4,349, while conservative evangelical, Pentecostal, and independent agencies built up an impressive eightfold advantage, supporting 35,386 missionaries.[38]

Make no mistake, this new wave of U.S. missionaries has been phenomenally successful.[39] Early in the twentieth century, the Jehovah's Witnesses' "Watchtower" movement began to take its peculiar mix of conservative theology mixed with absolute religious freedom around the world.[40] The Seventh-Day Adventists were also early starters, especially in Latin America, where they arrived from first the United Kingdom and then the United States. But the subsequent Protestant explosion in Latin America[41] has been so great that various Protestant churches and sects, plus the Mormons, now claim a fifth of the population and are engaged in a fierce battle for numbers with Catholic churches, who have begun to pay them the flattery of imitation by adopting their own charismatic worship techniques and finding increasing roles for women. Much the same dynamic is underway in Africa, where new converts number up to 25,000 a day in Christianity's contest with Islam. Again, it is worth citing Philip Jenkins's conclusion that, contrary to fear-mongered stereotypes and despite Islam's admittedly massive increases, Christianity has more than kept pace in global terms. Jenkins estimates that "by 2050, there should still be about three Christians for every two Muslims worldwide."[42] In fact, Christians have reason to be more concerned about a split in their own ranks than about losing market shares to Muslims. Over the same period as above, Christianity's balance will have tipped away from Europe and the United States in the North and West and toward Latin America, Africa, and Asia in the South and East. As noted earlier, the implications go far beyond changing demographics.

Meanwhile, if the new forms of U.S. missionizing are winning in many areas, they are anathema in others—at least from the standpoint of their host governments. I recall a plane trip out of Jakarta, Indonesia, sitting across the aisle from a young American Pentecostal missionary. He had just been evicted from the country with his wife and children for aggressive proselytization, although his mainline Protestant counterparts had been allowed to stay. Of course, Indonesia is by no means alone in implementing stern measures against outside missionaries and movements who seem to be rocking the local religious boat. In India, a number of Christians have been killed by Hindu "mobs" who resent their conversion techniques and see any religious switching on the part of "untouchables" as a violation of their cosmic duty to endure the cards reincarnation has dealt them. If the Indian authorities have been said to turn their backs on such violence, in China it is the government itself that has harassed and arrested members of the Falun Gong, a movement that was once a group of elderly exercisers, part of which has been appropriated and given religious significance by a Chinese leader now living in the United States. And by 1997, the Russian government had become so anxious about "outside" religious evangelism, mostly from the United States, that it passed a severe law that greatly hobbled all religions, including the Russian Orthodox Church it was partly meant to protect. Finally, France and Germany have taken similarly firm steps against several "new age" movements. Scientology has only recently begun to gain victories in European courts after years of litigation.

The U.S. Congress responded to the suppression of religious rights around the world by passing the International Religious Freedom Act (IRFA) in 1998.[43] This provided for an Ambassador for International Religious Freedom to work with a new Office of International Religious Freedom in making annual reports concerning countries where religious rights had been abused and where diplomatic intervention or stronger measures from the United States, such as reductions in foreign aid, might be appropriate. The bill was not a high-profile product of the Clinton years, and its final version was less extreme that the Wolf-Specter version initially proposed by a coalition of mostly western congressmen who made a point of their loyalties to the Christian right. But those who followed the legislation were split in assessing it. Proponents presented it as a shining example of the traditional U.S. concern for religious freedom everywhere. But there have been critics too, including France itself, which objected strenuously through diplomatic channels to a message faulting its treatment of several American religious groups.[44]

In fact, skeptics here at home have wondered if, in its day-to-day implementation, the only religious freedom the bill was likely to protect zealously was that of U.S. Christian evangelists and proselytizers abroad—and this at the cost of alienating host nations concerned to walk a blurred line between protecting religious freedom, on the one hand, and protecting their confused citizens from the kind of conversional arm-twisting that gives religion everywhere a bad name. As one observer explained his reservations privately, "Many of those involved in the implementation process do not draw the church-state line where I do. I draw the line between the U.S. promoting 'freedom of religion or belief' which is good, and promoting 'religion,' which is not right."

IRFA reminds us that the U.S. global religious influence may take myriad forms. Strangely, our religious reputation abroad is contradictory. On the one hand, we are often regarded as the most religious of all of the world's complex societies, though this version of "American exceptionalism," as the previous chapter suggests, is more mythical and simplistic than a closer look would sustain.[45] On the other hand, our often equally exaggerated "separation of church and state" has led some to regard us as among the world's most secular nations. Our First Amendment provisions concerning religion—as quoted earlier—have been widely cited, if not always admired. As Bruce Mazlish has suggested, "Into the void left by religion and science . . . has stepped a global concept: human rights."[46]

"Rights talk" is a staple of various treaties and declarations of collective intent over the last half-century. And as the European Union struggled with the issue of religion in developing its own constitution, its final decision not to mention God or Christianity no doubt took our own separationist tradition into account. Virtually every country makes at least a formal nod in the direction of religious free exercise. However, this sometimes applies only to private belief rather than public behavior, or it is honored as much in the breach as in the observance. And if the real brilliance of our First Amendment comes in its first (anti) "Establishment clause," it is telling that this clause has been adopted far less frequently around the globe than the "free exercise clause" that follows it. Even where it has been approximated, approval has not been unanimous. For example, a number of India's Hindu intellectuals blame us for the rise of its Hindutva extremism and violence on the grounds that, having for the most part banned an officially established Hindu government in India's 1950 constitution, Hinduism has been forced to the political sidelines, where it has had to resort to aggressive, even violent, measures to regain its natural position as the country's dominant faith.[47]

At least indirectly, the United States has exported secularization as well as its particular versions of the sacred. Although the Enlightenment is often portrayed as a European development of the eighteenth century, there is no question that America's experiments in democracy and church-state separation added an important dimension to it. There is also no question that beginning with the country's nineteenth-century industrialization, America's economic, scientific, educational, and mass media products have all spanned the globe with secularizing consequences. Earlier I suggested that secularization is an important precondition for globalization, and insofar as this is the case, it may represent the greatest U.S. contribution to the cause. But it comes at a cost. It is arguable that proponents of other world religions now have greater objections to America's secularity than to its Christianity. In addition to the Hindutva movement mentioned previously, this is also true of al-Qaeda and its expressed resentment of the way in which America's various secular exports to the Middle East have muscled aside basic Muslim values and lifestyles through the corruptions of Western capitalism and pop culture. It is true that al-Qaeda is deeply resentful of the support that U.S. foreign policy gives to Jews as opposed to Palestinians in Israel and to the House of Saud plutocracy in Saudi Arabia. But if al-Qaeda had been primarily concerned with attacking American Christianity, it would have selected different targets than the World Trade Center and the Pentagon—though America's separationist secularity coupled with its comparative youth as a nation means that it lacks religious structures on a par with Britain's Westminster Abbey, France's Notre Dame, or Italy's Vatican City.

Clearly, much of our world influence on cultural and religious matters—both positive and negative—is a function of our politics. Perhaps it is too much to trace a line from America's late–eighteenth-century Revolutionary War to India's early–twentieth-century nonviolent struggles against the British Raj, then back to the United States for its nonviolent Civil Rights Movement of the 1960s, which in turn influenced the more violent political-religious movements of Catholic Republicanism in Northern Ireland, the Palestinian *intifada* in Israel, and the terrorism of al-Qaeda. Ironically, any such line would ultimately reverse itself following America's Iraq initiative and our transformation from a victim to a bully according to recent surveys of world opinion.

It is hard to overlook religion's role in the Bush administration's post-9/11 "war to end all terror and evil," its messianic effort to restore freedom to Iraq, and the strong support it has had from American Christian Zionists for allying with the Sharon administration in Israel in order to prepare for Christ's return. Indeed, if one asks who is a real fundamentalist on the current world scene—meaning a doctrinal literalist and aggressive regressor in seeking a return to an earlier interpretation of the world—the answer is more George W. Bush than either of the more visionary men Ayatollah Khomeini or Osama bin Laden. Journalists have reported with varying degrees of credibility that Bush sees himself as God's chosen agent to right the wrongs of the world, although some suspect that his handlers are too astute to allow him to emphasize this publicly and prefer that he use encoded terminology that reaches his evangelical supporters without alienating others.[48]

Just as American politicians may be faulted for not being religious enough, they may also make voters uncomfortable in seeming too religious, as we saw with Jimmy Carter and his born-again confessions of lust in a *Playboy* interview. Ronald Reagan seemed to have it just about right in ending his first nomination acceptance speech with a prayer that he "just couldn't hold back," and professing his religious faith even though he rarely attended church. Many Americans may have voted for Reagan as the political equivalent of attending church on Christmas and Easter. But this may become much less the case with Bush. When religious zeal overtakes religious pluralism in this country, trouble lurks in the political wings. Unilateral coercion serves neither salvation nor globalization well. To the limited degree that Samuel Huntington was right in prophesying a "clash of civilizations," the United States has contributed amply to bringing it about.

Conclusion

As I arrived at the conference that spawned this volume, it occurred to me that somewhere, somehow, other conferences were convening to consider globalization's dialectical opposite: nationalism. In some sense, globalization and nationalism have long competed for scholarly attention even as they have competed for world prominence. To many, they represent the future's optimistic and pessimistic poles. At least this is so in the United States and the West. After all, globalization is largely a process of Westernization, and it is hard for us to imagine why or how non-Westerners might respond negatively—though the events since 9/11 in the Middle East and Iraq provide a hint.

Globalization's relation to peace and violence is by no means nonproblematic and linear. As suggested earlier, it is, if anything, curvilinear. Thus, societies with no overlap are just as unlikely to conflict as societies with total overlap. Problems really arise only with societies in the middle—that is, societies that have sufficient overlap to compete for shared ends while using unshared means or possibly use the same means to pursue different and clashing ends. Though restricting conflict to societies in the middle with only partial overlaps may sound optimistic, it really is not, because this is where the overwhelming majority of societies cluster. In a perverse way, then, some degree of globalization is necessary for conflict, and further attainments of the globalization necessary to inhibit conflict remain all too rare.

My perspective on the U.S. role in globalization may differ at points from this volume's premise. First, insofar as this is a country more eager to globalize than be globalized, this has been the pattern for virtually all societies with hegemonic ambitions and responsibilities. Second, while one might argue that the United States has been more successful than most in getting away with it, any society that has attained a structural power advantage over others is likely to exploit it culturally. But third, with regard to culture overall and religion specifically, I think the U.S. record shows a remarkably balanced set of exchanges and trade-offs over the years, especially where culture and religion are concerned, and this is a balance that is healthy for societies generally. Fourth, as I have demonstrated above, it is often tempting to focus attention on the political administration currently in power—in this case George W. Bush's administration—as somehow representative of the United States overall and over time. But clearly, one must be wary of both reifying and personalizing any society as complex as the United States and any phenomenon as complex as globalization. Finally, I hope it is apparent that I am a convert to and strong proponent of a new global history as a way of breaking out of old boundaries and making multicomparativism a new way of scholarly life.

7 Reverse Flow: European Media in the United States

Roberta E. Pearson and Nicola Simpson Khullar

IN THE 1980S, when the U.S. Congress was debating the pros and cons of foreign ownership of Hollywood studios (Sony had recently purchased Columbia/TriStar), notable film director Milos Forman (*Amadeus*, 1985; *One Flew Over the Cuckoo's Nest*, 1974) pointed out that if a German company acquired Twentieth Century Fox, the war films in its library might be "slightly corrected."[1] The American Film Institute expressed concern about what might happen to "local drama" if scripts were approved based on predicted international appeal, even fearing the challenge of "understated drama and subtle entertainment" from European imports.[2] The Americans' fear of foreigners and their media points to the paradoxical nature of the globalization of media industries: globalization is good when it benefits you and bad when it benefits the other guy. The U.S. government consistently insists on the inclusion of audiovisual media in international free trade agreements, arguing that films, television programs, and so forth should circulate as freely as any other industrial product. European governments consistently insist on the exclusion of audiovisual media, arguing that Hollywood products spread American culture around the globe and that trade restrictions might permit indigenous media to compete. But when European media products benefit from free trade agreements, and especially when they penetrate the lucrative American market, European audiovisual policymakers rejoice.

Sympathetic to the European (and other non-American) perspectives, scholars have ignored this paradox, focusing almost exclusively upon the one-way flow of media from the United States to the rest of the world, a process that has been labeled "cultural imperialism." In contrast to the preponderance of scholarship on transnational media circulation, this chapter discusses what we term "reverse flow." We investigate the importation of European media into the United States from both a historical and a contemporary perspective. European film and television have always flowed, or perhaps more accurately, trickled into the United States. These European imports have appealed primarily to a relatively restricted elite and reinforced the notion of European cultural superiority prevalent in the American republic since its founding. Perhaps for this reason, European films and television numbers have had a disproportionate impact upon the development of American media industries, influential in the rise of the feature film, the auteurist cinema of the 1970s, and the prime-time television serial. The historical importance of European media to the changing American "mediascape" leads us to focus upon European imports rather than upon the now flourishing foreign-language media primarily directed at fairly recent immigrant populations.[3] Our argument begins with a summary of the cultural imperialist argument and its contradictions. Following from this, we justify our concentration upon Europe, upon the screen media (film and television), and upon fiction. Next, we provide a historical summary of the importation of European film and television into the United States. Then, we document the present reverse flow by sketching the European media currently in circulation in the United States. Finally, we outline the current barriers to the importation of European (or indeed any foreign) film and television that now impede reverse flow.

Cultural Imperialism

Lenin claimed that the logic of capitalism led inexorably to imperialism: firms could fuel constant expansion and reap continually larger profits only by exploiting international markets. Media scholar Nicholas Garnham, not unsympathetic to Marxist analysis, describes the logic of media production.

> The particular economic nature of the cultural industries can be explained in terms of the general tendencies of commodity production within the capitalist mode of production. . . . There is a very marked drive towards expanding the market share or the form this takes in the cultural sector, audiences. . . . The drive to audience maximisation leads to the observed tendency towards a high level of concentration, internationalisation and cross-media ownership in the cultural industries.[4]

The tendencies Garnham identifies manifest themselves in the domination of the global mediascape by six transnational media corporations, three of which are American in origin (Time/Warner/AOL, Paramount/Viacom, Disney). True to the imperialist model, these American firms now, in many instances, take the majority of profits from the overseas rather than the domestic market. The speed and immediacy of electronic communication and satellite technology has brought into being Marshall McLuhan's global village, but the village shop stocks an overwhelming preponderance of American media products. The sheer quantity of American cinema and television in global circulation has led some to equate American media firms' expansion with imperialism of a cultural kind: in this model, a presumed one-way flow of media products from the United States to the rest of the world colonizes the minds and hearts of unsuspecting foreigners in hundreds of countries. The term "cultural imperialism" was coined by critics concerned that the diffusion of American taste and values has a detrimental effect upon national and cultural identity.[5] By contrast, the critics believed that indigenous media preserve local identity by reinforcing commitment to regional languages, customs, values, material culture, religion, and all the paraphernalia associated with "culture."

Hollywood cinema constitutes the most prominent manifestation of this supposed cultural imperialism. American movies continue to increase in popularity in foreign markets, with international sales consistently outpacing domestic receipts for Hollywood movies since 1993.[6] The 2004 blockbuster *The Day after Tomorrow* garnered 61 percent of its profits from international distribution, the figure not including subsequent sales of videos and DVDs.[7] American movies accounted for 70 percent of film imports to India (home of the most productive film studios in the world), 72 percent in Australia, and more than 90 percent in several other countries, including Mexico, Brazil, and the Netherlands. U.S. control of the European market increased from 56 percent to 70 percent from 1987 to 1996, and in the face of the flourishing U.K. production industry, 95 percent of British filmgoers were watching American products.[8] The reach of U.S. television programming was just as impressive. From 1958 to 1991, the European market for American television programming increased 9,000 percent, with a value of U.S.$1.3 billion in the European Union alone.[9] Equally disturbing is the fact that the locus of much of this popularity was in markets that had robust domestic production, such as Canada and Japan.[10]

Foreign elites have worried for years about the cultural implications of constant exposure to American media. The threat of Hollywood and the American tastes and values its products supposedly inculcate gave rise to the protectionist schemes many European nations put into effect after World War I to limit exposure to American cinema and encourage domestic production. The debate continues today, most recently in the 1993 controversy over audiovisual products in the last round of negotiations over the General Agreement on Tariffs and Trade. While countries such as France and Britain lobbied for recognition of films and television shows as artifacts of their unique cultures deserving of trade protection, the United States protested that entertainment resources were simply industrial products, no different than the proverbial widget. The agreement eventually ignored the "cultural exemptions" and "specificity" argued for by the European Union, an argument based on implicit assumptions about the relative values of European and American culture. As Hans Mommaas put it:

> The opposition against the deregulation of audio-visual trade became linked to issues of national identity, and national cultural sovereignty, generalized to the level of the opposition between a European and an American cultural space. The disagreement became couched in oppositions such as those between the refined and the vulgar, the cultural and the commercial, the creative and the superficial.[11]

European consumers, however, do not necessarily support elite dismissal of American popular culture. State-protectionist attitudes disguise the fact that many of the world's citizens may not wish to be "protected" from American media. The seeming preference for American media poses a chicken-and-egg dilemma—do people watch Hollywood movies because they truly want to or because American dominance of exhibition and marketing overtakes most alternatives?[12] Do audiences eschew indigenously produced films because they lack Hollywood production values or because they simply are not "good enough"? Greater complications arise when one distinguishes between film and television; national film industries collapse in the face of Hollywood's might, but national television industries continue to thrive. Despite the fact that the United States accounts for "three-quarters of the global trade in television by value,"[13] the great majority of British viewers would still rather watch British television programming.[14] Audiences are generally a complicating factor for the cultural imperialism hypothesis, predicated as it is upon an outdated model of media effects that assumes that exposure equals change in behavior or attitudes. As several researchers have now shown, active audiences derive meanings from Hollywood products that are quite different from those constructed by their domestic audiences or intended by their producers.[15] Critics of the cultural imperialist hypothesis have also pointed out that a model of one-way flow from the United States to the rest of the world fails to account for exchanges of media products among countries and geographic regions other than the United States, such as the Brazilian and Mexican *telenovelas* distributed to the rest of Latin America and elsewhere.[16]

In this chapter we wish to further complicate the cultural imperialism hypothesis by documenting the reverse flow of European media products into the United States.

Why Europe?

The United States may now be the world's sole superpower, enjoying political and cultural hegemony, but it was once a young nation suffering from the cultural cringe common to postcolonial countries. Whether envied, emulated, or despised, Europe has always been America's most significant cultural other, seen as the locus and arbiter of cultural value. Since the founding of the republic, American artists, musicians, and writers, as well as mere consumers of culture, have either embraced or contested European aesthetic mores. As Andrew Ross put it, "'Intellectuals' debate about national culture has been governed, at least until the early [nineteen] sixties, by the influence of European categories of taste and value, saturated with a precapitalist prestige that is 'foreign' but essential nonetheless to the American cultural apparatus."[17] Europe has had both positive and negative connotations. Writers such as Herman Melville and Mark Twain sought to create truly American art forms that reflected the vibrancy of the new world rather than the aristocratic decadence of the old. But for many nineteenth-century intellectuals, Europe represented political, social, and cultural maturity and, for their twentieth-century counterparts, the possibility of liberation from stifling American conformity and convention.[18] During the greater part of the twentieth century, as we discuss below, the positive valuation of European culture in the form of film and television imports had important influences upon the American film and television industries.

By the end of the twentieth century, however, Europe was importing more American screen media than any other part of the world. "Europe is the main destination with 65.5% of all exports in 1999, followed by Asia and the Pacific region with 17.4. Britain, Germany, the Netherlands, France and Japan are the top individual importers."[19] In 2000, the European Audiovisual Observatory reported that Europe's deficit in the balance of audiovisual trade with North America amounted to $8.2 billion, an increase of more than 14 percent from

1999. North American revenues in Europe had been steadily increasing and European revenues in North American steadily declining since 1998.[20] In that same year, the observatory's Andre Lang authored a preface to the annual report of the Eurofiction project stating that indicators such as "market shares, global volume of fiction and films imported as well as those diffused through television, monies received by American distributors in the European market" show "that the American [film] industry not only remains economically dominant at a global level but that it continues to expand its market share and its revenue within the European market."[21] The media trade deficit troubles those in European media industries and the state-funded infrastructures that support them. From the domestic perspective, the deficit attests to the constant, and often losing, battle for audiences with American products. From the international perspective, the deficit attests to the failure of most European producers to break into the extremely lucrative American market.

Why Screen Media?

We first envisioned this chapter as mapping the presence of myriad foreign cultural artifacts in the United States (newspapers, magazines, CDs, video games, films, television programs, and even Internet sites) but quickly realized that a team of several researchers would take several years to complete such an ambitious project. Most of the international debate surrounding trade in cultural products has focused on film and television, and we opted for the same approach because the screen media are more likely to circulate beyond their own borders than other media products. Popular music, whose meaning is very dependent on language, rarely converts as readily from culture to culture as audiovisual entertainment. The global hegemony of the English language ensures a ready market for American (and British, of course) pop songs abroad, but reverse flow is largely restricted to the niche market of "world music," a much more recent phenomenon than the importation of foreign films and television programs. Foreign language newspapers and magazines—even print media from English-speaking countries—circulate quite narrowly, available by subscription or for purchase at newsstands in the larger metropolitan centers.[22] In contrast to music and print, film and television offer a visual narrative that can be followed to some extent without linguistic access. Hollywood takes advantage of the film medium's visual appeal by producing blockbuster films replete with action and spectacle to appeal to non–English-speaking global audiences. There is as yet little statistical evidence concerning foreign video game penetration of the U.S. market, and the Internet is not a traditional media product exportable across defined geographical and cultural borders.[23]

Why Fiction?

We concentrate primarily on fiction partly because it is the "most heavily traded genre" in the international media market, responsible in 1996–97 for 37 percent of dramas, 23 percent of feature films, and 6 percent of television movies.[24] But more importantly, European elites and others who buy into the cultural imperialism hypothesis worry most about the ideological effects of fiction rather than documentaries, game shows, or home makeover programs. Fictional narratives embody a society's unique values, mores, and conflicts and have been a means of forging national cultures. The screen media now perform the bardic function once performed by national sagas. Italian media scholar Milly Buonanno speaks of the importance of indigenous television drama to a nation's viewers:

> As a popular story telling system, television fiction is engaged with the narration/representation of the social worlds of everyday life—though never actually working as a mirror-like reflex. . . . The stories that turn out to be more capable of attracting the viewers and keeping them enthralled are those which focus on and comment on conditions, situations, relationships and moods . . . that are part of our experience, expectations or imagination, and in which therefore we recognise ourselves and the world in which we live.[25]

Buonanno speaks as a long-term member of the Eurofiction research team, a project sponsored by the European Audiovisual Observatory to track the presence or absence of European television drama over the years. The observatory claims that both television drama and the fictional feature film are vitally important components of European culture. "Feature film as both a very influential and the most vulnerable of media is a primary preoccupation of European (both national and EU) cultural policies. [Financial support] takes the form of direct subsidies and other public aid measures, granted mainly to film production but also to cinematographic services (film distribution and exhibition)."[26] The threat of American incursion, of course, partially warrants this financial support, as policymakers seek to level the playing field to engender fair competition between domestic and American products. The question that we pose, however, is whether Eurofictions have ever penetrated the American market to such an extent as to affect American audiences.

Historical Overview of European Screen Media in the United States

Just as tracking all foreign media currently circulating in the United States would require several researchers several years, so would writing a complete history of the importation of European media into the United States. Instead, we look at three key moments when the circulation of foreign film and television had important consequences for the American media industries: (1) the pre–World War I transition to the feature film, (2) the post–World War II rise of the art cinema, and (3) the impact of British television programs upon American television. In each of these instances, European media helped to initiate change by setting a standard that American industries and audiences perceived as superior to their own.

The Pre–World War I Transition to the Feature Film

Since the late teens of the last century, audiences have been accustomed to feature films with a standard length of from seventy-five minutes to two hours. Prior to this, however, in the tens and early teens, films ran from ten to fifteen minutes, the projection time of a reel of 1,000 feet of 35-millimeter film. Distribution and exhibition practices, dictated by the two oligopolies that together controlled the industry, favored these so-called one-reelers and militated against the American film industry's producing longer films. The one-reelers were exhibited primarily at the famous nickelodeons, whose limited seating required short programs featuring a variety of subjects in order to ensure rapid audience turnover and a profit. To meet the nickelodeons' needs, the American film studios turned out a regular number of films of standardized length, selling them to distributors at a fixed price of so many cents per foot.

The impetus for the transition to the feature film came from the European, and specifically Italian, films imported into the country. Multireel foreign imports were distributed outside the control of the two oligopolies, with rental prices keyed to both negative costs and box office receipts. Instead of playing the nickelodeons, these features were "roadshowed" as a theatrical attraction, exhibited in legitimate theaters and opera houses. The spectacular Italian costume films' profits and popularity persuaded the American industry to compete with longer films of its own. In 1911, three Italian productions—the five-reel *Dante's Inferno* (1909), the two-reel *Fall of Troy* (1910), and the four-reel *The Crusaders or Jerusalem Delivered* (1911)—treated American audiences to a pictorial splendor seldom seen in domestic productions, with elaborate sets and huge casts enhanced through the use of deep space. Released in the United States in the spring of 1913, the nine-reel *Quo Vadis* (1913), running for more than two hours and exhibited exclusively in legitimate theaters, sparked the craze for the spectacular feature film. Adapted from the best-selling novel by Henryk Sienkiewicz, the film boasted 5,000 extras, a chariot race, and real lions, as well as detailed set design, clever lighting, and deep space. The 1914 *Cabiria* capped the trend, the twelve-reel depiction of the Second Punic War containing such visually stunning scenes as the burning of the Roman fleet and Hannibal's crossing the Alps. Director Giovanni Pastrone enhanced the film's spectacle through extended tracking shots (unusual at this time) that created a sense of depth through movement rather than through set design.

Cultural elites, many of whom still looked with disdain upon moving pictures, responded positively to the historical spectacle being offered in the Italian features. The papers of George C. Kleine, the period's premier importer of foreign films, contain numerous endorsements from social and cultural elites, such as the president of the Chicago Board of Education and the chancellor of the University of Pittsburgh, of the *Quo Vadis*–like films that Kleine brought to the United States.[27] Inspired by the positive response to *Cabiria* and the other Italian imports, D. W. Griffith, who desperately wished to establish the still fledgling American film industry as a respectable middle-class medium, made the three-hour-plus *The Birth of a Nation* (1915), the spectacular success of which guaranteed the death of the one-reeler and the ascendance of the feature film. The European imports contributed to a lasting transformation of the American cinema by demonstrating decisively that the oft-despised movies could appeal to the "right" audiences—those with social and cultural capital.

The Post–World War II Rise of the Art House Cinema

The so-called art house cinema, consisting primarily of foreign imports, emerged in the postwar United States at another moment of transition in the American industry when a variety of factors threatened the studios' oligopolistic control, including (1) the Paramount antitrust decision requiring divestiture of exhibition chains and the end of vertical integration, (2) the move to the suburbs that shrunk audiences for the vital first-run urban theaters, and (3) the increasing popularity of television. As with the rise of the feature film, imported Italian films played a crucial role in the rise of the art house cinema. Roberto Rossellini's 1946 *Roma, Città Aperta* (*Rome, Open City*) told, in semidocumentary style, a story of the Italian resistance. The film's unexpectedly robust performance at the box office led to the importation of one hundred foreign films in 1947, among them Rossellini's *Paisan*, which grossed more than a million dollars and broke all previous records for foreign films in the United States. Cinema owners threatened with closure were now able to exploit a profitable niche in the market by adopting an art film policy. By 1956, there were 200 art house cinemas; by 1966, 500; and by the late 1960s, over 1,000 (although they still constituted a small proportion of overall screens).[28] The majority of foreign films came from Britain, France, and Italy. British films had a better chance of breaking out of the art house circuit into mainstream theaters, but foreign language films had to be phenomenally successful in the art house circuit before getting a wider release.[29]

As had the Italian feature films several decades earlier, the postwar wave of European imports attracted audiences with high social and cultural capital. As a result, they had a much greater impact upon the American film industry than might have been predicted from their relatively small percentage of a box office still dominated by Hollywood movies. Concentrated in the major cities and university towns, the art house cinemas appealed to a high-income and well-educated audience who attended opera, the theater, and the ballet; listened to classical music; and read publications devoted to fine arts and literature.[30] As Douglas Gomery puts it, "In the 1960s . . . it was *de rigueur* in university circles to have seen the latest Fellini or Bergman film and to be able to discuss it intelligently."[31] Art house managers consciously sought to appeal to this audience, exploiting notions of high culture and art and attempting, according to Barbara Wilensky, to "offer patrons a sense of prestige and status by promoting art houses as sites of intellectual, artistic, and high culture leisure."[32] Young viewers, whose first and most important encounters with the cinema occurred in the elite, high-culture venues of the art houses, went on to effect major changes upon the American mediascape, helping to establish both the so-called new Hollywood cinema of the 1960s and 1970s and the discipline of film studies. A new generation of "auteur" directors (Martin Scorsese, Francis Ford Coppola, Robert Altman, and the like), drawing inspiration from the foreign films they had seen in their youth and conceiving of the cinema as art, made films that played with and undercut Hollywood conventions, as had those of their role models, such as Federico Fellini, Vittorio de Sica, and Jean-Luc Godard. Other cineastes, who had also spent much of their youth in the art house cinemas but now occupied the nation's lecture halls, began including film in their classes and eventually founded film studies as a separate and legitimate academic subject.

While the sensibilities of the art cinema became integrated into the American mainstream, the number of art house cinemas began to decline. According to Gomery, by 1980 the number of art houses was down to less than one hundred, all located in the core markets of the large urban centers.[33] Wilensky, however, asserts that the number of screens for specialty films has grown since the 1970s, with even multiplexes setting aside screens for specialized films.[34] What is certain is that the foreign film percentage of the American box office has precipitously declined, and the Italian films that helped to launch the art house movement have all but disappeared from American screens. In the late 1950s and early 1960s, all foreign films accounted for as much as 20 percent of the American box office, including a 3 to 4 percent share for Italian films. From 1993 to 1997, however, Italian films averaged only 0.1 percent of U.S. box office takings. The same general trend toward obscurity has also characterized other foreign films in the United States. Since 1980, domestic American films have consistently earned 95 to 98 percent of the U.S. box office income.[35]

The Impact of British Television Programs upon American Television

In *Something Completely Different: British Television and American Culture*, Jeffrey Miller tracks the importation of British television into the United States from the 1950s to the present day, asserting that British imports have always been "shaped for a specific audience wealthy in educational, cultural, and, eventually, financial capital."[36] For much of this time also, American critics hailed the British product as superior to the American networks' output. The trend began in the mid-fifties with the showing of costume drama children's programs such as *The Adventures of Robin Hood* and *The Adventures of Sir Lancelot*; continued with such innovative shows as *Secret Agent, The Prisoner,* and *The Avengers*, all of which still enjoy American cult status today; and manifested itself most spectacularly in *The Forsyte Saga*.[37] In 1969, Granada Television's twenty-six episode adaptation of John Galsworthy's lengthy Edwardian family epic was sold to the fledgling Public Broadcasting Service, which, Miller argues, the Nixon administration had fostered "in the elitist image of the early BBC"—another instance of European influence.[38] Just as the Italian feature films and the art house cinema had done, *The Forsyte Saga* attracted socially and culturally privileged viewers. According to Miller,

> The members of the "quality" audience of the *Saga* possessed educational and cultural capital that placed them . . . on a social stratum above many of the

show's potential viewers, a fact visible in the location of intertexual messages about the show and about the network—*The New Yorker, Vogue, The New York Times Magazine*, and other publications aimed almost exclusively at an upscale audience.[39]

The Forsyte Saga's high profile *succès d'estime* had consequences for both commercial and public service broadcasting in the United States. Miller argues that the *Saga's* serial nature, together with its story of a dysfunctional rather than an ideal family, served as a model for such commercial successes as *Roots* (1977) and *Dallas* (1978).[40] The program also led directly to the 1971 launching of *Masterpiece Theatre* as PBS's Sunday night showcase for British imports, at first primarily those based on canonical literature. Miller points out that the use of the word "*theatre* (as opposed to the ignoble *television*) with its British spelling in the show's title," together with sponsor Mobil Oil's "rhetoric about the 'cultural excellence' and 'quality' of *Masterpiece Theatre*," implicitly signaled to desired viewers the presumed superiority of British television.[41] *The Forsyte Saga* established PBS's strong reliance on British programming that continues to this day.

At the beginning of the twenty-first century, the United States accounts for a third of all British television exports, and yet these imports have a very particular profile and appeal to very particular sorts of audiences. Jeanette Steemers tells us that British television is perceived by American audiences as a

complementary public service alternative, as a nice purveyor of "high" culture in the form of documentaries, innovative "oddball" comedy, complex thrillers and period drama. This type of programming is "accessible" and attractive to an educated elite endowed with educational, financial and cultural capital. . . . Yet this idea of a complementary, distinctly British "quality" alternative compared to the broader appeal of American entertainment and fiction has tended to restrict acceptance to the margins. It restricts circulation to those outlets that have been influenced by and share a public service ethos with British broadcasting, particularly the BBC. Such outlets are exemplified by the geocultural and institutional proximity of the minority-appeal Public Broadcasting System [sic] (PBS) in America.[42]

Implicit in our investigation of reverse flow is the hope that the notoriously insular and provincial American public might learn something about other countries from their film and television screens. As Steemers shows in her book, America constitutes Britain's most lucrative and dependable overseas market, but as she concluded in a conference presentation, the "average American has no knowledge of British drama."[43] Nonaverage—that is, socially and culturally privileged—Americans may have knowledge of British drama, but the costume dramas and detective series they watch are not likely to impart much knowledge of a contemporary, multicultural, and urban Britain. Our three mini–case studies have shown that imported European media can have significant impact upon American media industries, yet how much impact do they have upon American audiences' views of the world? The imports that we have discussed have all appealed primarily to elites and have all reinforced the notion of European cultural superiority without doing much to illuminate contemporary European realities (with a few honorable exceptions amongst the art house films).

Current Circulation of European Screen Media

We have included our historical case studies partly to compensate for our difficulty in locating contemporary qualitative or quantitative information on American consumption of European media.[44] Those data that are available will not prove encouraging to European policymakers seeking to redress the media trade deficit with the United States. Between 1989 and 1993, 70 percent of nondomestic films shown in American theaters were European, but foreign titles still constitute only a tiny fraction of all films shown.[45] In 2001, European films accounted for 5.7 percent of the U.S. market, with British and British–American co-productions taking 2.8 percent, German productions 0.6 percent, Spanish productions 1.2 percent, French productions 1 percent, and Italian productions 0.1 percent. But the next year, the overall market share of European films declined to 4.4 percent. Total admissions amounted to around 69.2 million, a 19 percent drop in relation to the estimated 85.7 million admissions registered in 2001.[46] Exceptionally and very occasionally, a European film becomes a breakaway hit. In 1999, the Oscar-winning Italian film *La Vita è Bella* (*Life Is Beautiful*) grossed U.S.$57 million, making it one of the biggest foreign moneymakers in U.S. history.[47] In 2000, France's *Le Fabuleux Destin d'Amélie Poulain* also did well, bringing in more than U.S.$33 million in ticket sales. These films, along with other good performers such as *Gosford Park* and *Four Weddings and a Funeral* may attract American audiences precisely by bearing little resemblance to the present-day realities of their countries of origin. But even those rare films that do engage with current social conditions, such as *The Full Monty* (1997) or *Brassed Off* (1996), still compromise their social critiques with feel-good endings.

We know even less about European television's American circulation than about that of European film. Toby Miller estimates that 2 percent of American television is of foreign origin, though Jeanette Steemers estimates that European programming accounts for less than 2 percent of American transmissions.[48] Yet Jonathan Levy speculates that the enlarged, multichannel universe's insatiable need for programming might increase these percentages.

> The expansion in US demand for programming has also created opportunities for foreign producers to sell into the US market, but the cable networks, rather than the broadcast networks, are probably the most likely buyers. . . . [A] strategy that may be . . . successful in the multichannel US marketplace is for foreign producers to concentrate on what they do best and aim for the more narrowly focused cable channels.[49]

Levy's prediction has come true in one respect: the launch of BBC America in 1998. BBC America, the first foreign-owned, English-language cable channel in the United States, is available in 34.5 million homes and offers 24 hours a day of British programs not otherwise seen on American television: gardening and lifestyle makeover shows, factual entertainment, sitcoms, contemporary dramas.[50] BBC America was intended to raise the profile of the BBC with a "younger, urban, upscale audience who were felt to want 'edgier' television than that provided by the US channels"[51] and aimed "to push the boundaries to deliver high quality, highly addictive original programming to viewers who demand more."[52] This demand has not been as high as initially hoped for: the "sophisticated and discerning audience" apparently tunes out most of the programming except the news (watched particularly avidly during the Iraq War). And some demanding viewers never made it to BBC America in the first place because the proliferation of British programs on other channels (PBS, A&E, Bravo, USA Network, Discovery Network, National Geographic, and the History Channel) has diluted the brand identity.[53]

Aside from the British programs scattered around the dial and concentrated in BBC America, which, as always, appeal to relatively elite viewers, there remains little foreign television available to even large cable markets in the United States, as demonstrated by a simple content analysis of the programming bible, *TV Guide*. Comcast is one of the biggest communications service providers in the United States, with 21.5 million subscribers nationwide. Of the approximately 2,100 feature films it offered on basic and extended cable, along with premium service and pay-per-view channels, in the greater Philadelphia area the first week of November 2004, 145 would be classified as "foreign."[54] Of those, approximately one hundred are "European" films, mostly coming from Britain, France, Italy, and Scandinavia, ranging in original release date from 1948 (*The Red Shoes*) to 2003 (*The Triplets of Belleville*). While these statistics coincide with current market share estimates in the United States, they hardly bolster Levy's prediction of a more vibrant marketplace for European film in the American multichannel universe. The fact that many of these films date from ten, twenty, or thirty years ago means that American audiences, even the elite ones likely to watch these films, are being denied representations of contemporary Europe on the small screen as they are on the large.

Barriers to Distribution and Circulation of European Film and Television in the United States

The structural, fiscal, legal, and political strength of the American domestic industry constitutes the greatest barrier to entry to the American media market, as fewer and fewer companies own more and more media properties.[55] Vertically integrated, transnational corporations such as Paramount/Viacom and Disney own major motion picture studios, cable channels, television networks, record labels, and publishers, creating a synergistic environment of self-sufficiency, enabling "control and ownership over all aspects of their business, across different windows, and increasingly on a global scale."[56] The strength of the American transnationals, whose size and synergy gives them advantages across production, distribution, and exhibition, not only enables them to stifle domestic competition and to penetrate foreign markets, it also ensures that very little foreign television or film enters the American market.

Surprisingly, Europe consistently produces more movies each year than the United States (595:460 in 2000) but with such comparatively anemic budgets that their production pales in comparison to that of the Hollywood studios.[57] Media scholars take it as a truism that the huge size of the American domestic market permits studios to invest more heavily in films than foreign competitors with smaller domestic markets, confident that theatrical exhibition will at least recoup negative costs (the price for producing a film up to the point of distribution), if not make a profit. David Waterman's and Krishna P. Jayakar's comparison of the Italian and American movie businesses refines this perspective, showing that the Hollywood studios have maximized their return on investment through pay television and home video, which now earn more significant profit points than theatrical exhibitions, the primary purpose of which is often merely to provide publicity for subsequent release windows. In contrast, Italian (and other European) film industries have relied on exhibition through domestic broadcast television, which is "relatively inefficient in its ability to support theatrical film investment."[58] Waterman and Jayakar conclude that the imbalance in investment in production between the United States and Italy results in the continued growth of the American share of the Italian market and the continued decline of the Italian share of the domestic market.

It would seem that American and Italian audiences alike prefer Hollywood films with glossy production values to the competition, although so many factors overdetermine the exclusion of foreign media from the United States market that any conclusion about American audience preferences remains sheer speculation. Even when European producers do break into the U.S. exhibition market, they often find it impossible to compete with escalating Hollywood marketing campaigns, which create a "product differentiation barrier to entry."[59] Rival studios spend millions of dollars to distinguish their products from other competitive releases, building on advertising slogans such as "from the creative genius of Walt Disney." This accumulation of consumer preferences gives the studios a hypothetical monopoly over consumer awareness.[60] In theory, smaller distributors can challenge the majors, but few have succeeded without an innovative advertising campaign (e.g., *The Blair Witch Project,* 1999). In reality, competitive promotion requires investment that is generally even harder for smaller companies to match than the cost of production. Gramercy Pictures, for example, spent twice as much on marketing *Four Weddings and a Funeral* (1994) in the United States than on the entire production budget.[61] Though the average negative cost for a Hollywood feature film is upwards of U.S.$60 million, the budget for prints and advertising averages nearly U.S.$40 million. The increasing proportion of cost attributed to marketing is striking and is creating what Jack Valenti, former Motion Picture Association of America president, called a "cost tapeworm."[62]

Even if production and publicity budgets magically were increased to match Hollywood's, European producers would still have difficulty finding exhibition outlets for their films. One might think that the nearly geometric rate of multiplication for new movie theater complexes would make more screens available, but even high-profile European movies are mainly restricted to the diminishing art house circuit.[63] Since deregulation and the de facto return of vertical integration, the major United States exhibition chains have developed strong ties to the major studios to whose products they have a first commitment. Most theater managers still consider foreign cinema a risk unless the picture is accompanied by favorable mainstream press and awards. Independent distributors and exhibitors who might be interested in releasing foreign pictures are less willing to take risks in the face of competition from the major exhibition chains and increasing real estate and promotion costs.[64] As we have seen in the case of British television programs, European media fare no better on the small screen than on the large. Deregulation plays a role here too, permitting the powerful American networks to provide the great majority of their own programming. In 1995, the Federal Communications Commission repealed the financial interest and syndication rules ("fin syn") that limited the percentage of its own in-house productions that a network could air, effectively merging the network's production and distribution arms and shutting out any non–network-produced programming.[65] In 2001, CBS acquired 70 percent of its prime-time programming from its in-house production arm; in 2002–03, twenty-six out of ABC's twenty-nine pilots were produced by fellow Disney subsidiary Touchstone Productions. In the 2002 season, twenty-seven of the thirty-two new prime-time programs were produced either by the networks' in-house production companies or by a producing studio also owned by the network's owner.[66]

Other factors not so directly related to the stranglehold of the multinationals upon the U.S. domestic market militate against the importation and circulation of European film and television. Not least among these is language. It is hardly surprising that the most successful European media imports in the United States come from Britain and Ireland, with which Americans share a common language. Translation devices and dubbing can be prohibitively expensive for smaller producers and broadcasters, who are much more likely to rely on programming that requires little work to become acceptable to American audiences. American audiences who shy away from European movies and television generally do so for one reason above all others—they hate subtitles. Though cultural purists prefer subtitling foreign language audiovisual media to dubbing, there are many people who prefer not to process visual images, sound, and text all at the same time. Trying to overcome the language barrier, European filmmakers sometimes pursue the unwise strategy of remaking their movies in Hollywood. Classic examples of this are Luc Besson's *La*

Femme Nikita (1990) with Anne Parillaud, which was remodeled into a Bridget Fonda vehicle called *Point of No Return* (John Badham, 1993), and Dutch director George Sluizer's 1988 thriller *Spoorloos* (*The Vanishing*), which fizzled in its Hollywood version only a few years later (the latter failing despite the retention of the original director). French film provides the fodder for most Hollywood makeovers, including *La Cage aux Folles* (1978; *The Birdcage*, 1996), *Le Retour de Martin Guerre* (1982; *Sommersby*, 1993), *Les Diaboliques* (1955; *Diabolique*, 1996), and *Trois Hommes et un Couffin* (1985; *Three Men and a Baby*, 1987).

The remaking of foreign language films and the television industry's embrace of licensed formats such as *Big Brother* (Endemol Productions, the Netherlands) and *Who Wants to Be a Millionaire?* (Celador Productions, U.K.), together with its adaptations of British programs such as *Queer as Folk* and *The Office*, suggest that media industry insiders believe that the undiluted foreign product has little attraction for the American audience. A report prepared for the European Union on trade and investment barriers facing EU media products suggests that Americans aged 18 to 35, the biggest portion of the ticket-buying public, have little inclination to see foreign films.[67] Jeanette Steemers conducted interviews with American program buyers and reported that they "assume that audiences are intolerant and this colours their decisions."[68] Other cultural barriers include the American–European divergence on matters of sexual morality and technological differences between the two continents, such as DVD encoding and varying standards for HDTV and resolution for television broadcast and recording.[69]

Conclusion

This chapter contributes to debates about media globalization and cultural imperialism by documenting the existence of some degree of reverse flow of foreign media into the United States, although at least in the case of European media, this flow might more accurately be called a trickle and, as barriers to entry strengthen, even a slow drip. We have demonstrated that European media have, since the early twentieth century, appealed primarily to audiences with high social and cultural capital and that even recent innovations such as BBC America continue this tradition. We have hypothesized that European imports' elite appeal has enabled a greater impact upon American media industries than might otherwise be expected, with key foreign films and television programs contributing to the rise of the feature film, the auteurist cinema of the 1970s, and the rise of the prime-time serials such as *Dallas* and *Dynasty*. We have also suggested that the impact upon American media industries may have been greater than that upon American audiences. European media have often reinforced their elite audiences' visions of an old world of Roman monuments and English country houses rather than introducing them to contemporary and contested social realities. The restricted appeal and often backward-looking content of European media imports ensures that, in this case at least, the United States has little to fear from reverse cultural imperialism.

8

Weary Titan, Assertive Hegemon: Military Strategy, Globalization, and U.S. Preponderance

Ian Roxborough

ABOUT A CENTURY AGO, structural changes in the world economy and the rise of other countries to great power status had undermined Britain's position of unchallenged global hegemony. In military terms, this meant the de facto dropping of the two-power standard of naval strength and an acute awareness that the strategic balance between a continental commitment and the defense of empire could no longer be maintained. Neither the army nor the navy could simultaneously defend the empire and intervene in a major European war. The Pax Britannica had eroded. As Joseph Chamberlain said in 1902, "The weary Titan staggers under the too vast orb of his fate." Taking this as the title of his book on British economic and strategic dilemmas at the turn of the century, Aaron Friedberg has noted, "The moment Britain surrendered naval supremacy, its empire was living on borrowed time." [1]

Britain's crisis of imperial decline a century ago coincided with (indeed, was part of) America's emergence as a great power. In 1884, the Naval War College was established. In 1886, Congress authorized the building of the first modern battleships that were to be the foundation of America's rise as a great naval power. The Spanish-American War of 1898 gave America its first colonial possessions. The Great White Fleet set out on its world cruise in 1907.

Part I: Conceptual Framework

The American Paradox

The central paradox addressed in this volume—the apparent resistance of the United States to globalization—is readily apparent in the military sphere. It takes three forms.

First, globalization has produced not a diffusion but a marked concentration—almost a monopoly—of military power in the hands of the United States. In 2003, the United States spent as much on its military as the next twenty-four countries combined, ranked by military expenditure. Many of these are America's allies or friends. If the Royal Navy sought to maintain a two-power standard, the U.S. military now operates on a twenty-four–power standard. Each of America's four military services is more powerful than the armed forces of any other country. Nor is the difference merely quantitative: the United States has the capability to wage war in ways that no other country can match. America alone has the ability to project power across the globe. America leads the world in modern military technology. All of this is unprecedented in modern history.

Second, this preponderance of military means is matched by an assertive grand strategy of seeking to maintain this preponderance indefinitely. There is a sentence in the National Security Strategy of 2002: "We must build and maintain our defenses beyond challenge." By aggressively pursuing a profound transformation in the manner in which it conducts military operations, the United States hopes to deter would-be peer competitors from even attempting to match American strength. This strategy may be described as one of "preclusive preponderance": the maintenance of military preponderance is designed to preclude any possible challenge to American hegemony.

Third, since 2001 the United States has found itself embroiled in a new (and unplanned) global war: a global war against terror. This, as I shall argue, is no metaphor. The architects of American strategy see the war on terror as a real war. It is expected to be a protracted war involving subordinate campaigns.

These three phenomena—military preponderance, a strategy of preclusive preponderance, and the prosecution of a global war—are the military manifestations of our paradox.

There is a way to banish the paradox. Hegemonic powers throughout history have sought to set the rules, not necessarily to abide by them. They have attempted to create the institutions and enforce the rules that govern the global political economy and that regulate relations among states and peoples. This means that they generally act differently from the rest of the world. For example, hegemonic powers typically protect their citizens from the judicial proceedings of other powers. In the current American instance, the objection to the International Criminal Court is that it may result in "frivolous" proceedings against U.S. soldiers or policymakers. The unilateralism in American foreign policy that many observers decry has, at least in part, its roots in America's unique position as rule-setter rather than rule-follower.

Hegemony and Globalization

Let us step back a moment and reflect on the notion of globalization. When we employ the term, we generally have in mind a decentered social process. In this sense, globalization is not the result of the conscious intent of some group of policymakers. It is not the policy of a particular state. Rather, it is a diffuse, many-sided process. Globalization is spread via pop music, McDonald's, Nike, and the Internet. Military strategy, by contrast, is the deliberate policy of definable agents. It is the familiar terrain of international—not global—relations. Or so it may seem.

These diffuse, decentered processes of globalization are, however, shaped by the context of power politics, empire, and hegemony. The two dynamics are not contradictory or paradoxical but complementary sides of a single process. The power projection that undergirds empire and hegemony is a key facilitator of globalization. It does so in large part by establishing the institutional order and regulative framework for transnational interactions. This, in turn, constrains domestic processes in numerous ways, most obviously in countries of the periphery. Hegemonic powers set the rules and establish the parameters under which the decentered social processes can occur.[2]

Globalization, understood as a diffusion of cultural norms and as increased transnational economic integration, does not happen on its own. It takes place within a global system of political and economic norms and regulations, an institutional framework. This institutional framework may be developed to a greater or lesser degree. The global institutional framework is underpinned in large part by the political and military power of one or more dominant powers. What makes these powers globally dominant is their capacity to project military power globally.

The general strategic problems facing hegemonic powers may be grouped into three analytic categories: (1) the need to define and take measures to deal with the principal enemy, usually but not always a peer competitor; (2) the need to establish and maintain a global institutional order; and (3) the suppression of unrest on the periphery of the global system. At any given time there is a frontier or borderland where globalization processes actively impinge on a relatively "backward" zone. The inevitable resistance to the globalization project sometimes requires imperial policing and constabulary operations.

Global hegemons typically must address all three of these strategic problems simultaneously. Many of their strategic dilemmas arise from the difficulties of balancing the three concerns. Moreover, military force must be paid for, and the trade-offs in strategy generally appear first as economic and budgetary issues.

It is frequently the case that each of these three strategic problems requires a different kind of military response and different kinds of military forces. Britain, for example, needed a powerful force of capital ships to guard against a peer competitor and a large fleet of cruisers to patrol the oceans of the world to ensure free trade. She needed far-flung and relatively lightly equipped forces for colonial constabulary duty and a navy to transport, protect, and resupply these troops. She also needed a highly professional, technologically advanced army for possible intervention in European wars and a powerful battle fleet to protect the British Isles and dominate the coastal waters of Europe. Large numbers of small escort vessels (destroyers and corvettes) were required to protect the life-sustaining convoys crossing the Atlantic.

Balancing these different kinds of military requirements, particularly during long periods of peace (and hence of restricted budgets), is difficult. There is never enough money to go around for everything. Pressures to increase military spending as a percentage of gross national product are likely to initiate the self-defeating process, so elegantly described by Paul Kennedy, whereby increased military spending leads to a slowdown in economic growth and, eventually, to the hegemonic power's being displaced by its rivals.[3]

Of course, at times the tasks are complementary. Sea control, for example, contributes to all three strategic tasks. The sea is both a global commons and the great enabler of operations on land. Suppressing resistance on the periphery, fighting other states, and ensuring free trade on the oceans of the world all require a powerful navy.

The Analogy with Britain

This chapter began with an analogy to the British strategic dilemmas during the period of imperial decline. The implications are perhaps worth dwelling on. For much of the modern period, British strategy sought two objectives: intervention in European wars in order to prevent a single great power from dominating the continent; and the pursuit and protection of empire.

Control of the sea was required for power projection both in imperial expansion and defense and in the ability to intervene in continental wars. But sea power had another important effect: by making the oceans safe for naval forces, Britain secured the freedom of the commons. As Bruce Mazlish has said, "Central to the whole story is the sea."[4] By making the oceans safe for commerce, Great Britain provided a collective good. As the leading maritime nation, Britain was in an unrivaled position to take advantage of this and was therefore willing to bear the cost of maintaining peaceful commerce. Others benefited as well. This the Pax Britannica was the central institutional foundation of the great burst of globalization in the second half of the nineteenth century and the first decade of the twentieth.

The Pax Britannica presupposed a distribution of state power, such that Britain could act as an offshore balancer in European politics and a global political economy in which she was preeminent. Structural shifts in global power would eventually undermine these foundations of the global institutional order maintained by Britain. The question for those who seek to understand the future of American hegemony must be whether shifts in global power will do the same for the United States.

America's Enduring Grand Strategy

At the most general level, American grand strategy in the twentieth century has consisted of efforts to promote a liberal world order characterized by democracy, free markets, and adherence to nonaggression. From Woodrow Wilson (at least) through Franklin Roosevelt to the current Bush administration, these have been the stated goals of American strategy. At a minimum, the grand strategic interest of the United States has been defined as the defense and promotion of market democracy against various kinds of tyranny.[5] At a maximum, it has involved efforts to spread the American way of life across the globe.

Today, in its maximalist and most triumphalist formulation, American strategy is seen as the promotion of a new "American century." This, unsurprisingly, is the name of the project to which key figures in the current Bush administration signed on.[6] This vision celebrates Republican virtue, distrusts supranational institutions, and sees a providential role for America in the world. It asserts the

> need to strengthen our ties to democratic allies and to challenge regimes hostile to our interests and values; we need to promote the cause of political and economic freedom abroad; we need to accept responsibility for America's unique role in preserving and extending an international order friendly to our security, our prosperity, and our principles.[7]

The National Security Strategy of 2002 is best known for its emphasis on the need for preemptive strikes. What is less well appreciated is the clear declaration of purpose. The first paragraph reads:

> The great struggles of the twentieth century between liberty and totalitarianism ended with a decisive victory for the forces of freedom. . . . These values of freedom are right and true for every person, in every society—and the duty of protecting these values against their enemies is the common calling of freedom-loving people across the globe and across the ages. . . . We will extend the peace by encouraging free and open societies on every continent.

This is certainly a globalizing mission.

The inevitable tensions between the market and the democracy sides of this equation, and the frequent defense of dictators for strategic reasons, created a perennial debate about the relationship between "ideals" and "interests" as determinants of American strategy. The debate continues today.

The Historical Experience of the United States with the Three Strategic Tasks

The story of the rise of the United States to global predominance has been thoroughly detailed by diplomatic historians. It involved the sudden emergence of the United States as an imperial power in the 1890s; a period of relative quiescence in the period between the two world wars, followed by America's dramatic growth as a military–industrial power in the Second World War; its leadership of the "Free World" during the Cold War; and with the collapse of the Soviet Union, America's new position as sole superpower.

Emergence   As the United States emerged as a global power in the last decades of the nineteenth century, it had necessarily to confront major strategic choices. With regard to the first task of strategy, definition of the principal enemy, the United States faced a relatively benign but confusing and rapidly changing environment. There were no immediate threats to America; at the same time, realignments in global economic and political power were eroding British hegemony and the Pax Britannica, replacing these with a situation of great power rivalry, exacerbated by the rapid rise of new powers—Japan, Germany, and the United States itself. This rivalry was most manifested in the scramble for colonies and the naval arms races at the turn of the century.

To the most fundamental of the three strategic questions facing America as she emerged as a world power, who the principal enemy was, there was no clear answer. American diplomacy in the nineteenth century had aimed at keeping European influence in the Americas to a minimum. European threats were important, and American troops would be sent to the European front in the First World War but only in the face of widespread domestic opposition and German ineptitude.

On the other hand, America's imperial expansion across the Pacific had brought America face to face with another rising imperial power: Japan. When, in the Russo Japanese War of 1904–05, the Japanese showed that they could defeat a major European power and that, moreover, they possessed a capable modern navy, American strategists turned to the Asian threat. Prevailing notions of racial superiority, the desirability of imperialism, and a sense that the closing of the American frontier somehow required further expansion overseas all merged to channel strategic thinking into a concern with Japan. American strategists were thus torn in two directions: they could see emerging threats in both the Atlantic and the Pacific. As an instance of this, we might note that the most common adversaries in the war games played at the Naval War College in this period were Red (the United Kingdom) and Orange (Japan).[8]

In these circumstances, American ability to project power globally as a result of naval expansion was a marker of its great power status. The voyage of the Great White Fleet in 1907–09 was the symbolic assertion of this new ability to project power.

The second strategic task, that of establishing and maintaining a global institutional order, was still, though residually, undertaken by Great Britain. The United States was willing, along with other powers, to support this order with minor military contributions. This was a period in which Britain's global order was eroding and would not be replaced with a more stable institutional order until the United States assumed this responsibility at the beginning of the Cold War.

The third strategic task, that of suppression of resistance in the periphery, had become a new burden to the United States with its acquisition of the Philippines and its effort to maintain order in the Caribbean. The Marine Corps was given the task of waging "small wars," and the Army assumed constabulary duties in the Philippines.

Toward the Second World War   The collapse of international order in the wake of the First World War created two strategic threats to the United States. The most serious of these, Nazi Germany, surfaced relatively later; the lesser threat, that of Japan, had become apparent as early as 1905.

Britain's declining naval power in the Pacific had led to the alliance with Japan in 1902. The Japanese naval victories in the war with Russia in 1904–05 had shown the world that Japan was now a modern power. There was a major shift in strategic balance in the Pacific. With the end of the First World War, there were calls in the United States for a navy "second to none." Gradually, the conflict between the three empires in the Pacific sharpened and, by the end of 1941, America found itself at war with Japan (and with Germany).

The Pacific, however, continued to be only one aspect of America's strategic problem. The growing storm clouds in Europe would eventually bring American troops back to that continent. American strategists were forced to develop "Rainbow" plans that contemplated global war with several adversaries. The focus on Japan, generally favored by the Navy and Marine Corps, had to be balanced with attention to the larger threat posed by Germany. Official policy, constantly subverted by Admiral Ernest King, was one of "Germany first."

American naval thinking from the early years of the twentieth century wrestled with the problems posed by the emergence of Japan as a serious naval power. It centered on the difficulties of projecting and sustaining power across the Pacific. The solution came in the development of methods to seize islands and use them as forward operating bases.

This required the establishment of local air and sea control (for which the new aircraft carriers were central) and amphibious invasion by Marines (and sometimes the Army) using new types of landing craft (Higgins Boats). These forward operating bases could establish airfields and refitting and resupply centers for naval vessels. In this way, American power leapfrogged across the vast expanses of the Pacific until airpower could be brought directly to bear on the Japanese homeland. In the Pacific campaigns to push American forces ever closer to the Japanese homeland, carrier aviation was crucial to the establishment of local sea control.

Underpinning American victory, of course, was the stupendous power of the American economy. Fordist production techniques and the now-mature oil-automobile complex had supplemented the Taylorist steel-railway complex. This huge, underutilized economy turned out vast numbers of tanks, ships, and aircraft. Fordist techniques were also used to produce a mass army of interchangeable parts. This military–industrial complex would remain in place after 1945 as the foundation of American global mastery.

Turning to the second strategic task, that of creating and maintaining a global institutional order, the interwar period saw the working out of the results of the collapse of the Pax Britannica. Whether in the form of the collapse of collective security or in the form of the economic recession of the 1930s and the rise of autarky, global order—and with it globalization—receded. This dismal story is all too familiar.

By the middle of the Second World War, the United States, determined not to repeat the mistakes of the past, had begun serious planning for a new international order in which it was to be the key player.[9] This would involve an assumption of responsibility for creating a global institutional framework and a vastly increased role in suppressing resistance in the periphery.

Cold War   Prior to the division of the world into two antagonistic blocs, American planners, aiming at the prevention of a new global war, had given thought to the need for a new global institutional order. Partly as a result of these understandings and partly as a result of the emergence of the Cold War, a complex, multilayered set of regional and global institutions was created. This set of institutions established complex entanglements and understandings that stimulated a second great wave of globalization. World economic growth in the postwar period was dramatic.

This "globalization" was, of course, confined to part of the globe. America dominated its half of a bipolar system—its institutional order was confined to the "Free World"—and globalization during the Cold War was largely (though by no means entirely) restricted to the noncommunist bloc. In this semi-global world, defining the principal enemy—the USSR—and developing the strategy of containment were relatively straightforward tasks.[10]

The military underpinning of this new institutional order was the American commitment to leadership in the Cold War against the Soviet Union. This involved, in addition to the creation of the North Atlantic Treaty Organization, the establishment of the Department of Defense in 1948, the creation of a global Unified Command Plan, the formation of a vast arc of military bases on the communist periphery, and the development of a huge nuclear arsenal. It required forward-based Army forces in both Europe and Asia, a global warning system to detect Soviet missile attack, and the creation of a bomber force (and later a missile force) that could reach deep into Soviet territory.

As part of its responsibility as leader of the Free World, the United States now assumed the burden of maintaining and defending the system and of suppressing resistance in the periphery. The threats were twofold but were often so intertwined that they were indistinguishable. On the one hand, countries located on the perimeters and weak spots of the Free World had to be pre-

vented from moving into the communist camp. On the other hand, decolonization, Third World nationalism, and the stresses of development generated
the potential for widespread revolutionary movements. At the end of the Second World War, as Gabriel Kolko has argued, the United States confronted
nationalist and revolutionary movements in much of the periphery and found
itself playing a largely counterrevolutionary role.[11] The United States was unable to prevent the Chinese revolution, but it sought, successfully, to turn
back nationalist, reformist, and revolutionary movements in the Philippines,
Greece, Guatemala, and elsewhere. The military costs of this were high. However, American success in its counterinsurgency efforts was mixed. Success
in the Philippines was balanced by failure in Vietnam. In those cases where
counterinsurgency worked, as in Central America in the 1980s, it was often a
bloody and destructive business.

During the Cold War, there was a clear tension between the focus on the
task of confronting the main enemy on the European central front and the conduct of war in the hot zones of contact along the periphery where proxy forces
clashed and where insurgencies and conflicts unrelated to Cold War issues constantly boiled up. On the one hand, vast resources were poured into nuclear deterrence. Yet the hot wars were fought in Korea, Vietnam, and Central America.
In Vietnam in particular, as Andrew Krepinevich has shown, the focus on the
need to fight the Soviets on the North German plain led to a series of debilitat-
ing distortions in American military thinking as to the nature of the war.[12] (By
contrast, later U.S. efforts in Central America were more efficacious.)[13]

The costs, military and otherwise, of maintaining hegemony during the
Cold War were high. At times, they led to concern about American economic
decline and displacement, as in the popularity of Paul Kennedy's *The Rise and
Fall of the Great Powers*, or anxiety about Japanese industrial efficiency. But
in the end, our judgment must be that American grand strategy worked. It
produced the globalization that was behind much of world economic growth
during the Cold War. Though the greater part of the credit should be given
to efforts at institution-building, the determined containment of the Soviet
Union and the efforts to repress popular insurgency in the Third World also
played important parts in the eventual American triumph. Underpinning
it all was a dynamic American economy and an associated global economic
expansion.

Beyond the Cold War   The fourth period of American globalism, the period of unipolar hegemony since 1991, began on a note of strategic uncertainty.

The principal enemy had collapsed, and no new adversary had emerged to take its place. There was a brief moment of euphoria. The collapse of communism raised the prospect that history had come to an end and that a new era of liberal peace and the obsolescence of major war was beginning. All that was required was the continued maintenance, and possible extension, of the Bretton Woods–Marshall Plan–NATO institutional order.

On the other hand, as defense intellectuals insistently pointed out, the world was still "a dangerous place." The Soviet enemy might have disappeared, but this would not guarantee a peaceful and prosperous world. A wide-ranging debate about American strategy and the nature of the new global order began. There was something of a search for enemies as the defense establishment tried to take its bearings in the new situation.

One should bear in mind how rapidly the mood of Washington, D.C., can change on strategic matters. Toward the end of the Cold War there was a general pessimism. Then there was the triumphalism of the end of history—which still continues—followed by a concern about an eventual threat from China. Now an anxious tone has crept into discussions of strategy as the United States faces the combined threat of Islamism and weapons of mass destruction. The world has staggered from the optimism of the Clinton years—globalization will bring about a peaceful world (the Golden Arches theory of peace)—to the apocalyptic anxieties of the George W. Bush presidency. The next section discusses these strategic debates in more detail.

Part II: The Strategic Debates of the 1990s

Defining the Main Enemy

The first question for a strategist always is, Who is the principal enemy? Focusing on a central threat is not always a simple task. There is a tendency to think about this through the optic of the Cold War, when the definition of the central enemy (the USSR) was quite simple. For many global hegemons, and even for many great powers, there are long periods when it is hard to arrive at an institutional consensus about who the central enemy will be.

In such circumstances, there is a tendency to focus on the day-to-day tasks of maintaining stability in the system. Inertia explains, to some considerable extent, the adoption of the two-major-regional-conflict paradigm (later the two-major-theater-war paradigm). In this construct, America's armed forces were sized and organized to be able to fight simultaneous wars against two familiar enemies: Iraq and North Korea.

The strategy of the Clinton administration assumed that there was no central enemy on the near-term horizon. However, those within the strategy community that subscribed to realist notions of international politics believed that, sooner or later, a potential peer competitor or aspiring regional hegemon would challenge American power. Although there were several candidates for this dubious distinction, China came to be seen as the most likely threat of this kind.

Realists argue that a preponderance of power will call forth balancing effects whereby other powers will gang up on the hegemon to reduce relative power disparities. The most likely balancer is China. However, as yet there is little sign that China is seeking either to balance against the United States on her own or that she is attempting to build a coalition to do so. Charles Kupchan and Robert Kagan have each, in rather different ways, argued that Europe may act as a balancer against the United States.[14] Certainly the U.S. invasion of Iraq in 2003 did a great deal to fray relations with many NATO allies. It also had the effect, however, of deeply dividing Europe itself. (The notion that this division fell along "new" and "old" lines seems ludicrous. Certainly, the newly independent states of Eastern Europe were eager to win favor with their new hegemonic protector, but neither Spain nor Britain can easily be described as part of "new" Europe.) John Ikenberry argues that we have not yet seen the balancing or bandwagoning that realist theories of international relations would predict.[15] It is, however, simply too early to tell whether there will be efforts at balancing and whether they will succeed. Much depends on the adroitness of American diplomacy.

Insofar as some in the Clinton administration began to consider the rise of a peer competitor as a serious possibility, its preferred strategy was one of engagement in the hope not only that Chinese behavior would be moderated but that someday China would become a democracy (what was optimistically referred to as enlargement).

The Office of Net Assessment in the Office of the Secretary of Defense has, since the end of the Cold War, advanced three propositions: that the strategic situation is best seen as an interwar period; that a rising peer, probably China, will emerge as the central strategic threat in the future; and that innovation (the Revolution in Military Affairs, or RMA) is urgently needed to deal with this threat. These views spread through an increasing constituency in the late 1990s.

As Paul Bracken has noted, the issues in the Asia-Pacific region are larger than simply the rise of China.[16] The region contains a number of large states, many of which have large military forces and several of which (India, Pakistan, China, Russia, the United States) have nuclear weapons. Others (Japan, North Korea) are in a position to rapidly acquire nuclear weapons. Given the differential economic growth rates in the region, power asymmetries are likely to produce a destabilizing strategic competition. How nuclear deterrence will work when several states of quite different military capacity and different institutional forms have nuclear weapons is unclear. Multiplayer nuclear stability is much harder to achieve than the two-player, mutually-assured-destruction stability finally arrived at between the United States and the Soviet Union. This is a potentially very dangerous situation. Whether alliance formation, treaties, confidence building, and other measures can stabilize the situation is an open question.

The Bush administration came into office determined to deal with this threat of potential military competition by a strategy of preponderance, marking the shift from the containment and engagement of the Clinton administration. Would-be competitors were to be discouraged from even attempting to compete with the United States. They would, in effect, be locked out from competition. This was to be effected by military superiority. During the presidential campaign, Bush promised to make this a reality and leap ahead a generation in the acquisition of new weapons. The long-building pressures toward a radical transformation of the defense establishment were now officially blessed by Secretary of Defense Donald Rumsfeld.

Key to modern American military operations is control of space. Satellites are the physical backbone enabling masses of data of all kinds to be relayed back and forth. Like the sea before it, space is the great enabler of military operations, the basis of power projection and therefore, at least in the eyes of military strategists, a point of great vulnerability for the United States. Space is paradoxically simultaneously a great globalizing agent and now potentially the scene of new global military conflict. The United States wages war through the medium of space; it may not be long before war is waged in space.

The American decision to make the RMA a reality is at least as revolutionary as Britain's decision to build the Dreadnoughts. Like the earlier Dreadnought decision, the RMA has the potential to stimulate a new arms race. American strategists are counting on the fact that the United States has a dramatic lead in this new way of war to deter would-be competitors from attempting to match it. Although this may appear to be a form of arms racing against oneself, it is in fact intended as a form of preclusive deterrence.

The attacks on the World Trade Center and the Pentagon in the fall of 2001 appeared to change this. Suddenly, global terrorism was defined as the main enemy. Concerns about a rising China appeared to be forgotten. Yet the military component of the preclusive strategy remained in place. The efforts at transformation continued without skipping a beat. Moreover, China has not gone away, and sooner or later American strategists will have to turn their attention back to the question of how to deal with a potential peer competitor. After the attacks, it seemed as if the administration had adopted a dual-track strategy with two main enemies: China and global terror. This has been the source of considerable strategic confusion. It is simply very hard for the massive complex bureaucracy of the defense establishment to focus on more than one central enemy at a time.

Creating a Global Institutional Order

Despite modifications, the American institutional order was basically intact when the Soviet Union collapsed in 1991. Most global institutional orders are established in the wake of global wars; the generally unanticipated implosion of the Soviet Union was markedly different in this respect. Despite heady rhetoric, the United States had no blueprint in place for the new world order. Instead, it relied on a continuation of the "Washington Consensus" on the need for liberalization of markets as the recipe for global growth and economic stability. Again, there was to be institutional continuity and perhaps some extension.[17]

President Clinton and the new gurus of globalization reaffirmed the eternal validity of what might be called the liberal peace theory: market democracies open to international trade do not go to war with one another.[18] In part, this was a deliberate choice of strategy; in part, it was driven by inertia. The Clintonian strategy was to hope that continuing engagement and the ubiquitous forces of the market and the Internet would lead other countries to become market democracies. Although there was some effort at promoting democracy in failed states, by and large, the Clintonian approach was a hands-off one. Rogues would be contained, China would be engaged, and it was hoped that the forces of history would do the rest. Managing global economic crises and promoting international trade were the cornerstones of institutional management.

Because the Cold War ended with a whimper rather than a bang, there were few immediate incentives for the U.S. military apparatus to change its shape or orientation. Indeed, the reverse was the case, as the armed services sought to fight off the inevitable downsizing that was part of the peace dividend.

The vast inertia retained Cold War notions concerning the nature of military operations. These were seen as high-intensity, high-tech contests (like the Gulf War of 1991) with adversaries who fought in an approximately similar manner to the United States. Reacting to this, change advocates within the military argued for a major reorientation in military posture: some wanted the U.S. military to be better prepared for constabulary operations and small, dirty wars against low-tech foes, and others were concerned about the need for further technological innovation to deter or defeat an emerging peer competitor. The strategic implications of these distinct postures and their meaning for the global institutional framework were seldom spelled out in detail.

The result was that no radical change was attempted either in American military posture or in the global institutional order. The debates on this issue in the last decade have been poorly articulated in the policy community. In principle, there are three positions. There are the continuists—those like John Ikenberry who seek either a continuation of the existing institutional order or an expansion of the community of market democracies in order to achieve a more global liberal order. The continuists are a large and diverse group. Second, there are the militant optimists who think that America can reorder the world. In this view, the peace settlement that was due at the end of the Cold War remains to be written. The writers of the Project for the New American Century are the best known of the assertive optimists. For these thinkers, the appropriate analogy is with Britain in 1815. The third group comprises congenital pessimists. Some in this camp are realists, and they confidently expect balancing and a return to great power politics to set in. They disagree amongst themselves about where the stimulus for balancing will come from: China, Europe, or elsewhere. Other pessimists point to American diplomatic unilateralism, overextension, and hubris as routes to the deterioration of American hegemony. Some focus on the American economy as the Achilles' heel of the process. Still others see the task of "civilizing" the rest of the world as simply too great: whether in the form of a clash of civilizations or in the form of backlash to American globalization, the resistance to the new American hegemony will simply overwhelm the United States. Pessimists worry that 1903 has already returned and that America is the new "weary titan."

The continuists argue that better diplomacy is required to strengthen existing institutions of global governance. The objection to this position is that if, indeed, the global order has changed in some fundamental way with the end of the Cold War, then there is an *a priori* expectation that radical changes in the institutional order of global governance will be required to meet the new challenges.

This line of reasoning underpins the thinking of the second camp, that of the militant optimists. The incoming Bush administration was determined that the global institutional order would be one that would sustain a new American century. Quite what this would mean had not been clarified before the attacks of September 11, 2001. What seems like foreign policy unilateralism on the part of the Bush administration is better conceptualized as a search for a new global institutional order. This would be one that significantly reduced the role of the United Nations, that legitimized American military intervention around the globe, that transformed the purpose of existing military alliances such as NATO, and that created a second tier of client states that would support American policy. Although they may at first appear to be neglectful of the need for global institution-building, the relative absence of concern for nation-building and the exaggerated reliance on free markets (and American corporations) to deal with postconflict reconstruction are part and parcel of this new institutional order.

The increased foreign policy activism resulting from 9/11 turned out to be favorable to a more muscular version of the democratic peace theory. In strategic terms, this was the key innovation of the war with Iraq. In 2003, the Bush administration made the conscious decision to attempt to spread democracy to the Middle East directly.

The global war on terrorism thereby became assimilated to the tasks of global institutionalism via the invasion of Iraq in 2003. One of the several justifications for that war, the one presented most coherently by Deputy Secretary of Defense Paul Wolfowitz, was a version of the liberal peace theory. At least for the Middle East, there was a strategy of massive institutional reordering. The administration appeared to have bought into a democratic domino theory.

Liberal internationalists (the continuists) are dismayed when they see no equivalent of the Marshall Plan, of global Keynesianism, or of a global strategy for economic growth. The market ideology espoused by many on the right seriously downplays any attention to the need for an institutional order. The same is true for the rhetoric of "totalitarianism" and "liberation" that some policymakers have recently adopted. But behind the rhetoric of free markets, there is an effort to reshape the global economy along lines that favor the United States. This is institution-building; it is just that liberal internationalists do not like the institutions that are being built.

Pessimists argue that the Bush administration's plans for recasting the global institutional order are inappropriate or inadequate and bound to fail. There is considerable substance to liberal concerns about the current "unilateralism" and disparagement of existing institutions by the Bush administration. The neoconservative ideology of free markets and liberty obfuscates any serious analysis of global institutions. Indeed, the hostility toward the UN is the most manifest symptom. The grand strategy to deal with terrorism, akin to the grand strategy of the Cold War with the Marshall Plan, economic growth, and so forth, has yet to emerge. There is no serious effort to deal with the social basis of radical Islamic hostility to the United States. There is no program, for example, to finance secular alternatives to the *madrassas*.

Controlling the Periphery

The end of the Cold War greatly relieved America's strategic burdens with respect to the principal enemy but extended American commitments laterally as new zones came under American hegemony. This was manifested in the sudden rash of peace operations and humanitarian interventions that marked the 1990s. Despite considerable inertia on the part of the defense establishment, there was a gradual reorientation of military forces toward an expeditionary posture. The absence of a peer competitor enabled the United States to shift forces to dealing with the other two strategic tasks. This was summarized in notions of the United States as global policeman. Spokesmen for the Clinton administration were more likely to describe American posture as that of a "reluctant sheriff."[19]

The practical question is how the periphery is to be policed. What sorts of forces will conduct peace operations in the littorals and the border zones? Globalization has not put an end to the bloody and intractable wars fought, often with relatively low-tech weapons, in the periphery. Indeed, globalization, through the diffusion of small arms and through its destabilizing impact on certain kinds of states, may well have exacerbated the problem. A truly global optic, rather than an America-centered discussion of globalization (as intended in this volume), might well focus on such conflicts rather than the high-tech wizardry of the U.S. military. Suffice it to say that the questions of whether or not to intervene in such conflicts, and how to provide the necessary manpower, are central strategic problems for the United States. There is no reason to assume that this strategic demand will lessen in the future.

In the past, colonial wars could be a serious drain on manpower. Efforts were often made to supplement troops sent out from the center by local levies. These could be more or less satisfactory but could never be taken for granted. Today, the analogical equivalent for the United States is the process of cajoling other nations to provide peacekeeping troops. This was done more or less successfully during the Clinton presidency. However, the poor diplomacy of the American invasion of Iraq has seriously compromised the system that had evolved since the end of the Cold War. It has led administration officials to begin a search for new mechanisms to deal with the need for constabulary forces.

American Power Projection Capabilities Today

At the dawn of the twenty-first century, the United States stands practically alone in its ability to project power globally.[20] These power-projection capabilities serve all three strategic purposes. The ability to conduct global precision strikes together with national missile defense is intended to deter would-be peer competitors from even attempting to match American military capabilities. Power projection is also central in a way that previous imperial powers such as Great Britain would appreciate: it enables the swift suppression of trouble on the periphery, and it rapidly stifles threats to the smooth functioning of the global system. American power projection also reassures allies and can act as a regional stabilizer. This is an increasingly problematic issue in East Asia. The structural shifts in both economy and military capabilities in the region make it potentially quite unstable.

American power projection has meant increasing reliance on long-range precision strike, on the development of an expeditionary orientation, and on the development of new forward bases.

The long-range precision strike complex has been developing over the decades. It now consists of ballistic and cruise missiles; bombers based in the continental United States, Guam, and elsewhere; and naval striking power. Like all forms of American military power, long-range precision strike depends heavily on space satellites for its operation. This area of military capabilities is constantly evolving but presents few conceptual or strategic challenges.

The situation is quite different with regard to the newly adopted expeditionary orientation of America's armed forces. Reliance on forward basing during the Cold War meant that ground forces would be in place when a conflict started. They could then be reinforced over a matter of months through sealift. The reliance on forward basing also meant that the United States could field large numbers of fighter aircraft with relatively short ranges. This was true for naval aviation as well as for ground-based fighters. The shift to an expeditionary orientation involved pulling back many U.S. forces to home bases in the United States. It also implied that the United States could no longer count on the availability of permanent, well-established bases in distant theaters from which it could mount operations. Instead, U.S. forces would have to mobilize and deploy rapidly to the theater and possibly effect a forced entry in a hostile environment.

In response to these changed strategic circumstances, the Air Force has created a number of expeditionary wings. There is now a heavy reliance on air refueling. At the same time, the Air Force now relies more on long-range bombers based in the United States. The Army has begun to move away from its reliance on heavy armor and artillery by fielding the Stryker Brigades. The Marines have accentuated their already-existing amphibious capabilities, and the Navy is currently considering how best to organize for support of land operations.

Though there have been considerable changes with regard to expeditionary operations, the U.S. military continues, however, to face certain limitations and does not yet posses anything like the kind of rapid global reach that some strategists seek.

Its fleets of transport aircraft and refueling tankers are barely adequate. The Army still moves its equipment by sea, and fast sealift capabilities are in short supply. Moreover, sealift depends on adequate port facilities in the staging area, something that can act as a serious constraint on operations. The Army and the Air Force compete for limited logistical assets as they deploy overseas.

In terms of power projection, the United States can normally expect only one-third of its carriers to be on station at any given time. With but a dozen carriers, this means that only four areas of the globe can be regularly patrolled by a carrier battle group. There is, of course, considerable surge capacity in the carrier fleet, but even this is limited by the vast distances that must be transited and by the relatively limited staying power of carriers in the theater of operations.

Moreover, there are serious doubts about the viability of American power projection either in a contested environment or in a protracted war. American military strategists worry about a series of relatively low-tech antiaccess and area-denial measures that an adversary could deploy. These measures—for example, naval mines—could slow down American forces and raise casualties to a perhaps unacceptable level.

The vulnerability of American space assets is a matter of great concern. Finally, there is the question of sanctuaries in an age where adversaries may also be able to strike anywhere in the globe. One source of the recent interest in national missile defense is the notion that a limited form of missile defense is required to prevent "rogue states" from deterring attack by the United States. Because the number of intercontinental ballistic missiles that such states can field is small, even a limited national missile defense system should be adequate. It should be noted that such a missile defense system, if successful, would also have the effect of negating China's nuclear deterrent and would ease constraints on American military operations in the Asia-Pacific region.

Today, the uses of space have grown enormously. It continues to be an important source of surveillance. Indeed, the surveillance capacity of space has improved steadily, and satellites can now provide all sorts of information about terrestrial activities that were unavailable even a couple of decades ago. Space has become the backbone for global communications. The importance of this for military operations cannot be exaggerated. Space, with the Global Positioning System (GPS), now provides very precise information on terrestrial location. This makes an enormous difference to ground troops, who can now know exactly where they are. Perhaps more importantly, it enables a new kind of precision targeting: GPS-guided munitions (GGM). It is no exaggeration to say that the conduct of military operations by the United States is practically unthinkable in the absence of the space enabler.

Satellites have thus increased the capabilities of all terrestrial forces—on the sea, on land, or in the air—but most notably have increased the capabilities of aircraft. This of course raises concerns about the vulnerability of U.S. space assets and is one driver for the weaponization of space.

At the same time that air and space have become the new enablers, they have also become the new global commons. This, as in the case of sea control, raises possible conflicts between the rights of nonbelligerents and the efforts of belligerent powers to achieve sea control and deny it to the enemy.

Integral to the issue of power projection is basing policy: where should a global hegemon, in this case the United States, establish bases for its ground, air, and naval forces? (Increasingly, it is important to include considerations of command and control complexes in basing policy.) Even with long-range precision strike assets and a (relatively) impressive logistics capability, the United

States still needs to move enormous amounts of equipment to distant theaters as rapidly as possible. Even in the current phase of globalization, the tyranny of distance has not been overcome, merely recast.

In the late nineteenth century, naval power projection required secure coaling stations for battleships. For Alfred Thayer Mahan and other navalists, this was an important motive in the pursuit of empire. Today, power projection requires four things: (1) forward bases and prepositioned stocks of equipment, (2) long-range precision strike from bases in the continental United States, (3) secure access to space (and denial of space access to an adversary), and (4) the ability to deploy (and sustain) carrier battle groups and other naval assets in sufficient quantities in a timely manner.

This raises the question of "Where is forward?" For some years now, the United States has maintained bases and stocks of equipment in the Middle East and on the periphery of the Asian landmass. With the operations in Afghanistan, new bases were created in some of the ex-Soviet, central Asian republics. Current plans are for the United States to develop a series of military bases in Eastern Europe and Central Asia. These are intended to be relatively austere launching pads for military operations in Asia. The strategic implication of these bases is not entirely clear. They can be seen as part of the global war on terrorism, with a focus on the arc of instability running from the Middle East to South Asia. Alternatively, these bases can be seen as the beginning of an encirclement of China.

Part III: The Global War on Terrorism

How Does the Global War on Terrorism Fit into the Picture?

Well before the attacks of September 11, 2001, a number of policymakers and defense intellectuals had drawn attention to the threat posed by the combination of terrorists and weapons of mass destruction. Both Secretary of Defense William Cohen and Secretary of State Madeleine Albright made forceful public statements about this. President Clinton issued a number of presidential decision directives on the topic. And the prestigious Hart–Rudman Commission singled it out as the number one problem for the early twenty-first century.[21]

The official phrase to describe the current conflict is "the global war on terrorism." Time will tell whether this is merely a passing rhetorical flourish that will eventually fade away and be replaced by some other concept. I believe that the global war on terrorism is the contemporary equivalent of the Cold War concept of the "containment of communism." This simple phrase, "containment of communism," served as conceptual shorthand for a well-elaborated set of understandings (and misunderstandings) about the nature of the security environment. The global war on terrorism has come to replace containment as the central organizing concept of American strategy. The global war on terrorism is a real war, not a metaphor or rhetorical hyperbole.

There is, however, considerable ambiguity and implicit debate about the relationship between the global war on terrorism and the three strategic tasks facing the American hegemon. The global war on terrorism seems to be conceptualized along all three dimensions of the security concerns of a global hegemon. In principle, it is defined as "the main threat;" at the same time, it is assimilated to the tasks of maintenance of the system, particularly through the linkage with the invasion of Iraq in 2003 and the effort to create democracy in the Middle East. It is also seen as a new form of colonial warfare.

The global war on terrorism by definition singles out "terrorism" as the main enemy. But it is a peculiar strategic enemy. It is certainly not a peer competitor. This is not merely a rhetorical difficulty. "Terrorism" is a vague and diffuse term. Defining a war against a technique or method is strange. It is using "war" as a metaphor. Wars are conducted against peoples or states, not against methods of fighting.

American thinking is torn between defining the adversary as "terrorism" as such and targeting militant Islam as the central threat. In this second view, the specter currently haunting official Washington is, indeed, jihad. To define Islam (or any other religion) as the adversary is, for the American polity, quite impossible. It is hard even to identify radical Islam or religious fundamentalism as the enemy. This is simply unacceptable in American society.

Hence, spokesmen for the United States government are compelled to assert repeatedly that the global war on terrorism is not a conflict with Islam.[22] It is not a war of religion. However, it is a war against radical Islamism. It is a war against Islamic terrorists. The religious dimension of the conflict will not go away.[23]

The problem is that to ignore the fact that al-Qaeda is a religious movement, to ignore the fact that many Muslims have already defined the conflict as one between Islam and America, is to ignore reality. To argue that the enemy is terrorism, without tackling the question of the religious origins of this terrorism, is to create cognitive disconnects and shortcuts in strategic thinking. These disconnects are so blatant that they cannot be kept suppressed. The tensions keep reappearing.[24]

A further conceptual problem inherent in the global war on terrorism is the difficulty American strategists have in dealing with an adversary of a non-state kind. States generally deal with other states, and it is not surprising that the emphasis in U.S. strategic thinking is on state sponsors of terrorism rather than on the terrorists themselves.[25] Although U.S. military forces have directly targeted terrorists (and continue to do so) and although there are extensive ongoing police and intelligence efforts to apprehend terrorists, the central strategic thrust is to reduce state sponsorship of terrorism. This has led to a concern not only for rogue states but also for weak states and "ungoverned spaces" where terrorists can find sanctuary. This line of reasoning means that the United States must now be concerned about the internal activities of numerous foreign states in all parts of the world. This is the "global" part of the global war on terrorism. It not only involves a vast dispersion of effort but also makes it difficult to identify a clear intellectual focus for strategy.

The global war on terrorism leads, more or less inevitably, into a concern with ungoverned spaces, arcs of instability, the challenge of radical Islam, and so on into a form of global micromanagement. It leads to a diffusion of military effort. The situation is not unlike the British dilemma prior to the two world wars of how to divide their attention between the needs of imperial policing and a continental commitment. Though British strategists had little doubt that the continental balance was the central issue,[26] the force structure and doctrine they developed was largely oriented to the needs of imperial policing. The contemporary United States now faces a similar dilemma, compounded by the uncertainty about whether or not the main enemy is also to be found in the periphery. The irony is that the force structure currently possessed by the United States is—at least in the view of military radicals—inappropriate to the tasks of policing the periphery.

Summary: Military Strategy and the Meaning of Globalization

The expansion of America overseas in the age of Mahan was part of the process whereby the Pax Britannica was undermined by structural changes in the global economy and by the emergence of new powers. The result was a reversal of globalization, understood as the increasing economic integration of the world economy. Instead, there were tendencies toward protectionism and formal colonialism. In the aftermath of the First World War and the collapse of the Wilsonian project for global order, these autarkic tendencies were exacerbated. In the eyes of many American policymakers, this was a principal cause of the renewal of hostilities in 1939 (and earlier in Asia).

It was partly a desire to prevent a return to this situation that inspired American planning for postwar reconstruction in the 1940s. The immediate aftermath of the Second World War saw the creation of the institutional order that would generate a new round of globalization, at least in the Free World. The phase of globalization that was much commented on in the 1990s had its origins not in the Internet but in Bretton Woods. It had been ongoing since 1945. It was sustained by a largely liberal world order. It was underpinned by Fordism, by high mass consumption in the core, and by (uneven and often problematic) economic development in the periphery.

The functioning of the global system was not without its problems. Economic growth of the periphery was startling in some cases but often erratic and subject to crisis. Some parts of the periphery failed to grow or experienced economic decline and political instability. Moreover, the strategic considerations of the Cold War prompted repeated American intervention in contested areas. The tension between the desire to promote markets and the goal of promoting democracy was resolved in favor of the former.

Initially, the collapse of the Soviet Union seemed to signal both a lateral expansion and a deepening of globalization as liberal capitalism triumphed. There was a consensus that a liberal peace was within grasp. Variants of a liberal peace theory were articulated by a wide range of policymakers, and the Clintonian strategy of engagement and enlargement reflected this kind of thinking. It seemed as if the United States could promote both free markets and democratic institutions without contradiction.

By 2003, this picture was considerably more ambiguous. American military strategy, partly in response to the attacks of September 11, 2001, seemed to be driving the dynamics of globalization in unexpected directions. Although the thinking of the Bush administration could also be characterized as informed by a liberal peace theory, it was of a more muscular and assertive kind than that espoused by the Clinton administration.

The core tenet of the current American grand strategy is the attempt to maintain its current military preponderance. The United States will seek to preserve the "unipolar moment" indefinitely. The method will be continual innovation in the art of war together with strenuous efforts to ensure that the international economic regime is as favorable to American enterprise as possible. At the same time, the United States will work to deal with a wide range of threats from rogue states, terrorists, failed states, and the like. What the global war on terrorism variant of American grand strategy does is involve the United States in detailed control of local politics in many parts of the globe.

The task that American strategists have set for themselves is the simultaneous maintenance of military preponderance and detailed local control on a global scale. The current mood in Washington is that if this sounds like empire, then so be it. The question must be whether the United States has the economic resources and the requisite strategic clarity to coherently and consistently pursue all three strategic imperatives simultaneously.

Because of this uncertainty, the shape of the global institutional order that would emerge in the early twenty-first century was unclear, and therefore the nature and content of globalization was unknowable.

Surveying America's strategic situation in 2003, there are similarities and differences with Britain's situation in 1903. Like Britain, the United States has vast global commitments that threaten her ability to cope with structural changes in the distribution of global power. Dealing with resistance on the periphery is likely to undermine America's ability to retain its military lead over state competitors. However, unlike Britain, America faces no serious challenge from peer competitors. Its military preponderance remains unchallenged. In this respect, America's current position is more like that of Britain in 1815. If this part of the analogy holds, then we may well witness another American century.

A Recipe for Failure

Whether or not this will be another American century will depend largely on factors beyond the control of American policymakers. Nevertheless, within the broad constraints of structural shifts in global power, American policymakers can make things better or worse for themselves (and others). This chapter has stressed, inter alia, the importance of inertia in slowing down a wholesale reassessment of America's global strategy. Such a reassessment is urgently required. It is not something that can be easily pulled out of a hat. It is not the property of some currently undiscovered George Kennan. Rethinking America's global strategy, including its strategy for transforming the institutions underpinning globalization, will require serious and sustained collective debate. Unfortunately, institutional complexes that have been successful in the past tend not to change.[27] As Aaron Friedberg notes, "Supremacy is seldom conducive to hard thinking."[28] It is hard, therefore, to be other than pessimistic about American prospects.

Very little has changed in the cluster of global institutions (the Bretton Woods–Marshall Plan–NATO complex) that constitutes the institutional order of globalization. Nor have American political institutions changed radically.

The currently most pressing illustration of the lack of institutional change is the inability of the United States to find enough constabulary troops to adequately deal with peripheral challenges. The poor diplomacy of the Bush administration has weakened alliances and made burden-sharing more problematic. The need for constabulary troops has been met by a series of unsatisfactory ad hoc arrangements. The need for a clear doctrine regarding peace operations, nation-building, postwar reconstruction, and so forth has received only scant attention, and the Army's Peacekeeping Institute (the only military organization dedicated to thinking about the tasks of peace operations) was only just saved from extinction. The inherently political nature of these military operations has hardly been addressed at all. Nor has the proper balance between military and civilian, between U.S. and transnational organizations been addressed. The political education of American officers remains primitive, and with a highly politicized and partisan officer corps,[29] there is every chance of trouble as a result. Civil affairs officers and area specialists and linguists in the military are in woefully short supply.[30] The general neglect of area studies in the university system in the last two decades has not helped. In general, the resort to ad hoc solutions to what are structural problems indicates a clear need for serious thinking and an institutional solution. I doubt whether this will be forthcoming.

Even on the economic aspect of nation-building, the government has resorted to insider deals and last-minute efforts. It has been unable to rise above a short-term faith in markets to think through the long-term institutional issues involved in generating sustainable economic growth and effective governance.

If the United States is to deal with the third strategic task, that of suppressing resistance on the periphery, it will need to develop new institutional structures. It shows no signs of doing so. Focused as ever on a high-tech war, the U.S. military has created a vast mismatch between its ability to overthrow a government and the ability to bring about a desired political end. The current administration has been unwilling to hand power to any allies except the most servile and unconditional, and it has been unable to reform its military machine. War has ceased to be the obedient servant of politics. This is a recipe for failure.

9 Globalization and Empire: The Effects of 9/11 and the Iraq War

James Kurth

THE 1990S WERE CLEARLY the decade of globalization. The period between the fall of the Berlin Wall on November 9, 1989 (11/9), and the fall of the twin towers on September 11, 2001 (9/11), comprised a "long decade" in which globalization, as promoted by the United States, seemed to be rational, desirable, and inevitable. There appeared to be so many winners from globalization—for example, the United States, Europe, East Asia, and even India—that all the losers together—Russia, the Muslim world, Africa, and perhaps Latin America—seemed to be, in the grand or global scheme of things, merely weak or marginalized.

This, of course, was not the first era when the spread of capitalism around the world had seemed to be rational, desirable, and inevitable. Much the same mentality characterized the period of 1896–1914, the two decades of "Belle Époque" before the First World War. This earlier era of globalization was also promoted by the leading world power of the day, in that case the British Empire.[1] But underlying and backing up the supposed economic rationality of Belle Époque globalization was the military force of the British Army and the Royal Navy. When the losers (or dissatisfied winners) of globalization welled up in resentment and rose up in resistance, it was the military forces of the British Empire (and of junior and friendly empires such as the French, the Dutch, and the Belgians) that put them down. Whatever the conceits of that time that economic rationality by itself would spread global capitalism, any serious historian in our own time knows that some kind of empire was a necessary condition for the globalization of a century ago.

Contemporary Globalization and the American Empire

It should not be surprising, then, that near the end of the long decade of contemporary globalization, analysts of world affairs began to think about the need for an American empire. Resentment and resistance to globalization, particularly to its American version, developed in the late 1990s in Russia, the Muslim world, and, after the Asian financial crisis of 1997–98, even in East and Southeast Asia. There were also those "rogue states" that had always rejected American foreign policies root and branch—particularly North Korea, Iran, and Iraq. The spread of resistance to globalization naturally concentrated the minds of U.S. policymakers upon the potential need to employ U.S. military force at a variety of points around the globe.

The Kosovo intervention of 1999 can be interpreted as the first conflict of the new global period. The Clinton administration went against one of the lesser (and least threatening to Americans) rogue states—the Serbia of Slobodan Milošević. Its objectives were not only to end the human rights abuses in Kosovo but to expand NATO's responsibilities "out of area" in the direction of the Middle East and to establish a precedent for quick and effective military operations there.[2] The methods used (extended use of precision bombing, no use of U.S. ground forces, and not a single combat fatality) were seen as a demonstration of what the United States could do to other rogue states and more serious adversaries if it chose to do so, particularly Iraq, Syria, and Iran. The U.S. victory in the Kosovo War consequently made it much more likely that the United States would soon seek a similar victory over the most troublesome of these rogue states, the Iraq of Saddam Hussein.

We now know that most of the people that the George W. Bush administration would appoint to high positions in the Department of Defense had already by 2000 set their sights upon the regime of Saddam Hussein and were determined to go to war with Iraq at the first convenient opportunity. (Of course, they said virtually nothing about their project during the 2000 presidential election campaign itself.) Indeed, given the growing focus upon the Saddam Hussein regime even within the Democratic Party by 2000, it seems wholly plausible that an Al Gore administration might have also sought to go to war against Iraq at a convenient opportunity. However, given the practice of the Clinton administration, it probably would have done so only after it had received the approval of either the United Nations or NATO.

In any event, three developments of the 1990s—the pervasive spread of globalization, the growing resistance to it, and the growing awareness of the potential need to use military force—logically culminated and combined by early 2001 into the idea that the time had come for some new kind of American ordering of the globe. Writers on world affairs began to apply a new term (actually an extremely old term) to America's role in the world: empire. A stream of books and articles announced the coming of the American empire.[3]

The Coming of the American Empire

This American empire was the logical culmination of America's supreme position on four dimensions of world affairs.[4] In addition to being (1) the largest and most advanced economy within the global economy and the driving force promoting globalization, the United States was also (2) the sole superpower and even a hyperpower, (3) the only high-tech military power and the leader in the "revolution in military affairs," and (4) the exemplar of "soft power" and the disseminator of popular culture throughout the globe.

America's rise to its supreme position on each of these four dimensions was already underway in the 1980s, but at that time its ascendancy was obscured by the formidable military challenge from the Soviet Union and by the formidable economic challenge from Japan. The collapse of the Soviet Union in 1991 and the stagnation of the Japanese economy since 1991, combined with the military and economic ascent of the United States in the 1990s, made the supreme position of the United States clear to all, and this supreme position became the most central and important reality of international politics. Indeed, it contributed greatly to a reinvention of international politics into global politics.

With the coming of the 2000s—and the coming of a new century and a new millennium—it seemed that we were witnessing the coming of a new empire as well. Of course, this empire was not the first global empire; the Spanish Empire of the sixteenth to eighteenth centuries and the British Empire of the nineteenth to twentieth centuries also had been empires with a global scope. However, the Spanish and British empires had always had to contend with challenges from other extensive empires or great powers. In contrast, the United States was now not only the sole superpower or hyperpower, it was the sole empire. For something approximating a sole empire, one had to go back to the Roman Empire, but that empire was not on a global scale.

In short, the United States was something that had never before existed in history: a sole empire that was global in scope and, indeed, that sought to reinvent the nations of the globe in its image. For, in the minds of the American political and economic elites, the American ideas are universal ideas. They are, in the words of the Declaration of Independence, the "self-evident truths" of the rights to "life, liberty, and the pursuit of happiness," or as worded in a 2002 reformulation by Michael Mandelbaum, they are "peace, democracy, and free markets," which are "the ideas which conquered the world."[5]

The American Empire as the Cause of Islamic Terrorism

At the very time of its proclamation, however, the American empire was suddenly shocked by an unprecedented threat to the very heart of America itself, manifested in the terrorist attacks on the World Trade Center and the Pentagon on September 11, 2001, and the fear ever since of new terrorist attacks upon the United States. The specter of Islamic terrorism was haunting the American empire.

The simultaneous occurrence of the coming of the global American empire and the coming of the global Islamic terrorist threat was not just an awful, indeed terrible, coincidence or irony, however. It appeared that there was a dialectical or symbiotic causal connection between the imperial and the terrorist trajectories. But in which direction did the causal connection go?

Immediately after the attacks of September 11, a great question went up: "Why do they hate us?" One of the answers, principally given by the anti-globalization movement, was that they (particularly Muslims) hate us (particularly Americans) because of the overwhelming American power that is intruding into their societies, that is, because of the oppressive expansion of globalization and of the American empire that imposes it. Although oversimplified, this is one useful notion of the causal connection between the American empire and Islamic terrorism.

The advocates of globalization often describe it as a process: steadily progressing over time, pervasively spreading over space, and clearly inevitable in its development. In this conception, the economics of globalization are all-important, and the politics of globalization are practically nonexistent. But globalization can also be seen as a revolution, one of the most profound revolutions the world has ever known. (It is certainly more of a *world* revolution than communism ever was.)

Like all revolutions, the globalization revolution has produced both winners and losers. The winners from globalization are the business, professional, and even working classes that are competitive in the global market. These winners are largely found in the United States, Europe, and Northeast Asia, where they comprise the dominant groups within the population. By 2001, these beneficiaries of globalization were led by the United States and were organized into the American empire. Similar classes that benefit from globalization are found in China and India, where they constitute a rapidly growing part of the population. In other regions of the globe, however—Russia, the Muslim world, Latin America, and Africa—the winners in the globalization revolution probably compose only a small elite, one that is deeply resented by the rest of the population.

Revolutions normally produce reactions, however. At first, the losers from the revolution have no theory or ideology with which to comprehend and critique the revolution, and relatedly they have no leaders or organizations with which to combat it. They are capable only of resentment. But if an ideology, leaders, and organizations should emerge, the losers can move to resistance. And if these elements should come together into a comprehensive movement, the losers become capable of a full-scale reaction to the revolution.

During the 1990s, there was no longer any obvious ideology available to the losers from globalization because the once-robust contender, Marxism, was now largely discredited and abandoned. There were also no obvious leaders of the losers. The national states that had resisted global capitalism in the past were now either too weak to do so (Russia and the rogue states) or were now winners themselves (China and India). And, given the absence of ideology and leadership, there was also no organization of the losers.

The Muslim world was the region that had one of the highest proportions of losers within its population, but it also was the region that was symbiotically interconnected with the winners in the greatest number of important ways (e.g., the global oil market, American military bases in the region, American support of Israel against the Palestinians, Muslim immigrants in Europe). It was natural, therefore, that it was the Muslim world that developed the most pronounced grievances against globalization and against the United States.

Consequently, it was the Muslim world that provided an antiglobalization ideology—Islamism—that could fill the void left by the discrediting of the prior antiglobalization ideology, Marxism.[6] Islamism is not the same as Islam; it is more ideological and less theological. Like the secular ideologies developed within the modern West, Islamism is explicitly methodical and political, not customary and spiritual. But Islamism is also not the same as Marxism; it is more communal and less universal. Like Islam, it can appeal only to Muslims around the globe, not to the workers of the world. In any event, for the Muslim losers from globalization—and for the dissatisfied Muslim winners who claim to represent these losers—Islamism is the ideology that fits, the system of ideas whose time has come, the hope for the wretched of the Earth of our own time. As they say, and say with conviction, "Islam is the answer."

Thus, by 2001, the ideological element for resistance to globalization and the United States by the Muslim world was widespread and well developed. It could be observed by anyone who had eyes to see.[7] The leadership and organization for the resistance were less evident, however; instead of these elements, there still appeared to be only a void. Of course, with the terrorist attacks of 9/11, this void suddenly seemed to be filled by Osama bin Laden and al-Qaeda, and more generally by transnational networks of Islamic terrorists with global reach.

Islamic Terrorism as the Cause of the American Empire

The Bush administration therefore formulated a different notion—indeed a reverse notion—of the causal connection between the coming of the American empire and the coming of Islamic terrorism. One year after the attacks, on September 17, 2002, the administration presented its new *National Security Strategy of the United States of America*.[8] This important document declared that the United States and the world confronted a new and unprecedented reality: the simultaneous existence of both terrorist networks with global reach and rogue states with weapons of mass destruction (WMD). This meant that very soon these terrorists might acquire these weapons from these states and then use them against the United States and its allies, with destruction that would be truly massive and terrible. Obviously, such a disaster had to be prevented; also obviously, according to this document, this unprecedented threat had to be met with unprecedented methods.

The Strategy of Unilateral Preemption

The unprecedented method announced by the Bush administration for the new global era—the era of both global American power and global Islamic terrorism—was preemptive military attacks (or more accurately, preventive war) by the United States upon any emerging threat that terrorist groups might receive weapons of mass destruction from rogue states. If possible, a U.S. preemptive attack would be undertaken in a multilateral way, in the sense that other nations (e.g., the United Nations or the NATO allies) would approve it;

if necessary, however, the U.S. action would be unilateral—that is, the United States would go it alone.[9]

The new U.S. strategy of preemption and unilateralism was supposed to govern the global era; it would replace the old U.S. strategy of containment and deterrence, which governed the Cold War era but which seemed to be incapable of dealing with terrorist groups. The "Bush doctrine" of 2002 was comparable in importance, therefore, to the Truman Doctrine of 1947.

Iraq as the Central Rogue State in the New American Strategy

At the time of the announcement of the new National Security Strategy, the rogue states that seemed to be developing WMD were Iraq, Iran, and North Korea. But it was also plausible that Islamic terrorist groups might receive WMD, including nuclear weapons from rogue elements within the military of America's putative ally, Pakistan. The new strategy of unilateral preemption might reasonably have been applied to any one of these rogue threats.

However, the Bush administration focused upon the threat from Iraq.[10] This suggested, even in 2002, that the true origin of the new strategy of unilateral preemption was not 9/11 and the threat that rogue states might provide WMD to terrorist groups. Something else was needed to fully explain the focus upon Iraq. Of course, when the U.S. military invaded and occupied that country in 2003, it was discovered that Iraq actually had no WMD at all. Conversely, during 2003–2004, it became clear that North Korea and Iran were far along in developing nuclear weapons and that Pakistan's rogue elements had already sold nuclear technology through the global underground economy.

Iraq as the Model Dominion in the New American Empire

The Bush administration wanted to do more to rogue states than to just disarm their weapons of mass destruction with a preemptive military attack. It also intended to implement "regime change," that is, to overthrow the existing government and to replace it with one that would become an American ally. It also intended to dismantle the existing political and economic system and to replace it with one that would be characterized by liberal democracy, free markets, and an open society. In short, the Bush administration envisioned that a preemptive military attack would initiate a process that would culminate in a new extension of "the ideas that conquered the world." It would also be a new extension of the American empire. The state targeted to become the first new dominion of the empire was Iraq.

In the minds of those involved in the antiglobalization movement, and in the rhetoric and perhaps the minds of Islamic terrorists themselves, the growth of the American empire had been the cause for the growth of Islamic terrorism. But in the minds of the American political and economic elites, and in the rhetoric and perhaps the minds of officials of the Bush administration, the growth of Islamic terrorism had become the cause for the growth of the American empire. As it happened, both causal theories were in some sense correct. There was a dialectical and symbiotic connection, even an escalating and vicious cycle, between the two global forces, and the world is now witnessing a titanic and explosive struggle between them.

Four Perspectives on American Foreign Policy

The coming of the American empire was not just an inevitable and automatic consequence of America's supremacy on the four dimensions of economic globalization, relative power, military strength, and cultural diffusion. As with much of American foreign policy, the global imperial project was the outcome of a domestic political struggle. In particular, it was a product of changes in the relative power of four different groups within the United States, each with its own distinct perspective on America's role in the world and particularly in the establishment of an American empire on a global scale. We can identify these groups as (1) traditional liberals, (2) traditional conservatives, (3) neoliberals, and (4) neoconservatives.

These four contemporary groups have some similarities and continuities with what Walter Russell Mead has called the four historical traditions of American foreign policy.[11] Mead names each tradition after a particular American historical figure, resulting in (1) the Jeffersonian, (2) the Jacksonian, (3) the Wilsonian, and (4) the Hamiltonian traditions. But the contemporary groups differ from the historical traditions in some important ways, particularly because of the new conditions and perspectives created by globalization.

The National Perspectives: Traditional Liberals and Traditional Conservatives

For much of the twentieth century, American politics was dominated by the agenda of the traditional liberals. The central concern of this group has been the American domestic economy, enhanced by domestic social reform. Consequently, the central purpose of American foreign policy should be to protect and promote this domestic economy; it is certainly not to engage in foreign interventions and undertakings that would disrupt economic prosperity and social progress. Among the more recent presidencies, the traditional liberal perspective was best represented by the Carter administration. And among the four historical approaches identified by Mead, the traditional liberal perspective has been virtually the same as the Jeffersonian tradition.

The central concern of traditional conservatives has been American national security, enhanced by national unity. Consequently, the central purpose of American foreign policy should be to protect and promote this security; it is certainly not to engage in foreign interventions and undertakings that are remote from American vital interests and that would drain America's strength or multiply its foreign enemies (which, in the view of some traditional conservatives, was a consequence of the Vietnam War). Among the more recent presidencies, the traditional conservative perspective was probably best represented by the administration of George H. W. Bush, although his idea of a "new world order" was remote from traditional conservative concerns. And among the four historical approaches of Mead, the traditional conservative perspective has been similar to the Jacksonian tradition in regard to its objectives, that is, the security of the American people, although perhaps it has been more like the Hamiltonian tradition in regard to its means, a regard for the discerning and prudent ("realistic") use of force.

Whatever their differences on a variety of liberal-conservative dimensions, the two traditional groups share a *national* perspective: they view the United States as a national state within a world of national states that engage in the conduct of *international* relations. American foreign policy toward these other national states should be governed by the principle of the national interest, which is the protection and promotion of the interests of Americans.

The Global Perspectives: Neoliberals and Neoconservatives

Conversely, the two "neo" groups share a *global* perspective: they view the United States as a unique power within a global arena. This arena is filled with many different kinds of actors, but all of them have much less power and influence than the United States.

The central concern of the neoliberals has been the American role in the global economy and in global society. They want the United States, with its great and unique power and influence, to be the leader in the grand project of globalization, which is the progressive elimination of borders and the liberalization of societies. The great goal is to establish a global order characterized by liberal democracies, free markets, and the "democratic peace."[12] Among the more recent presidencies, the neoliberal perspective was best represented by the Clinton administration, and among Mead's four historical approaches, it has been very similar to the Wilsonian tradition.

The central concern of the neoconservatives has been the American role in global security. They want the United States, with its great and unique power and influence, to be the leader in a grand project to eliminate military or terrorist threats to the security of America and its allies. These allies include one that finds itself in one of the least secure environments on the globe—Israel. This grand project entails the progressive reduction or elimination of such threats as rogue states, terrorist organizations, and above all, those with potential access to weapons of mass destruction. Among the more recent presidencies, the neoconservative perspective was present to a degree in the first Reagan administration, particularly in regard to its tough military policy directed at the Soviet Union and in regard to the "Reagan Doctrine," which promoted anticommunist guerrilla movements against Marxist regimes. However, it was under George W. Bush that the neoconservative perspective reached its greatest strength. This was particularly so in regard to the administration's foreign policy toward the Middle East, including its support of Israel and its war against Iraq, and in regard to the "Bush doctrine." As we have seen, this new doctrine advocated preemptive military action by the United States against states that pose a threat because of their weapons of mass destruction; if necessary, such action can be taken unilaterally. Among Mead's four historical approaches, the neoconservative perspective has been similar to the Hamiltonian tradition in regard to objectives—defining American security interests in expansive, even global terms—but similar to the Jacksonian tradition in regard to means—the intensive and decisive use of force.

From National Perspectives to Global Perspectives

When the largest American business enterprises looked mostly to the American or national market, there was a strong economic and political base for the traditional (i.e., national) conservative perspective. Similarly, when the largest American organizations that promoted social reform were industrial labor unions, there was a strong economic and political base for the traditional (i.e., national) liberal perspective. These two solid bases for national perspectives existed in America for much of the twentieth century.

Beginning in the 1960s, however, there came the great leap outward of American business, the transformation of national corporations first into multinational ones and then into global ones. Also beginning in the 1960s, there came the great upward advancement of American business, the transformation of an industrial economy first into a postindustrial one and then into an information one.[13] Both of these great transformations, from a national to a global economy and from an industrial to an information economy, greatly enlarged the scope of the perspective of business enterprises. They also greatly undermined the industrial labor unions and brought about a sharp decline in their membership and political strength. By the late 1980s, the economic and political bases for traditional or national perspectives had largely collapsed. Then, when the Soviet Union—that giant monument to statist and protectionist industry—also collapsed and the Cold War came to an end, the American multinational corporations and postindustrial enterprises had not just the Free World, but the whole world—the great globe itself—as their arena of operations. This quickly gave rise to the rhetoric of the new world order and to the reality of the grand project of globalization. The now-global corporations and information enterprises quickly became the strong and solid economic and political base for the neoliberal perspective. They were joined by many new nongovernmental organizations (NGOs) and Internet groups, which promoted universal human rights and which operated on a global scale. These all came together to form a grand coalition in the Clinton administration and largely shaped its foreign policies.[14]

Finally, in the George W. Bush administration, the neoconservatives and a good part of the neoliberals came together to form an even grander coalition. The neoconservative perspective was well represented by top civilian officials in the Defense Department, for example, Deputy Secretary of Defense Paul Wolfowitz, Undersecretary of Defense for Policy Douglas Feith, and at least a dozen of their immediate subordinates.[15] (In contrast, however, the top military officers largely continued to hold a traditional-conservative perspective.) In regard to the Middle East, the neoconservatives had a special interest in the security of Israel. Because Israel considered Iraq, Syria, and Iran to be the major threats to its security, the neoconservatives did also, and this led them to advocate "regime change" for these "rogue states." Moreover, because of its peculiar and vulnerable military position in the Middle East geography, Israel since 1948 had almost always adhered to a strategy of preemption. This led the neoconservatives to favor preemption too, as a strategy not only for Israel but for any realistic state, particularly the United States.[16] Finally, because of its peculiar and isolated diplomatic position in international organizations and in international law, Israel since 1967 had almost always adhered to a policy of unilateralism. This led the neoconservatives to favor unilateralism too, as a policy not only for Israel but for any realistic state, particularly the United States.

The neoconservatives were thus enthusiastic supporters of the Bush strategy of unilateral preemption. Indeed, Paul Wolfowitz was a prominent architect of it. From the Israeli-centric perspective of the neoconservatives, what was good for Israel was good for the United States, and what was true for Israel was true for the United States. Indeed, in its relationship to the rest of the world, the United States appeared to be more or less just a big Israel.

Conversely, the neoliberal perspective was well represented in the Bush administration by the Treasury Department and the State Department (but not by Secretary of State—and former army general—Colin Powell, who largely tried to hold onto a traditional-conservative perspective). In regard to the Middle East, the neoliberals had a special interest in increasing U.S. influence over the global oil market, as well as promoting liberal-democratic reforms in the region. As the most committed and consistent promoters of American-style globalization, they knew full well the central importance of both controlling the lifeblood of the global economy and creating more regimes open to globalization.

Both the neoconservatives and the neoliberals saw the overthrow of Saddam Hussein's rogue regime—which ruled an Iraq that might achieve weapons of mass destruction and was also rich in oil reserves—to be a fulfillment of their own central interests in the Middle East. Historically, pro-Israeli groups and the oil industry have often opposed each other in regard to U.S. policies toward that region. The fact that these two groups came together in the Bush administration around a policy of regime change in Iraq gave a new and extraordinary energy to that project. The drive toward war with Iraq and toward the new and expanded empire that was expected to follow in its wake was thus already underway before September 11, 2001. The terrorist attacks on that date, although they had no connection whatever with Saddam Hussein and his regime, provided the Bush administration with still more explosive energy, which it used to drive the United States down its predetermined path toward war and empire.

On its way toward war and empire, however, the Bush administration confronted a major obstacle along its path, and that was the very same American military that was supposed to win the war and secure the empire. As Secretary of Defense Donald Rumsfeld well knew, the new American empire did not fit well with the traditional American military. What military strategists and historians have called "the American way of war"[17] was deeply imbued with a *national* perspective. The U.S. military, especially the U.S. Army, defended the vital national interests of the United States, and it did so by fighting the regular militaries of other national states. For the United States to use its military for the new *global* and *imperial* purposes, a new—and very different—American way of war would have to be invented, and this was the notion that underlaid Rumsfeld's "project of military transformation."

The Classic American Way of War

Military strategists and historians have discerned in some nations a distinctive strategic culture or way of war.[18] In the last third of the twentieth century, there was a widespread understanding among these professionals that there was a particular American way of war and that it was characterized by a reliance upon such advantages as (1) overwhelming mass (i.e., a pronounced advantage in men and material), (2) wide-ranging mobility (i.e., a pronounced advantage in transportation and communication), (3) high-technology weapons systems, and, underlying and sustaining them all, (4) high public support of the war effort. The purest expression of this American way of war was, of course, World War II. Another excellent example was the Persian Gulf War. However, the origins of the American way of war lay in the greatest American war of all, the Civil War. The use of overwhelming mass was crucial to the final victory of the North; it was exemplified by the strategy of Ulysses S. Grant. Conversely, the use of wide-ranging mobility was crucial to the initial victories of the South; it was exemplified by the strategy of Robert E. Lee.[19]

On the rare but important occasions when the United States could not deploy its advantages in both mass and mobility, the U.S. military faced serious problems. Both the Korean War and the Vietnam War degenerated into wars of attrition in which the U.S. military had the advantage in firepower but no obvious advantage in the use of its ground combat forces. In the last two years of the Korean War, both the U.S. Army and the communist armies were trapped in a static war of position near the thirty-eighth parallel, and the end result was a stalemate. In the Vietnam War, the communist guerrilla forces had the advantage in mobility, and this contributed greatly to the U.S. defeat. Indeed, it is the nature of any guerrilla war that the insurgent forces have the advantage of mobility and the counterinsurgency forces have the advantage of mass. It seems that the classic American way of war has no obvious answer if the military challenge comes from guerrillas and insurgents.

In the aftermath of its Vietnam debacle, the U.S. Army painfully examined the lessons of that war, and it largely concluded that the classic American way of war was really the only right way of war for the Army.[20] The lessons learned were institutionalized in the curriculum of the Army War College, as well as several other military schools, and in the strategic doctrine, bureaucratic organization, and weapons procurement of the Army itself. Many of the lessons learned were crystallized in what became known as the Weinberger–Powell doctrine (after Caspar Weinberger, Secretary of Defense in the Reagan administration, and General Colin Powell, Chairman of the Joint Chiefs of Staff in the administration of George H. W. Bush).[21] Central to the classic American way of war and its recapitulation in the Weinberger–Powell doctrine is the idea that when the United States goes to war, it should do so as a *nation* defending its vital national interests against another nation, and that when the U.S. Army goes to war, it should do so as an army fighting another army. Because the interests being defended were vital national ones, they would be recognized as such by the American people, who would support the war. Conversely, wars to advance peripheral, imperial interests and wars against insurgent forces were violations of the American way of war. They would be unlikely to receive the sustained support of the American people.

The Rumsfeld Transformation Project

From the very beginning of the administration of George W. Bush, Secretary of Defense Donald Rumsfeld worked vigorously and systematically to overthrow the classic American way of war and the Weinberger–Powell doctrine and to replace them with a new program of military "transformation."[22] He moved to reduce the role of heavy weapons systems (armor and artillery) and large combat divisions in the U.S. Army and to increase the role of lighter and smaller forces (airborne and special operations); in effect, he sought to reduce the role of mass and to accentuate the role of mobility. To implement his transformation project, he canceled the Crusader heavy artillery system and appointed a retired Special Forces general to be the new Army chief of staff. Most importantly, however, Rumsfeld saw the Iraq War as the pilot case of his grand project of transformation. If the United States could win a war in Iraq with a transformed military and a transformed doctrine, it would also be a decisive victory in Washington for a thoroughly new American way of war in its bureaucratic struggles with the old, classic one.

The Rumsfeld transformation project gained credibility because there are indeed some serious problems with the classic American way of war—particularly with the idea that the U.S. Army should fight only another army. The most obvious difficulty is that there no longer seems to be any other real army to fight. Indeed, the Army, the Navy, and the Air Force of the United States lack any equivalent force or "peer competitor." Although the Chinese nation might become a peer competitor to the American nation in a couple of decades, the Chinese military probably will not become a peer competitor to the American military until far in the future, and the last peer competitor—the Soviet military—is now far in the past.

The United States still has enemies, however, most obviously in transnational networks of Islamic terrorists but also in particular rogue states that oppose globalization and the American empire, such as North Korea and Iran. These enemies will seek to attack the United States not with conventional military forces or an American-style way of war but with "asymmetrical warfare." At the upper end of the war spectrum will be weapons of mass destruction, particularly nuclear ones. At the lower end of the spectrum will be terrorist operations and guerrilla warfare. Of course, the most ominous threat comes from a diabolical synthesis of the upper end and the lower end—weapons of mass destruction in the hands of transnational terrorist networks. For all of these unconventional or asymmetrical threats, the classic American way of war has no credible strategy or solution.

However, neither did the notions of Secretary Rumsfeld. The Rumsfeld transformation project, along with the Bush doctrine of unilateral preemption, did not really address the challenge of North Korea, that is, of rogue states that have already acquired nuclear weapons. Hypothetically, some combination of highly accurate intelligence and highly effective weapons (e.g., nuclear "bunker bombs") could destroy an enemy's stock of WMD. However, the failure to find any such weapons in Iraq certainly cast doubt on the accuracy of United States intelligence. And even highly effective weapons systems would have a hard time destroying widely dispersed stocks of biological weapons. The only time that the Bush doctrine and the Rumsfeld project could deal with the WMD threat is when a rogue state had not yet acquired such weapons and a U.S. military operation could destroy the rogue regime before it did so. But this would really be a preventive war, not a preemptive one. This was the case with Iraq. Some advocates of the Bush administration's innovations, particularly neoconservatives, also thought that it could next become the case with Iran.

The Rumsfeld transformation project also did not really address the challenge of transnational terrorist networks, such as al-Qaeda. This threat is better dealt with by a multidimensional array of agencies and instruments (intelligence, security, and financial) working with their counterparts in other countries that face similar threats, particularly those in Europe. The war in Iraq certainly did not help to enhance these counterterrorist capabilities.

The Rumsfeld Army and Imperial Wars

Other than dealing with nonnuclear rogue states, the only task that the new Rumsfeld army—with its lighter, more mobile configuration—arguably could have performed better than the old classic army—with its heavy armor and artillery configuration—was in operations against an enemy that was even more mobile: guerrillas and insurgents. It appears that the new Rumsfeld army was really designed to engage in colonial kinds of war, with the U.S. Army putting down rogue states and insurgent movements who are resisting the American empire, rather than a national kind of war, with the U.S. Army fighting another nation's army. The Rumsfeld project can also be seen as providing the military dimension of the globalization project, the stick that must go along with the carrot. As such, the new American way of war is indeed the "neo" way of war because it is the way of war that is promoted by the holders of the two global perspectives—the neoliberals and (with particular enthusiasm) the neoconservatives.[23] These groups know that the old American way of war, with its large numbers of troops, requires the sustained support of the American people, and they know that the American people are unlikely to give that support to wars for their global and imperial purposes. These purposes can be achieved only with a new American way of war and with an American military that is so light and mobile that it doesn't need the support of the American people at all.

There are, however, several ironies attending the Rumsfeld transformation project. First, the origins of the Weinberger–Powell doctrine lay in the lessons learned from the Vietnam War, and its basic impetus was "no more Vietnams." Among other things, this meant that the regular units of the U.S. Army would fight no more counterinsurgency wars. The Rumsfeld transformation project amounted to a radical overthrow of the Weinberger–Powell doctrine, and it sought to return the Army to the period at the beginning of the Vietnam War—the era when Secretary of Defense Robert McNamara was engaged in his own radical program of military transformation and when other political appointees of the Kennedy and Johnson administrations were enthusiastic advocates of some major combination of high technology and counterinsurgency as the new way that the United States would fight its future wars.

Second, even before Rumsfeld began the construction of his new army and the deconstruction of the old one, the United States already had a long-established, lighter, and more mobile ground force, and that was the U.S. Marines. During the first half of the twentieth century, the Marines had far more experience and success with light and mobile operations than did the Army. This included operations against insurgents in the Caribbean Basin and in Central America.[24] With only minor modifications and some modest expansion, the Marines by themselves could perform many of the colonial tasks that Rumsfeld's lighter, more mobile, transformed army was supposed to perform (although not an invasion and conquest of large rogue states, such as Iraq and Iran). But his new army may not be able to perform some of the tasks that the old army could perform so well, such as quickly overwhelming another "peer competitor" army, if one should ever come into being and pose a threat to the vital national interests of the United States.

Third, it was not until the United States invaded Iraq and imposed a military occupation upon it that the United States faced any guerrilla or insurgent threat that it needed to deal with by regular U.S. military forces. (Almost everyone agreed that the guerrilla forces in Afghanistan and in Colombia would be better dealt with by a combination of U.S. Special Forces and local military forces.) The U.S. occupation of Iraq created, for the first time since the Vietnam War, the very problem that the Rumsfeld transformation project was supposed to solve.

The Rumsfeld Army and the Iraq War

When it invaded Iraq in March 2003, the new Rumsfeld army was spectacularly successful against the army of Saddam Hussein. (Of course, the old, American-way-of-war army had been similarly successful against Saddam Hussein's army back in 1991.) The "shock-and-awe" tactics of the U.S. Air Force and the fluid and flexible tactics of the unusually light and highly mobile U.S. Army and Marines quickly won the conventional war so that President Bush on May 1, 2003, famously (and as it turned out, fatuously) declared "mission accomplished" and the end of "major combat operations." But it soon became clear that the real war, the counterinsurgency war, had just begun.

The United States Army had anticipated that its real challenge in Iraq would come *after* its defeat of Saddam Hussein's conventional forces. The Army had conducted a series of studies of previous U.S. military occupations, and these had produced some sophisticated conclusions.[25] But one simple ground rule for occupations was that, in order to establish security and deter insurgency, it was necessary to have a ratio of about 20 soldiers for every 1,000 civilians within the occupied population. These soldiers could include collaborating units drawn from the occupied country, but of course the core forces had to be provided by the U.S. military. Given that Iraq had a population of about 25 million, the number of occupation troops would have to be about 500,000. This is why the chief of staff of the Army, General Eric Shinseki, had stated on the eve of the war that the forces required for establishing the peace would have to consist of "several hundred thousand" soldiers for several years. For this, he was publicly rebuked and ridiculed by Rumsfeld and Wolfowitz as being "wildly off the mark."[26] The conclusions of the Army studies and the statement of Shinseki did not conform to the transformation project's notion of a light and lean U.S. Army.

The United States invaded Iraq with about 140,000 troops (not all of them combat personnel), and allied units—especially British forces—added another 40,000. These numbers were enough to defeat Iraq's conventional forces, but they were obviously not enough to establish security and deter insurgency. For that, other forces were needed. It was here, however, that the principles and practice of the Bush doctrine ushered in fatal consequences. Because of its doctrinal fixation on unilateralism, the Bush administration had insulted and marginalized many traditional American allies during the run-up to the war, and therefore it could not assemble troops from these allies to participate in the occupation. Further, because of its ideological fixation on liberal democracy and an open society, the Bush administration immediately abolished the Iraqi army and other security forces because they had been instruments of the Saddam Hussein regime, and therefore it could not draw upon Iraqi security units to collaborate in the occupation. In essence, the U.S. military, along with the British military, were left alone to provide law and order, and their forces were far too few to do so.

An interregnum—or rather, period of anarchy—of looting, sabotage, kidnappings, and murders immediately ensued. This in turn provided the conditions for the beginning and growth of a vigorous and organized insurgency. Moreover, since the U.S. military had too few forces to secure or destroy the vast stores of arms and ammunition that the old regime had distributed around Iraq, the insurgents had easy access to all the weapons that they needed.[27]

The Iraqi Insurgency and the American Dilemma

The insurgents quickly moved to confirm the isolation of U.S. occupation forces by attacking the few allies that they had. Using an array of classic insurgent tactics—bombings, ambushes, kidnappings, and beheadings—they repeatedly attacked the military units, civilian organizations, and simple individuals from every nation that was providing support to the occupation. In most cases, the governments of these nations had provided their support without mobilizing their own publics behind it, and in some cases they had done so despite the clear opposition of public opinion. The insurgents' attacks upon exposed allied personnel also exposed the gap that existed between the allied governments and their publics, which had hardly been a robust example of democracy in action. Of even more fundamental and fatal importance were the insurgents' attacks upon Iraqis who were working with the occupation. A particularly crucial target was the American effort to recruit and organize new Iraqi security forces (e.g., repeated insurgent bombings of police stations).

The United States military soon found that it had no good options for putting down the insurgency. If the ground forces engaged in direct assaults upon urban areas sheltering the insurgents (e.g., Fallujah and other cities in the "Sunni Triangle"), the resulting fatalities among American forces would arouse the opposition of American public opinion and the fatalities among local civilians would arouse the opposition of the Iraqi and allied publics. Similarly, air strikes upon these urban areas would inflame Iraqi and allied public opinion. Finally, if the United States military simply tried to maintain a defensible position in Iraq, it would suffer a slow but steady stream of fatalities, which would eventually arouse the opposition of the American public. More fundamentally, neither the classic American way of war nor the new American way of war, which Rumsfeld sought to establish with his transformation project, had any effective answer to the challenge posed by the insurgency in Iraq.

Some Americans thought that the Iraqi insurgency represented a different kind of war. Unlike the Vietnam War, it was more urban than rural. But the U.S. military had already had a recent experience with urban guerrilla warfare in Mogadishu, Somalia—hardly an encouraging example. In any event, the Iraqi insurgency was not really that different; indeed, it was merely a new example of another classic way of war, which was the guerrilla ("little war") or insurgent way of war. And as in most insurgent wars, the final solution had to be grounded not in the military operations but in the political process. The fundamental problem to be solved in Iraq, therefore, involved the U.S. political project for Iraq. The Bush administration made loud and repeated proclamations that it was bringing a liberal democracy, market economy, and open society to that country. But it soon became evident that there was very little connection between these proclamations and either the actual realities of Iraq or the actual policies of the administration.

The American Historical Experience with Democratization

The Bush administration claimed that it would convert Iraq into a liberal democracy, market economy, and open society. Iraq, in turn, would be a model for similar changes that would soon ensue in other countries of the Middle East (particularly Syria, Iran, and Saudi Arabia). For its vision of the future, the administration projected a sort of democratic domino theory. But for its models from the past, the administration repeatedly cited the successful American occupations and democratizations of West Germany and Japan after the Second World War. These nations became solid allies of the United States within the great system of alliances with which America fought and won the Cold War.

However, the Bush administration never mentioned the many other U.S. efforts in the course of the twentieth century to use military force to democratize countries, particularly within the Caribbean Basin and Central America during the 1900s to 1930s (Cuba, the Dominican Republic, Haiti, and Nicaragua) and again during the 1960s to 1990s (the Dominican Republic and Haiti again and also Grenada and Panama). Most of these efforts at democratization ended not only in failure but in the establishment of brutal dictatorial regimes (including Trujillo in the Dominican Republic and Somoza in Nicaragua). And of course the administration never mentioned the epic failure in South Vietnam. Nor did it mention the most recent, wide-ranging, and numerous efforts, without U.S. military forces, for democratization among the countries of the former Soviet Union and communist Eastern Europe. Together, these American and non-American efforts at democratization add up to about two dozen cases. If any honest discussion about the prospects for democratization in Iraq and other countries of the Middle East had included any analysis of a few of these cases, the discussion would have ended with a general consensus that the prospects were surely bleak.

The Democratization Project and the Iraq War

We have already noted that the Bush administration's ideology of democratization caused it to abolish the Iraqi army and other security forces that had functioned under the Saddam Hussein regime. The abolition of these forces and the anarchy that resulted were important contributors to the insurgency that followed. However, just because the United States destroyed the old authority, this did not mean that it really sought to establish a new democracy, as that term is normally defined. It did not do so because a real democracy would have contradicted the primary interests of the two globalist groups—the neoliberals and the neoconservatives—who had produced the war and who were now designing the occupation.

By the normal definition of democracy, one would have expected an electoral system based upon one person–one vote and majority rule. However, Shi'ites compose about 65 percent of the Iraqi population, and in such a system they could easily achieve a great preponderance of power and control of the Iraqi state. The Shi'ites took very seriously their version of Islam and Islamic law; this made them repugnant to the neoliberals, with their ideological fixation on such secular values as the free market, the open society, and Western conceptions of human rights. The Shi'ites of Iraq also had many close connections with the Shi'ites of Iran; this made them repugnant to the neoconservatives, with their primary interest in the security of Israel.

The Bush administration consequently was determined that, whatever kind of democracy might be established in Iraq, it could not result in Shi'ite rule. As a result, the administration would not allow a system of majority rule, that is, a simple democracy. Rather, the system would have to be some kind of *limited* democracy, be it a liberal, a federal, or an elite one, or some combination thereof. This explains why the U.S. occupation (the Coalition Provisional Authority, headed by the imperious but ineffective L. Paul Bremer III) persistently tried to marginalize Shi'ite religion leaders and political parties and why it persistently tried to inflate political groupings of secularized Shi'ites, which had no following at all among the vast Shi'ite population. This strategy had failed by June 2004, the time when the Coalition Provisional Authority was succeeded by the collaborating Iraqi government headed by Ayad Allawi, which also had little following among the Iraqi population.

Of course, the Sunni and Kurdish minorities in Iraq naturally opposed Shi'ite rule and therefore majority rule. The Sunnis really wanted minority rule of Iraq by themselves; that is, they wanted an authoritarian system like that which had served their interests under every regime since Iraq was created by the British in 1920. The Kurds really wanted an independent Kurdish state or, at most, a loose kind of federal system for Iraq. Neither the Sunnis nor the Kurds wanted an Iraq that was democratic, but the Shi'ites wanted an Iraq that was, from the American perspective, too democratic. For this three-part political problem, there was no stable democratic solution, and that is why the United States could not find one.

The neoliberals also insisted upon a radical transformation of the Iraqi economy and Iraqi society. Bremer promulgated a series of decrees and measures designed to dismantle the state-controlled Iraqi economy and to bring about privatization and openness to American investment. (These measures were illegal under international law because established international conventions forbid an occupying power from changing the economic structure of an occupied country.)[28] Bremer also promoted programs to increase the power of women in Iraqi society. The neoconservatives supported these neoliberal objectives for their own reasons. They wanted to ensure that Iraq could not again become a strong state that controlled an organized society based upon an Arab or Muslim collectivist identity. However, these radical economic and social measures were largely abortive because their institutionalization was made impossible by the growing insurgency. Indeed, because they were so offensive to the traditional Iraqi way of life, they helped to generate support for that insurgency.

The neoconservative civilians in the Defense Department sometimes demonstrated how little they cared about any real democratization in Iraq. Defense officials allowed a series of acts of commission and omission that assaulted Iraqi public opinion and that therefore undermined the legitimacy of any promises about democratization. These included the initial period of anarchy (dismissed by Rumsfeld as "stuff happens"); the perverted and illegal interrogation methods at Abu Ghraib prison, which would inevitably become common knowledge among the Iraqi public; and the failure to spend already-appropriated funds to provide such basic physical necessities as sewers and electricity. For some Defense Department neoconservatives, it was not really necessary that Iraq be democratic, merely that it be weak.

In short, because of the primary interests and insistent demands of both the neoliberals and the neoconservatives, the proclamations of the Bush administration soon lost whatever credibility they had had in the first weeks of the occupation. Iraqis saw the United States objective of liberal democracy to be phony, its objective of free markets to be self-serving, its objective of an open society to be offensive, and all three objectives to be illegitimate. The global perspectives, indeed the universal conceits and imperial arrogance, of the two "neo" groups utterly ignored the local, intractable realities within Iraq and thereby ensured that the American democratization project would end as a failure.

The Effect of the Iraq War on the American Empire

By the spring of 2004, the unfolding failure in Iraq had already had a major impact upon the great expectations about the American empire. On the eve of the Iraq War and during its first months, there was a good deal of earnest discussion about the future development of the empire. But the steady growth of the Iraqi insurgency brought about a rapid decline in these expectations. Books about the American empire, which had been begun in 2001–2003, were brought to completion and published in 2004, but by that time, the agonies of the U.S. war in Iraq had already made proclamations of empire incongruous and obsolete. As it turned out, the golden age of speculations about the American empire was very brief, from 2001 to 2003.

There may come wars in the Middle East or in the broader Muslim world, but there will hardly be an American empire there. The post-Vietnam military was a volunteer military; underlying it was a steady and sufficient stream of volunteers. At some level, the recruits to the U.S. military assumed that they would be defending the vital, national interests of the United States, or at least that they would be sent into war according to reasonable principles like those articulated by the Weinberger–Powell doctrine. The Iraq War violated these assumptions, and the consequence was a decline in Army and Marine recruitment and retention, a decline that made it exceedingly difficult to launch a new war in some other country. This military reality was evident for all to see, including the enemies of the United States, and this greatly diminished the U.S. ability to deter its enemies with the threat to invade and occupy their countries with ground forces. And because all empires must be able to threaten invasions and occupations, the Iraq adventure greatly diminished America's ability to extend its empire, particularly into the Middle East or the broader Muslim world.

The Effect of the Iraq War on Globalization

The demise of the American imperial project in the Muslim world will probably also mean the demise of the American globalization project there. The imperial project was greatly energized by 9/11 and the specter of Islamic terrorism. The course of the Iraq War may have aborted the American empire, but the threat from transnational networks of Islamic terrorists remains; indeed, that threat is probably greater after the war than it was before, and it remains directed both at globalization and at the United States that promotes it.

The actions of the United States military in Iraq have angered many people throughout the Muslim world, and the failures of the counterinsurgency in Iraq have emboldened many Islamic militants. One obvious danger is that the insurgency against U.S. forces in Iraq is likely to become a model for Islamic insurgents against U.S. forces elsewhere (rather like the insurgency against Israeli forces in Lebanon in the 1980s and 1990s became a model for Palestinian insurgents in Israel itself in the 2000s). An even greater danger is that the Iraqi insurgency is likely to become a recruiting network for Islamic terrorists who seek to directly attack the homelands of the United States and other Western nations.

Much of the Muslim world will likely become off-limits to Americans. American military bases, American business interests, and even individual American travelers will be under constant threat from insurgents or terrorists. The presence of Americans, if not any American presence at all, will become unviable. Globalization may continue elsewhere, but it will be contained and even rolled back in Muslim lands. In effect, the Muslim world will secede from the American version of globalization. Of course, if the Muslim world separates itself from American globalization, this globalization would no longer be truly global, and therefore it would no longer be globalization in the literal sense. Moreover, a series of successful terrorist attacks within America and within Europe will likely bring an end first to open borders and then, if necessary, to open societies. This would go a long way to slow or even stop the putatively inevitable process of globalization.

Globalization was a world revolution, one whose chief promoter and defender was the United States. Although in the 1990s the spread of this world revolution to the very limits of the globe seemed inevitable, a world reaction to it was already beginning to develop, or at least a reaction within the Muslim world. Islamism also represented a kind of globalization, and so did Islamic terrorists with global reach. The terrorist attacks of 9/11 were a quantum leap in the reach of Islamic terrorists, and the Iraqi insurgency provided a compelling model for military actions by Islamist movements. Together, they demonstrated the strength of the new, Islamist version of globalization against the old, American one. Like the last decade, the next decade is likely to be defined by globalization. But this time it will be defined by a titanic and bloody struggle between two warring globalizations, that of America and that of Islamism. Together, they may bring an end to any kind of globalization at all.

10 Conclusion

Bruce Mazlish

GLOBALIZATION TENDS to produce a global society. The form of that so-ciety is, however, a matter of chance and contestation. As indicated in the introduction, as a concept globalization can function as an ideal, or vision, possibly leading to what its supporters call a global civil society. Such a so-ciety has among its aims justice, peace, and economic well-being for all, to be achieved by institutions that transcend national boundaries. Among them might be numbered the United Nations, various international courts, all sorts of nongovernmental structures, and manifold global treaties and accords, for example, those on global warming, land mines, and so forth.

Reality, however, is messy, and even at its best the institutions of global civil society generally fall far short of their ideals. Moreover, many countries and polities are hostile to the very concept of global civil society. Instead of supporting the initiatives that favor such a development, they seek to hinder it or, just as frequently, to substitute their own version of what a global society should look like. Often, this is not "civil." Instead, it may be in the image of a religion, for example, Christian or Islamic, with universal pretensions. Or it may be pursuing a more "national" ideal.

Is this what the United States is aiming for? The United States, in the first decades after the end of World War II, bolstered this movement toward a new world order in the context of an international system based on nation-states and moving to a global order, however vague its nature. It lent support to the Nuremberg trials and its extension of war crimes to crimes against human-ity, to the founding of the UN, to the Declaration of Human Rights, to global treaties in regard to the environment, and to other such "global" initiatives.[1]

Then, sometime in the late sixties, possibly in relation to the Vietnam War, the United States turned away from the ideal of a global civil society and pursued another path, mostly unilateral actions to protect its own national sovereignty and security. September 11, 2001, seemed to accelerate this turn. Was this, as many of our chapters show, mere appearance, with the United States a reluctant and highly ambivalent "citizen" of the world from its beginnings and on into the present?

That question restates the paradox at the core of this book. To put it another way, it appears that the United States has contributed powerfully to globalizing the world, thus changing the nature of society on the international level but without a comparable change in the country's consciousness. It can be argued that, though marked by ambivalence and contradictions, the American reaction to globalization is basically hostile unless that globalization is on its terms and perceived as being in its interests (defined in narrow, nationalistic terms). Putting this thesis in the most hyperbolic terms, American empire can consequently be viewed as implementing the particular vision of a global society being pursued by the hegemonic power of our times. Other versions, especially that of global civil society, are then seen as the "enemy."

Are there any other contenders besides the United States and some aspects of Islam who wish to give global form to their own image? The European Union is preoccupied with its own expansion and the concomitant effort to hold together and achieve its own identity. When it has time and resources, it seems to favor some version of global civil society. Japan has been and is a major force in the globalization process and, despite a rising nationalism, generally supportive of moves toward global civil society. But it obviously has little aspiration to throw its weight around politically outside of Asia or to dominate global society. In the eyes of some, China has global aspirations. These may be achieved in some future time, but the evidence runs against China's ascension in the present. Though China is on its way to being an economic powerhouse whose shadow casts itself across the globe, nothing in its ideology or history suggests a desire to establish a global China, with bases and forces scattered abroad adequate to such a mission.

At this point, the fight seems to be between an emerging global civil society and global America. The issue, of course, is more complicated than this Manichean division, and further research and thought should be addressed to the possibilities, aside from Islamic radicalism, of serious rivals to the United States as the global hegemon. This situation suggests that the potential for derailing some sort of global civil society, which attempts to address global prob-lems, lies very much in the hands of the United States.[2] An incipient global civil society, developing in a painful, inadequate, and stumbling fashion, may be wiped out by the direction taken by the American behemoth.

I

Accepting the centrality of the United States in its paradoxical relation to global society, we are led to inquire into the conditions that shape America's behavior—a task attempted in the volume as a whole—and then to speculate about the possibilities of change in these conditions that would favor the coun-try's becoming a better global citizen. Consequently, this project may be said to entail certain policy implications. Needless to say, both the notion of a global civil society and the politics to which this notion leads are controversial.

With this notion in mind, let us examine what changes in America might come to favor a continuing movement toward a realistically envisioned global civil society. Such a society is certainly not a teleology and definitely not an aim shared by all the contributors to this volume, but it does seem to be in tune with the thrust of globalization itself. It accords with the fact that globaliza-tion is not the result simply of economic forces but of a human desire for a bet-ter, more humane world based on values such as peace, justice, freedom, and locally based democracy. In becoming more integrated and interdependent than ever before, human beings are moving consciously to such a world—and not in pie-in-the-sky terms but as grounded in day-to-day events of the glo-balization process.

There appears to be much continuity in American attitudes, values, inter-ests, and commitments over its entire history. Though their expression and intensity vary over time, they seem to persist even in the midst of change. Al-though the same might be said of all countries, an American claim to unique-ness and a sense of exceptionalism stand in back of much of its actions. This claim finds expression in its pulsating sense of mission, frequently in the form of Christian evangelism, which shades imperceptibly into the patriotic view of America as the beacon to the world and the carrier of freedom and democracy. What may seem like hypocrisy in this regard to others in the world is a matter of conviction in the United States. It then follows that if one is unique and ex-ceptional, one is implicitly detached from the rest of humanity and ought not to be subjected to its laws—for example, an international criminal court—nor to its needs—for example, a common and farsighted energy policy.[3]

How might one change this situation? How to bring home the fact that the United States is subject to the "laws" of both history and humanity and not exceptional in their regard? How to break through the barriers of amnesia as to past actions and willful ignorance regarding how one's acts are perceived by others? These traits reflect natural human tendencies and are found in many other countries, but they take on special significance in the globalizing world and America's paradoxical role in relation to it. To effect change here means to change the consciousness of a people, and that is an extremely difficult task to achieve without cataclysmic occurrences.

The Manichean tendency is strong in the United States. Can the search for an enemy be diverted in a useful direction? One possibility is finding an enemy in, say, environmental threats. This is a major feature in today's globalization, caused increasingly by its economics of production, made more evident by satellites conveying information about the transnational effects, and combated more and more on a global scale. However, many American institutions, especially political and military ones, prefer to target other countries as the "enemy." This is obviously a more traditional way of choosing an enemy. It is less impersonal than finding one in the environment or in other global challenges. It is also in accord with "national" needs and serves the self-interested forces that defend the country against these traditional threats.

All of these attitudes and interests find expression in politics, which, as the cliché has it, are always local. In a representational democracy, politicians are there to respond to their constituencies' demands, which generally tend not to be global. To go further on this topic, however, is to engage in all the problems as to how representative the American political system is. Obviously, the rich get more representation than the poor. The fight over campaign reform, gerrymandering, and such is never ending and all too frequently not successful: how to get the guardians to reform themselves? There are the structural problems such as an electoral college that tilts the field. There are the media influences, mostly under the control of multinational giants with a conservative and national agenda. One major effect, as the Pearson and Simpson Khullar chapter confirms, is a reinforcement of the parochialism that shuts off Americans from the globalization to which they are otherwise contributing.

The possibilities of change in these areas seem small at the moment. In an America that seems an exception to class analysis—"there are no classes" is the refrain, only rich and poor with "equal" opportunity to rotate positions—

political change, barring a major depression, appears unlikely. Polls constantly show that Americans ignore the reality of class division—blue collar families remain blue collar—and the fact that the top 1 percent of the population holds an astounding percentage of the wealth. The cult of rugged individualism apparently obscures this reality or accepts it without thinking on the grounds that the individual responding to the poll will shortly become part of that top 1 percent. There is a spillover, of course, of such attitudes in respect to corporate power and its behavior in the world. Property rights attached to individuals are worshipped—and in America, corporations are conceived in law as individuals. When the corporations use their lobbying power to achieve exceptional representation, that, too, often seems to accord with dominant beliefs. Change in this area comes hard.

Much of American religion, in the form of Christianity, reinforces the cult of unrestrained individualism. What matters is individual salvation. "Jesus loves *me*" is a frequent refrain. When the Rapture believed in by so many evangelical Christians comes, it will be for individuals. Little or no regard is given to the damnation and destruction of millions of other humans or to the Earth itself. These religious beliefs then animate political convictions and parties, with results that seem heavily opposed to any form of global civil society. Perhaps Professor Demerath is right in his chapter on religion: globalization requires some form of secularism. Where pronounced religious concerns press on American foreign policy—for example, in regard to attitudes on abortion short-circuiting foreign aid—it appears that domestic national issues take precedence over global population conditions. If Demerath's analysis is right, a look at religious trends in America offers little ground for believing that change favoring globalization will occur.[4]

What of the military that plays such a large and increasing role in extending America's global power, a military that makes the United States the sole power with global reach aside from terrorist networks that approach commensurability in reach but not in power now or in the foreseeable future? What are the attitudes toward globalization and a global society to be found in the ranks? The available data suggests that the military is to the right of most Americans politically, with all that that implies for understanding their global mission. Here lies an important research goal: to use survey data combined with historical and sociological analysis to establish the facts firmly. Then on that basis, having inquired into current education in the service academies, for example, translate this evidence into educational recommendations. Is this one possible way of responding to Roxborough's analysis of U.S. strategic doctrine and its need for an enemy?

II

It is fashionable to speak of the conflict between modernizing and antimodernizing forces in Middle Eastern countries. Now we speak of globalizing and antiglobalizing forces. It is important to realize that the same struggle goes on in the United States. To an almost overwhelming extent, America's role in the globalizing process is subject to a political contest. The odds are heavily weighted in the local and "national" direction and against global citizenship. This is a fact of current life and America's past conditions. In general terms, the odds are not promising for the proglobal forces.

Yet this bleak picture is not all. The strength of the currents pushing in the direction of globalization's producing a kind of global civil society are strong in the sense of such a society being an unintended consequence. Multinational corporations (MNCs) and nongovernmental organizations (NGOs), though flawed agents, are key factors in globalization. MNCs are a prime cause, the economic agent, pushing the world toward greater integration as well as interdependence. NGOs are both an effect and, in part, a further cause of this shift. Indeed, the NGO movement (flawed as it is) can be said to be a form of global civil society or, more credibly, a part, substituting for more formal global institutions and means of democratic representation. In one sense conscious agents and in another simply part of the process, but having unintended consequences, NGOs have been growing exponentially.

A key to almost all of the problems is education, taken in the broadest sense (education has already been mentioned in regard to the military). Schools and media play a major role in shaping the public's attitude toward the world America is helping to bring into existence, like it or not. They are deeply implicated in the politics, both local and national, of the country. It is hard to be optimistic about the media. More and more a corporate operation, dedicated to blurring the boundaries of entertainment and news, and congenitally tending to conservatism, the media seem impervious to conscious efforts to improve them. Education, on the other hand, because of the people who tend to be involved in it, seems a more promising venue in which to change consciousness. Alas, with the increasing "media-ization" of education in so many ways, the promise dims.

These comments are intended to spark further thinking about what changes might be introduced into the continuity of American attitudes in regard to global society, to stimulate thoughts about a possible continuing research project. It must be recognized that the problem/project is all of a piece. Each part, education or politics, for example, is related to every other part. Each reinforces the other. The up-side of this reinforcement is that once some change is introduced, it causes a chain reaction. There is no guarantee that such change will be in the direction desired by the forces pushing for that change, but it does offer some possibility of a successful outcome, that is, greater global citizenship.

III

Thinking about what is and what should be is inevitably influenced by the state of the social sciences being applied to the matter. This volume has employed a historical perspective in which history is conceived as a multidisciplinary inquiry. The focus, of course, has been on the United States and its paradoxical position in a globalizing world. The globalization setting itself has been studied holistically, as befitting the nature of the phenomenon. As far as it goes, this approach is fine, but it is still parochial in its procedures. It still stays within the disciplines, as they have been shaped by the nation-state system in which they have arisen.

A revolution in the social sciences is necessary in the sense that they must be reconceived in terms of the globalizing world whose nature and problems they try to understand and to address.[5] Such a revolution will take place only in the doing. The fact is that globalization at this time is studied in a largely nonglobal manner. Scholars and thinkers in the disciplines of the various social sciences rarely cross the boundaries of their own specialties. (In the present project, we have been as bold as we could be in this regard.)

Just open a journal or book on international relations (IR). When globalization is treated, the references are almost entirely restricted to other IR publications, scholars, and citations. The rhetoric (jargon in the minds of outsiders) is that of the discipline. Do the same with works in political science, anthropology, or sociology. Each exhibits the same general disregard of the other toilers in the field. History, of course, is no better. There is no global discourse across the professional boundaries.

How, we may ask, can we strive for an understanding of globalization, whose present-day manifestations are new, when the very ways we study it are so compartmentalized, so unglobal? Realistic measures to decrease the career investments that partition the field in an unhealthy manner can at least be envisioned. Even action might be possible. New structures and institutions can emerge once there is a growing consciousness of the situation.

Would that the situation were as obvious in regard to the needed rethinking of social science concepts! Here we need an original and pioneering mentality. By this very fact—such rethinking doesn't yet exist—it is more or less futile at this place to talk further about it. Here, then, we must settle for exhortation and the appeal for fresh minds with new thoughts.

IV

Descending from the disciplines, we need to consider afresh the significance of a particular event, the destruction wrought on September 11, 2001. Did the United States and the world change on that day in a "revolutionary" manner? Much has been written on this topic. James Kurth in this volume concludes, "The imperial project was greatly energized by 9/11 and the specter of Islamic terrorism. The course of the Iraq War may have aborted the American empire, but the threat from transnational networks of Islamic terrorism remains; indeed, that threat is probably greater after the war than it was before, and it remains directed both at globalization and the United States that promotes it." To have been both energized and aborted makes for clumsy dancing by the global hegemon.

Did the events of 9/11 mark a change in America's role with the global community or a continuance of the previous relation? Will the response to 9/11 entail unintended consequences, pushing the country toward the global society it consciously opposes? Is America actually in a domestic fight, politically and culturally, that will help determine the answer to this last question? At one point during our conference, Michael Adas said, "The apparent, and selective, move to a more genuine multilateralism under the first Bush and early Clinton administrations has been decisively reversed by the Middle East policies pursued in the wake of 9/11 by the current Bush regime." Or is it that, as many of the articles in this volume suggest, *plus ça change, plus ça reste*? In this case, it is the move to multilateralism that is out of character and therefore bound to be ephemeral.

These are early days, and, to turn to the cliché, only time will tell. Meanwhile, short-term effects are observable. It can be argued that the terrorists have succeeded in many of their objectives. They have disrupted daily life in the developed countries, ranging from airport security searches to treatment of immigrants. They have forced restraints on the exercise of freedom, ranging from speech to movement. They have pushed the Western countries to expenditures of money that have been disruptive to the general economy.

All in all, the terrorists have caused liberty to retreat in the United States while discrediting its efforts to change the Iraqi regime in that direction. In fact, as is now known, Iraq, as Afghanistan before it, has become a breeding ground for the supporters of jihad. In the process, the American military has been overstretched and made to appear perilously close to being a piteous giant, able to wreak enormous destruction but not to create a new, democratic regime. If this be global war, little is clear but that the terrorists can be said so far to be winning it in important ways.

Insofar as U.S. actions in Iraq have stimulated the spread of terrorism, America can be seen as fostering that particular brand of globalization: global Islam. The latter, in its radical fundamentalist form, has also provoked a global antiterrorist response. Thus, 9/11 must be reckoned in these terms as well as the more familiar ones.

Strictly speaking, the loss of life at the World Trade Center was small in comparison with other disasters. What made it so traumatic was, first, the audacity involved. Second, of course, was the potential of other and worse attacks, a very realistic concern. The upshot was that the United States was rudely made aware of its existence in a globalizing world, where it was not the only player able to exert force globally.

V

In this volume, we have attempted to give information and views that will help in answering such questions. We have oriented ourselves around the paradox of the United States as the major country pushing globalization in economic terms—to which we could add military as well—yet, on balance, disinclined to be a good citizen in the society that results from the globalization process. Consciousness is a "soft" power, yet it is a constituent part of any behavior. Having tried to delineate the conditions of the United States, past and present, that determine that consciousness and hence influence action, and having much in mind my colleagues' work, I have personally also tried in this conclusion to speculate gingerly on how those conditions might be changed.

To go further would be to enter into the uncertain future. In the short present, it appears, however, that the United States is "hijacking" globalization away from a possible global civil society and pointing it in the direction of an American empire. This attempt, it can be argued, is rooted in the history of the country along with gestures toward a more civil international system. Alongside the American attempt to shape the globe in its own image can be placed the hijacking engaged in by global Islam. Both are related dialectically and can be seen as part of the same process.[6] Yet the present-day globalization process continues to stumble toward a global society. Inasmuch as there are many other actors besides the United States and global Islam, the kind of society the process will produce is up for grabs. National will plays the central role in this situation. This is especially true in regard to the United States, which is for better or worse the hegemon of our present global epoch.

Reference Matter

Notes

Chapter 1

1. For further details, see the Web site www.newglobalhistory.com.

2. Cf., for example, *Rethinking American History in a Global Age*, ed. Thomas Bender (Berkeley: University of California Press, 2002).

3. John Gerard Ruggie, "Reconstituting the Global Public Domain—Issues, Actors, and Practices," *European Journal of International Relations*, 10 (2004): p. 519.

4. Sylvia Walby, "The Myth of the Nation-State: Theorizing Society and Politics in a Global Era," *Sociology*, 36 (2003), p. 5.

5. C. A. Bayly, "'Archaic' and 'Modern' Globalization in the Eurasian and African Arena, c. 1750–1850," in *Globalization in World History*, ed. A. G. Hopkins (London: Pimlico, 2002), pp. 48–49.

6. I have myself tried to deal with this subject in my new book, *The New Global History* (New York: Routledge, 2006), in a chapter titled "Cold War and Globalization: Unintended Consequences."

7. A leader in the attempt to treat global civil society in these terms is the project responsible for the *Global Civil Society Yearbook*, started in 2000, and published annually under the auspices of the London School of Economics and Political Science and the University of California, Los Angeles.

Chapter 2

1. See, for example, Michael Hardt and Antonio Negri, *Empire* (Cambridge, Mass: Harvard University Press, 2000); Niall Ferguson, *Empire* (Oxford: Oxford University Press, 2003).

2. Kenichi Ohmae, *The Borderless World* (London: Collins, 1990).

3. Paul Hirst and Graham Thompson, *Globalization in Question* (Cambridge: Polity Press, 1996).

4. Peter Gowan, *The Global Gamble: Washington's Faustian Bid for World Dominance* (London: Verso, 1999).

5. David Held, Anthony McGrew, David Goldblatt, and Jonathan Perraton, *Global Transformations* (Cambridge: Polity Press, 1999).

6. Martin Shaw, "The Historical Sociology of the Future," *Review of International Political Economy*, 5 (1998), pp. 322–27.

7. Immanuel Wallerstein, *The Modern World-System* (New York: Academic Press, 1974).

8. Andre Gunder Frank and Barry K. Gills, eds. *The World System: Five Hundred Years or Five Thousand?* (London: Routledge, 1993).

9. Anthony Giddens, *The Consequences of Modernity* (Polity: Cambridge, 1990).

10. The following is based on my *Theory of the Global State: Globality as an Unfinished Revolution* (Cambridge: Cambridge University Press, 2000), Chapter 1.

11. Giddens, *Consequences*, p. 64.

12. Jan Aart Scholte, "Globalisation: Prospects for a Paradigm Shift," in Martin Shaw, ed., *Politics and Globalisation: Knowledge, Ethics and Agency* (London: Routledge, 1999), pp. 11–14. Held and Anthony McGrew also provide a suggestive amplification of the spatial concept when they write: "Globalization refers to an historical process which transforms the spatial organization of social relations and transactions, generating transcontinental or inter-regional networks of interaction *and the exercise of power.*" (David Held and Anthony McGrew, "The End of the Old Order? Globalization and the Prospects for World Order," *Review of International Studies*, 24, Special Issue, p. 220, emphasis added.) As my emphasis suggests, the novel aspect of their definition is not the specification of worldwide as "transcontinental or inter-regional"—a formulation that amplifies the spatial conception into a specific hierarchy of nations, continents, and regions and world—but the introduction of power into the definition. However, once again the content of the global transformation of power is not defined except in spatial terms.

13. I use "twenty-first century" here in a sense that is not strictly chronological. Eric Hobsbawm, *The Age of Extremes: A History of the World, 1914–1991* (London: Joseph, 1994), is surely right that the "twentieth century" should be considered as the "short" century between 1914 and 1989. So the beginning of the new century, in a meaningful historical sense, can be dated to the end of the Cold War.

14. Mazlish, *The New Global History* (New York and Oxford: Routledge, 2006), p. 9.

15. See Andrew Bacevich, *American Empire: The Realities and Consequences of U.S. Diplomacy* (Cambridge, Mass.: Harvard University Press, 2002).

16. United States dominance is stronger in military than in political, economic, or ideological terms: see Michael Mann, *Incoherent Empire* (London: Verso, 2003).

17. Geir Lundestad, *"Empire" by Integration: The United States and European Integration, 1945–1997* (Oxford: Oxford University Press, 1998).

18. Michael Mann, *The Sources of Social Power: The Rise of Classes and Nation-States, 1760–1914*, Volume II (Cambridge: Cambridge University Press, 1993), p. 76.

19. Martin Shaw, "The Global Transformation of the Social Sciences," *Global Civil Society Yearbook 2003* (Oxford: Oxford University Press, 2003).

20. Mann, *Incoherent Empire*.

21. George Monbiot, *The Age of Consent: A Manifesto for a New World Order* (London: Penguin, 2003).

Chapter 3

1. Oscar and Lilian Handlin, eds., *From the Outer World* (Cambridge, Mass.: Harvard University Press, 1997), p. 191.

2. Quoted in W. T. Stead, *The Americanization of the World: The Trend of the Twentieth Century* (New York and London, 1902), pp. 191, 354–55, 357.

3. Quoted in Julius W. Pratt, *Expansionists of 1898: The Acquisition of Hawaii and the Spanish Islands* (Baltimore: Johns Hopkins University Press, 1936), p. 228.

4. L. T. Hobhouse, *Morals in Evolution: A Study of Comparative Ethics*, Part I (London, 1908), p. 331.

5. Cited in Stephen Kern, *The Culture of Time and Space, 1880–1918* (Cambridge, Mass.: Harvard University Press, 1983), p. 183.

6. Norman Naimark, *Fires of Hatred: Ethnic Cleansing in Twentieth-Century Europe* (Cambridge, Mass.: Harvard University Press, 2001).

7. On the development of cosmopolitan visions during the 1920s, see Akira Iriye, *Cultural Internationalism and World Order* (Baltimore: Johns Hopkins University Press, 1997).

8. Dorothy Jones, *Toward a Just World: The Critical Years in the Search for International Justice* (Chicago: University of Chicago Press, 2002).

9. Victor Klemperer, *I Will Bear Witness: 1933–1941, A Diary of the Nazi Years* (New York: Random House, 1998), p. 282.

10. On the idea of "one world" and its implications, see David Reynolds, *One World Divisible: A Global History since 1945* (New York: W.W. Norton, 2000).

11. Ibid.

12. Bureau of Census, *Historical Statistics of the United States: Colonial Times to 1970*, Part 2 (Washington, D.C.: U.S. Government Printing Office, 1975).

13. Frank Ninkovich, *The Diplomacy of Ideas: U.S. Foreign Policy and Cultural Relations, 1938–1950* (Cambridge and New York: Cambridge University Press, 1981); Walter L. Hixson, *Parting the Curtain: Propaganda, Culture, and the Cold War, 1945–1961* (New York: St. Martin's Press, 1997); Volker Berghahn, *America and the Intellectual Cold Wars in Europe: Shepherd Stone between Philanthropy, Academy, and Diplomacy* (Princeton, N.J.: Princeton University Press, 2001).

14. Ford Foundation internal memos. I am grateful for copies of these memos that were provided to me by Kim Gould Ashizawa of the Japan Center for International Exchange.

15. See Akira Iriye, *Global Community: The Role of International Organizations in the Making of the Contemporary World* (Berkeley: University of California Press, 2002).

16. I have discussed turn-of-the-century discourses on racial and civilizational issues in my essay, "Mistrust, Mistrust, Fear," in Geir Lundestad and Olav Njølstad, eds., *War and Peace in the 20th Century and Beyond* (River Edge, NJ: World Scientific, 2002).

17. The most recent such conference took place in New Delhi on July 9 and 10, 2003. The text of the New Delhi declaration that contained these ideas may be found online at http://www.unesco.org/dialogue2001/delhi/delhi_declaration.html.

18. Kristin Hoganson, "Cosmopolitan Domesticity: Importing the American Dream, 1865–1920," *American Historical Review*, 107 (February 2002).

19. Stead, *Americanization*, p. 316.

20. Jessica Gienow-Hecht, "Music, Emotions and Politics in German-American Relations since 1850" (Habilitationsschrift, Martin-Luther-Universität Halle-Wittenberg, 2003).

21. Daniel T. Rodgers, *Atlantic Crossings: Social Politics in a Progressive Age* (Cambridge, Mass.: Harvard University Press, 1998).

22. Warren Cohen, *The Asian American Century* (Cambridge, Mass.: Harvard University Press, 2002), p. 105.

23. Henry James, *Selected Letters*, Leon Edel, ed. (Cambridge, Mass.: Harvard University Press, 1987), p. 15.

24. Arthur Holitscher, *Amerika, Heute und Morgen: Reiseerlebnisse* (Berlin, 1912), pp. 322–34, quoted in George Blaustein, "*Amerika*, 1911: The Case of Arthur Holitscher," unpublished paper, April 2003.

25. For information on the National Council for History Education, the best source is its newsletter titled *History Matters!*

26. Carl Becker and Kenneth Cooper, *Modern History*, 11th edition (Morristown, N.J.: Silver Burdett, 1984), p. 1.

27. National Center for History in the Schools, ed., *National Standards for History* (Los Angeles, 1996), p. 1.

28. Joan Arno, ed., *Teacher's Guide: AP World History* (Princeton, N.J.: The College Entrance Examinations Board, 2000).

29. Richard Bulliet, et al., *The Earth and Its Peoples: A Global History* (Boston: Houghton Mifflin, 1997), pp. xxv, 944, 1014.

Chapter 4

For help in refining my ideas, I am grateful to members of the conference, particularly the commentator on my paper, Charles Bright.

1. On the very real limits of British imperial power—an issue of importance because of the popularity of analogies between Britain and America as hegemons—see David Reynolds, *Britannia Overruled: British Policy and World Power in the Twentieth Century* (2nd edn., London: Longman, 2000), esp. Chapter 1.

2. Statistics from Frank Thistlethwaite, *The Anglo-American Connection in the Early Nineteenth Century* (Philadelphia: University of Pennsylvania Press, 1959), p. 11.

3. Geoffrey Sherrington, *Australia's Immigrants, 1788–1988* (Sydney: Allen & Unwin, 1970), p. 149.

4. Stephan Thernstrom, ed., *Harvard Encyclopedia of American Ethnic Groups* (Cambridge, Mass.: Harvard University Press, 1980), p. 335.

5. Alexander Hamilton, James Madison, and John Jay, *The Federalist, with Letters of "Brutus,"* Terence Ball, ed. (Cambridge: Cambridge University Press, 2003), pp. 59–63, quoting from pp. 63, 60–61.

6. Quoted in Frederick Merk, *Albert Gallatin and the Oregon Problem: A Study in Anglo-American Diplomacy* (Cambridge, Mass.: Harvard University Press, 1950), p. 13.

7. Emphasized and graphically illustrated in Douglass C. North, *The Economic Growth of the United States, 1790–1860* (New York: W.W. Norton, 1966), pp. 99–100.

8. Quoted in Frederick Merk, *Manifest Destiny and Mission in American History: A Reinterpretation* (New York: Alfred A. Knopf, 1963), p. 32.

9. Merk, *Manifest Destiny*, p. 51.

10. Georg Wilhelm Friedrich Hegel, *The Philosophy of History*, J. Sibree, transl. (New York: Dover Publications, 1956), pp. 85–86.

11. D. P. Crook, *The North, the South, and the Powers, 1861–1865* (New York: John Wiley & Sons, 1974), pp. 227–30.

12. David H. Donald, *Lincoln* (New York: Simon & Schuster, 1995), pp. 328, 529.

13. James M. McPherson, *Battle Cry of Freedom: The Civil War Era* (New York: Penguin, 1990), p. 859.

14. This paragraph draws heavily on Michael Geyer and Charles Bright, "Global Violence and Nationalizing Wars in Eurasia and America: The Geopolitics of War in the Mid-Nineteenth Century," *Comparative Studies in Society and History*, 38 (1996), pp. 619–57, esp. pp. 638–48, 657, quoting from p. 647.

15. Michael Kammen, *People of Paradox: An Inquiry Concerning the Origins of American Civilization* (New York: Vintage Books, 1973), p. 4; cf. Benedict Anderson, *Imagined Communities: Reflections on the Origins and Spread of Nationalism* (2nd edn., London: Verso, 1991).

16. See Linda Colley, *Britons: Forging the Nation, 1707–1837* (New Haven, Conn.: Yale University Press, 1992).

17. A theme of David Campbell, *Writing Security: United States Foreign Policy and the Politics of Identity* (Manchester, U.K.: Manchester University Press, 1992).

18. Alexis de Tocqueville, *Democracy in America*, J. P. Mayer, ed. (New York: Anchor Books, 1969), pp. 394–95, 412–13.

19. Michel Chevalier, "La guerre et la crise européenne," *Revue des Deux Mondes*, 63 (June 1, 1866), pp. 784–85. On the larger theme see Geoffrey Barraclough, "Europa, Amerika und Russland in Vorstellung und Denken des 19. Jahrhunderts," *Historische Zeitschrift*, 203 (October 1966), pp. 280–315.

20. Statistics and quotation from Kevin H. O'Rourke and Jeffrey G. Williamson, *Globalization and History: The Evolution of a Nineteenth-Century Atlantic Economy* (Cambridge, Mass.: MIT Press, 1999), pp. 33–35.

21. Gavin Wright, "The Origins of American Industrial Success, 1879–1940," *American Economic Review*, 80 (1990), pp. 661, 664.

22. Statistics from R. W. Davies et al., eds., *The Economic Transformation of the Soviet Union, 1913–1945* (New York: Cambridge University Press, 1994), p. 305; Robert W. Campbell, *Soviet and Post-Soviet Telecommunications: An Industry under Reform* (Boulder, Colo.: Westview, 1995), p. 15.

23. Alfred D. Chandler Jr., *The Visible Hand: The Managerial Revolution in American Business* (Cambridge, Mass.: Harvard University Press, 1977), esp. Part II and Conclusion.

24. For this paragraph see Tino Balio, ed., *The American Film Industry* (Madison: University of Wisconsin, 1976), esp. pp. 65, 112–15, 187, 222–23, 326.

25. For this theme see David Reynolds, "Power and Superpower: The Impact of the Second World War on America's International Role," in Warren F. Kimball, ed., *America Unbound: World War II and the Making of a Superpower* (New York: St. Martin's Press, 1992), pp. 13–35.

26. The *Morning Post*, quoted in Edward Lowry, "Trade Follows the Film," *Saturday Evening Post* (Nov. 7, 1925), p. 12.

27. Carl Abbott, "The Federal Presence," in Clyde A. Milner II, Carol A. O'Connor, and Martha A. Sandweiss, eds., *The Oxford History of the American West* (New York: Oxford University Press, 1994), p. 496.

28. Letter of June 21, 1785, in Lester J. Cappon, ed., *The Adams–Jefferson Letters: The Complete Correspondence between Thomas Jefferson and Abigail and John Adams* (2 vols., Chapel Hill: University of North Carolina Press, 1959), vol. I, pp. 33–34.

29. Geoffrey Perret, *A Country Made by War: From the Revolution to Vietnam— The Story of America's Rise to Power* (New York: Vintage Books, 1990), p. 558.

30. Quotation and statistics from Walter Russell Mead, *Special Providence: American Foreign Policy and How It Changed the World* (New York: Alfred A. Knopf, 2001), pp. 218–19.

31. All quotations in this paragraph are from Chapter 13 of Albert K. Weinberg, *Manifest Destiny: A Study of Nationalist Expansionism in American History* (Baltimore: Johns Hopkins University Press, 1935), pp. 385, 388–89, 396. For the context of

the Washington quotation see his letter to John Trumbull, 25 June 1799, in John C. Fitz-patrick, ed., *The Writings of George Washington from the Original Manuscript Sources, 1745–1799*, vol. 37 (Washington, D.C.: Government Printing Office, 1940), p. 250.

32. Weinberg, *Manifest Destiny*, p. 451.

33. Fireside chat of February 23, 1942, in *The Public Papers and Addresses of President Franklin D. Roosevelt*, comp. Samuel I. Rosenman, vol. 11, 1942 (New York, 1950), pp. 107–78. More generally see David Reynolds, "The Origins of the Two 'World Wars': Historical Discourse and International Politics," *Journal of Contemporary History*, 38 (2003), pp. 29–44.

34. Melvyn P. Leffler, *A Preponderance of Power: National Security, the Truman Administration, and the Cold War* (Stanford: Stanford University Press, 1992), p. 56.

35. Thomas H. Etzold and John Lewis Gaddis, eds., *Containment: Documents on American Policy and Strategy, 1945–1950* (New York: Columbia University Press, 1978), p. 387.

36. I have developed this theme in David Reynolds, *One World Divisible: A Global History since 1945* (New York: W.W. Norton, 2000).

Chapter 5

1. Akira Iriye, "Transnational History," in *Contemporary European History*, 13 (2004), pp. 218–20; Bruce Mazlish, "An Introduction to Global History," in Bruce Mazlish and Ralph Buultjens, eds., *Conceptualizing Global History* (Boulder, Colo.: Westview, 1993), pp. 1–24.

2. C. A. Bayly, *The Birth of the Modern World, 1780–1914: Global Connections and Comparisons* (Oxford: Blackwell, 2003), p. 2; Arjun Appadurai, *Modernity at Large: Cultural Dimensions of Globalization* (Minneapolis: University of Minnesota Press, 1996); A. G. Hopkins, ed., *Globalization in World History* (London: Pimlico, 2002).

3. On the topic of American exceptionalism, the literature is vast. For an overview, see Daniel Rodgers, "Exceptionalism," in Anthony Molho and Gordon S. Wood, eds., *Imagined Histories: American Historians Interpret the Past* (Princeton, N.J.: Princeton University Press, 1998), pp. 21–40. See also Aristide R. Zolberg, "How Many Exceptionalisms?" in *Working-Class Formation: Nineteenth Century Patterns in Western Europe and the United States*, I. Katznelson and A. R. Zolberg, eds. (Princeton, N.J.: Princeton University Press, 1986), pp. 397–455; Byron Shafer, *Is America Different? A New Look at American Exceptionalism* (Oxford: Oxford University Press, 1991); Seymour Martin Lipset, *American Exceptionalism: A Double-Edged Sword* (New York: Norton, 1997); Elizabeth Glaser and Hermann Wellenreuther, eds., *Bridging the Atlantic: The Question of American Exceptionalism in Perspective*; Publications of the German Historical Institute Series (New York and Cambridge: Cambridge University Press, 2002); Jack Greene, *The Intellectual Construction of America: Exceptionalism and Identity from 1492 to 1800* (Chapel Hill: University of North Carolina Press, 1993).

4. Lipset, *American Exceptionalism*.

5. Zolberg, "How Many Exceptionalisms?" pp. 397–455; Peter Kruger, "Transatlantic History as National History: Thoughts on German Post-World War II Historiography," in Glaser and Wellenreuther, eds., *Bridging the Atlantic*, p. 268; Ric Halpern and Jonathan Morris, "The Persistence of Exceptionalism: Class Formation and the Comparative Method," in Halpern and Morris, eds., *American Exceptionalism? US Working-Class Formation in an International Context* (London: Macmillan, 1997), pp. 5–7.

6. Dorothy Ross, *The Origins of American Social Science* (New York: Cambridge University Press, 1991); Ross, "The New and Newer Histories: Social Theory and Historiography Win an American Key," in Molho and Wood, eds., *Imagined Histories*, p. 101.

7. Greene, *Intellectual Construction of America*.

8. Sacvan Bercovitch, *The Puritan Origins of the American Self* (New Haven: Yale University Press, 1975); Bercovitch, *The American Jeremiad* (Madison: University of Wisconsin Press, 1978).

9. Charles Gibson, *The Black Legend: Anti-Spanish Attitudes in the Old World and the New* (New York: Knopf, 1971); Greene, *Intellectual Construction of America*, pp. 35–36, only briefly touches on this theme.

10. Ari Hoogenboom, "American Exceptionalism: Republicanism as Ideology," in Glaser and Wellenreuther, eds., *Bridging the Atlantic*, pp. 43–53.

11. Frederick Jackson Turner, *The Frontier in American History* (New York: Holt, 1921).

12. Ian Tyrrell, "The Threat of De-provincializing US History in World War Two," in "Internationalizing U.S. History," Dirk Hoerder, ed., *Amerikastudien/American Studies* 48.1 (Spring 2003), pp. 41–59.

13. See Neil Smith, *American Empire: Roosevelt's Geographer and the Prelude to Globalization* (Berkeley: University of California Press, 2003).

14. See, for example, Louis Hartz, *The Liberal Tradition in America* (New York: Harcourt, Brace & World, 1955).

15. http://www.whitehouse.gov/news/releases/2004/07/20040702-8.html, accessed 12 August 2004.

16. http://www.whitehouse.gov/news/releases/2004/01/20040120-7.html, accessed 12 August 2004.

17. Rush Welter, *The Mind of America, 1820–1860* (New York: Columbia University Press, 1975), pp. 362–63.

18. David Reynolds, "American Globalism: Mass, Motion, and the Multiplier Effect," in Hopkins, *Globalization in World History*, p. 245.

19. Niall Ferguson, quoted in "The United States Is the Empire That Dare Not Speak Its Name," http://www.baja.com/ubb/Forum5/HTML/000118.html, accessed 24 October 2004.

20. *Internet Modern History Sourcebook*, http://www.fordham.edu/halsall/mod/1982reagan1.html, accessed 24 October 2004.

21. Stuart C. Miller, *"Benevolent Assimilation": The American Conquest of the Philippines, 1899–1903* (New Haven, Conn.: Yale University Press, 1982); Paul Kramer, "Empires, Exceptions, and Anglo-Saxons: Race and Rule between the British and United States Empires, 1880–1910," *Journal of American History*, 88 (March 2002), pp. 1314–53.

22. Samuel Flagg Bemis, *A Diplomatic History of the United States*, 4th ed. (New York: Holt, 1955).

23. Christopher Thorne, *Allies of a Kind: The United States, Britain, and the War Against Japan, 1941–1945* (Oxford: Oxford University Press, 1978); W. R. Louis, "American Anti-Colonialism and the Dissolution of the British Empire," *International Affairs*, 61 (1985), pp. 395–420; Gary R. Hess, "Franklin D. Roosevelt and Anti-Colonialism," *Indian Journal of American Studies*, 13 (1983), pp. 23–38; N. Gordon Levin Jr., *Woodrow Wilson and World Politics: America's Response to War and Revolution* (New York: Oxford University Press, 1968), esp. pp. 236–51; Arno J. Mayer, *Politics and Diplomacy of Peacemaking: Containment and Counterrevolution at Versailles, 1918–1919* (New York: Knopf, 1967).

24. W. A. Williams, *The Tragedy of American Diplomacy*, rev. ed. (1959; New York: Delta Books, 1961); Williams, *Empire as a Way of Life* (New York: Oxford University Press, 1980).

25. Geir Lundestad, *The American "Empire" and Other Studies of US Foreign Policy in a Comparative Perspective* (New York: Oxford University Press, 1990), pp. 54–61.

26. Catherine Beecher, *A Treatise on Domestic Economy* (1841; New York: Source Book Press, 1970); Ian Tyrrell, *Sobering Up: From Temperance to Prohibition in Antebellum America, 1800–1860* (Westport, Conn.: Greenwood Press, 1979), pp. 78–79.

27. Charles H. Hopkins, *History of the Y.M.C.A. in North America* (New York: Association Press, 1951); Hopkins, *John R. Mott, 1865–1955: A Biography* (Grand Rapids, Mich.: Eerdmans, 1979); Emily Rosenberg, *Spreading the American Dream: American Economic and Cultural Expansion, 1890–1945* (New York: Hill & Wang, 1982).

28. Timothy Marr, "Imagining Ishmael: Studies of Islamic Orientalism in America from Puritans to Melville," unpublished dissertation, American Studies Department, Yale University, 1998.

29. Sylvana Tomaselli, "The Enlightenment Debate on Women," *History Workshop Journal*, 20 (Autumn 1985), pp. 101–24.

30. Ian Tyrrell, *Woman's World/Woman's Empire: The Woman's Christian Temperance Union in International Perspective, 1880–1930* (Chapel Hill: University of North Carolina Press, 1991).

31. Michael F. Holt, *Forging a Majority: The Formation of the Republican Party in Pittsburgh, 1848–1860* (New Haven, Conn.: Yale University Press, 1969); Richard Jensen, *The Winning of the Midwest: Social and Political Conflict, 1888–1896* (Chicago:

University of Chicago Press, 1971); Ronald P. Formisano, *The Birth of Mass Political Parties, Michigan, 1827–1861* (Princeton, N.J.: Princeton University Press, 1971).

32. Tyrrell, *Woman's World*, pp. 140–41; Nancy Cott, *Public Vows: A History of Marriage and the Nation* (Cambridge, Mass.: Harvard University Press, 2000), p. 113.

33. Gaines M. Foster, *Moral Reconstruction: Christian Lobbyists and the Federal Legislation of Morality, 1865–1920* (Chapel Hill: University of North Carolina Press, 2002).

34. George M. Marsden, *Fundamentalism and American Culture: The Shaping of Twentieth-Century Evangelicalism, 1870–1925* (New York: Oxford University Press, 1980); Michael Lienesch, *Redeeming America: Piety and Politics in the New Christian Right* (Chapel Hill: University of North Carolina Press, 1993).

35. See John Sharpless, "World Population Growth, Family Planning, and American Foreign Policy," in Donald T. Critchlow, ed., *The Politics of Abortion and Birth Control in Historical Perspective* (University Park: Pennsylvania State University Press, 1996), pp. 103–27; Donald T. Critchlow, *Intended Consequences: Birth Control, Abortion, and the Federal Government in Modern America* (New York: Oxford University Press, 1999).

36. John Higham, "America in Person: The Evolution of National Symbols," *Amerikastudien/American Studies*, 36 (Spring 1991), pp. 473–93, quoted at 474.

37. Maldwyn Jones, *American Immigration* (Chicago: University of Chicago Press, 1960), pp. 248, 158, 175.

38. Formisano, *Birth of Mass Political Parties*; Holt, *Forging a Majority*.

39. Wilbur Zelinsky, *Nation into State: The Shifting Symbolic Foundations of American Nationalism* (Chapel Hill: University of North Carolina Press, 1988).

40. Higham, "America in Person," p. 486.

41. On the pledge see John W. Baer, "The Pledge of Allegiance: A Short History," http://history.vineyard.net/pledge.htm, accessed 23 March 2004.

42. John Bodnar, *Remaking America: Public Memory, Commemoration, and Patriotism in the Twentieth Century* (Princeton, N.J.: Princeton University Press, 1992).

43. Roderick Nash, *Wilderness and the American Mind* (New Haven, Conn.: Yale University Press, 1967).

44. Harold U. Faulkner, *The Decline of Laissez-Faire: The Economic History of the United States, 1897–1917* (New York: Holt, Reinhart & Winston, 1951), pp. 92–93.

45. The literature on the history of the frontier thesis long ago established this. For a review see Richard Hofstadter, *The Progressive Historians: Turner, Beard, Parrington* (New York: Alfred A. Knopf, 1968), pp. 474–75, 155–58.

46. Stephan Thernstrom, *The Other Bostonians: Poverty and Progress in the American Metropolis, 1880–1970* (Cambridge, Mass.: Harvard University Press, 1973).

47. The out-migration of African Americans to northern cities is the best known and studied example of this.

48. David Potter, *People of Plenty: Economic Abundance and the American Character* (Chicago: University of Chicago Press, 1954).

49. Richard P. Tucker, *Insatiable Appetite: The United States and the Ecological Degradation of the Tropical World* (Berkeley and London: University of California Press, 2000), pp. 190–91.

50. See the interview with Gabriel Kolko at http://multinationalmonitor.org/hyper/issues/1989/09/mm0989_09.html, accessed 10 August 2004; Kolko, *Confronting the Third World: United States Foreign Policy, 1945–1980* (New York: Pantheon Books, 1988); Kolko, *Main Currents in Modern American History* (New York: Harper & Row, 1976).

51. For land/labor ratios and economic development, see H. J. Habakkuk, *American and British Technology in the Nineteenth Century: The Search for Labor-Saving Inventions* (Cambridge: Cambridge University Press, 1962). For a different view, see Carville Earle and Ronald Hoffman, "The Foundation of the Modern Economy: Agriculture and the Costs of Labor in the United States and England, 1800–1860," *American Historical Review*, 85 (December 1980), pp. 1055–1094. On the exploitation of abundant resources giving the United States greater resource-intensive and capital-intensive industrialization from 1880 to 1940, see Gavin Wright, "The Origins of American Industrial Success, 1879–1940," *American Economic Review*, 80 (September 1990), pp. 651–68.

52. Samuel Hays, *Conservation and the Gospel of Efficiency: The Progressive Conservation Movement, 1890–1920* (Cambridge: Harvard University Press, 1959); Donald Pisani, "Forests and Conservation, 1865–1890," *Journal of American History*, 72 (September 1985), pp. 340–359.

53. Tucker, *Insatiable Appetite*, pp. 422–24.

54. http://www.eia.doe.gov/emeu/efficiency/wec98.htm, accessed 10 August 2004.

55. Ibid.

56. John C. Torpey, *The Invention of the Passport: Surveillance, Citizenship and the State* (Cambridge: Cambridge University Press, 1999), p. 95.

57. On the history of the American state structure, see especially the following influential works: Steven Skowronek, *Building a New American State: The Expansion of National Administrative Capacities, 1877–1920* (New York: Cambridge University Press, 1982); Richard F. Bensel, *Yankee Leviathan: The Origins of Central State Authority in America, 1859–1877* (New York: Cambridge University Press, 1990).

58. "How the Convention on Biodiversity Was Defeated," http://www.sovereignty.net/p/land/biotreatystop.htm; Union of Concerned Scientists, http://www.ucsusa.org/global_environment/archive/page.cfm?pageID=388, accessed 10 August 2004.

59. Arthur M. Schlesinger Jr., *The Age of Jackson* (Boston: Houghton Mifflin, 1945), p. 423; Robert Remini, *Andrew Jackson and the Course of American Freedom, 1822–1832* (New York: Harper & Row, 1981), pp. 68–71, 360–61.

60. Douglas A. Irwin, "Historical Perspectives on U.S. Trade Policy," http://grove.ship.edu/econ/trade/Irwin_on_us_trade.html, accessed 14 August 2004.

61. Walter LaFeber, *The New Empire: An Interpretation of American Expansion, 1860–1898* (Ithaca, N.Y.: Cornell University Press, 1963).

62. Cf. Walter LaFeber, *The American Search for Opportunity, 1865–1913*, vol. 2, *The Cambridge History of American Foreign Relations*, Warren I. Cohen, ed. (Cambridge: Cambridge University Press, 1993), pp. 77–78.

63. Irwin, "Historical Perspectives on U.S. Trade Policy."

64. See, for example, David Goodman and Michael Redclift, eds., *The International Farm Crisis* (New York: St. Martin's Press, 1989).

65. Douglas A. Irwin, "The GATT's Contribution to Economic Recovery in Post-War Europe," in B. Eichengreen, ed., *Europe's Postwar Recovery* (New York: Cambridge University Press, 1995), cited in http://grove.ship.edu/econ/trade/Irwin_on_us_trade.html, accessed 14 August 2004.

Chapter 6

1. N. J. Demerath III, *Crossing the Gods: World Religions and Worldly Politics* (New Brunswick, N.J.: Rutgers University Press, 2001).

2. Ulrich Beck, *What Is Globalization?* (Cambridge: Polity Press, 2000).

3. Clifford Geertz, *The Interpretation of Cultures* (New York: Basic Books, 1973).

4. See Mike Featherstone, Scott Lash, and Roland Robertson, eds., *Global Modernities* (London: Sage, 1995) and Roland Robertson, *Globalization: Social Theory and Global Culture* (London: Sage, 1992).

5. W. F. Ogburn, *W. F. Ogburn on Culture and Social Change: Selected Papers* (Chicago: University of Chicago Press, 1955).

6. Lewis S. Feuer, ed., *Marx and Engels: Basic Writings on Politics and Philosophy* (New York: Doubleday Anchor, 1959), pp. 256ff.

7. Alex Inkeles and David Smith, *Becoming Modern: Individual Change in Six Developing Countries* (Cambridge: Harvard University Press, 1974).

8. Robertson, *Globalization*.

9. Cf. Reinhard Bendix, *Max Weber: An Intellectual Portrait* (New York: Doubleday, 1960), and Steven Lukes, *Emile Durkheim: His Life and Work, a Historical and Critical Study* (New York: Harper & Row, 1972).

10. Robert N. Bellah, "Civil Religion in America," *Daedalus*, 96 (1967), pp. 1–21.

11. Samuel Huntington, *The Clash of Civilizations and the Remaking of World Order* (New York: Simon & Schuster, 1996).

12. Demerath, *Crossing the Gods*, pp. 228–46.

13. N. J. Demerath III, "Snatching Defeat from Victory in the Decline of Liberal Protestantism: Culture and Structure in Institutional Analysis," in N. J. Demerath,

P. H. Hall, T. Schmitt, and R. Williams, eds., *Sacred Companies* (New York: Oxford University Press, 1998), pp. 154–72.

14. Peter F. Beyer, *Religion and Globalization* (Newbury Park, Calif.: Sage, 1994).

15. Cf. H. R. Niebuhr, *The Social Sources of Denominationalism* (New York: Holt, Rinehart, & Winston, 1929); Nathan Glazer, *We Are All Multiculturists Now* (Cambridge, Mass.: Harvard University Press, 1997); Edwin S. Gaustad and Philip L. Barlow, *New Historical Atlas of Religion in America* (New York: Oxford University Press, 2001); William R. Hutchison, *Religious Pluralism in America: The Contentious History of a Founding Ideal* (New Haven: Yale University Press, 2003).

16. Niebuhr, *The Social Sources.*

17. Hutchison, *Religious Pluralism.*

18. W. E. B. DuBois, *The Souls of Black Folks* (New York: New American Library Edition, 1969).

19. C. Eric Lincoln and Lawrence H. Mamiya, *The Black Church in the African American Experience* (Durham, N.C.: Duke University Press, 1990).

20. N. J. Demerath III and Rhys H. Williams, *A Bridging of Faiths: Religion and Politics in a New England City* (Princeton, N.J.: Princeton University Press, 1992).

21. Quoted in Hutchison, *Religious Pluralism*, p. 225.

22. Rudolph J. Vecoli, "Immigration," in Paul S. Boyer, *The Oxford Companion to United States History* (New York: Oxford University Press), p. 361.

23. Fenggang Yang and Helen Rose Ebaugh, "Transformations in New Immigrant Religions and Their Global Implications," *American Sociological Review*, Vol. 66 (April, 2001: 269–88) p. 282.

24. R. Stephen Warner and Judith Wittner, *Gatherings in Diaspora: Religious Communities and the New Immigration* (Philadelphia: Temple University Press, 1998).

25. Diana Eck, *A New Religious America: How a "Christian Country" Has Become the World's Most Religiously Diverse Nation* (San Francisco: Harper San Francisco, 2001).

26. James A. Beckford. "Religious Movements and Globalization," in Robin Cohen and Shirin M. Rai, *Global Social Movements* (London: The Athlone Press, 2000), pp. 165–83.

27. The term originated in Japan but has globalized since; see Robertson, *Globalization*, pp. 173–74.

28. Philip Jenkins, *The Next Christendom: The Coming of Global Christianity* (New York: Oxford University Press, 2002), p. 105.

29. Hutchison, *Religious Pluralism.*

30. Robert Wuthnow, "The Challenge of Diversity," *Journal for the Scientific Study of Religion*, 43 (June 2004), pp. 159–70.

31. Ibid, p. 164.

32. Beyer, *Religion and Globalization.*

33. William R. Hutchison, *Errand to the World: American Protestant Thought and Foreign Missions* (Chicago: University of Chicago Press, 1987).

34. Terry Schmitt, "Representing the Faith." Unpublished Ph.D. Dissertation, Department of Sociology, Yale University, 1995.

35. Lamin Sanneh, *Encountering the West: Christianity and the Global Cultural Process* (Maryknoll, N.Y.: Orbis Books, 1993).

36. Niall Ferguson, *Empire: The Rise and Demise of the British World Order and the Lessons for Global Power* (New York: Harper Collins, 2002).

37. J. Bruce Nichols, *The Uneasy Alliance: Religion, Refugee Work, and U.S. Foreign Policy* (New York: Oxford University Press, 1988).

38. Steve Brouwer, Paul Gifford, and Susan Rose, *Exporting the American Gospel: Global Christian Fundamentalism* (London: Routledge, 1996).

39. Martin Marty and Scott Appleby, eds., *Fundamentalisms Observed*, 4 vols. (Chicago: University of Chicago Press, 1990–94).

40. Beckford, "Religious Movements and Globalization."

41. David Martin, *Tongues of Fire: The Explosion of Protestantism in Latin America* (London: Blackwell, 1990).

42. Jenkins, *The Next Christendom*, p. 5.

43. T. Jeremy Gunn, "American Exceptionalism and Globalist Double Standards: A More Balanced Alternative," *Columbia Journal of Transnational Law*, 41 (2002).

44. James A. Beckford, "Globalization and Religion," Chapter 4 of *Social Theory and Religion* (London: Blackwell, 2003).

45. N. J. Demerath III, "Taking Exception to American Exceptionalism," Chapter 8 of *Crossing the Gods.*

46. Bruce Mazlish, "An Introduction to Global History," in Bruce Mazlish and Ralph Buultjens, eds., *Conceptualizing Global History* (Boulder, Colo.: Westview, 1993).

47. Demerath, *Crossing the Gods*, esp. Chapters 4 and 7.

48. See, for example, Kevin Phillips, *American Dynasty: Aristocracy, Fortune, and the Politics of Deceit in the House of Bush* (New York: Viking Press, 2004).

Chapter 7

1. Toby Miller, "The Crime of Monsieur Lang: GATT, the Screen, and the New International Division of Cultural Labour," in Albert Moran, ed., *Film Policy: International, National and Regional Perspectives* (London: Routledge, 1996), p. 78. See also Bert R. Briller, "The Globalization of American TV," *Television Quarterly* 24 (1990), pp. 71–79 (Forman quoted on p. 77). In any event, an Australian company—Rupert Murdoch's News Corp—acquired Fox, with perhaps less deleterious cultural consequences.

2. Briller, pp. 75–78. See also George H. Quester, *The International Politics of Television* (Lexington, Mass.: Lexington Press, 1990), pp. 56–57.

3. Limitations of space also necessitate that we avoid discussion of certain foreign cultural imports into the American market, such as diasporic media. Since 2000, the Hispanic population of the United States has grown at a rate of four times that of the total population. While the impact of this market has been notable in the media, particularly Spanish-language television, newspapers, and magazines, we do not consider these examples of "European imports" for the purposes of this chapter.

4. Nicholas Garnham, "Concepts of Culture: Public Policy and the Cultural Industries," in Joanne Hollows, Peter Hutchings, and Mark Jancovich, eds., *The Film Studies Reader* (London: Arnold, 2000), pp. 19–20.

5. See, among others, Oliver Boyd-Barrett, "Media Imperialism: Towards an International Framework for the Analysis of Media Systems," in James Curran, Michael Gurevitch, and Janet Woollacott, eds., *Mass Communication and Society* (London: Arnold, 1977), pp. 116–35; Herbert Schiller, *Mass Communications and American Empire* (Boulder, Colo.: Westview, 1969); Schiller, "Not Yet the Post-Imperialist Era," *Critical Studies in Mass Communication*, 8(1)(1991), pp. 13–28; and Jeremy Tunstall, *The Media Are American: Anglo-American Media in the World* (London: Constable, 1977). For a critical overview, see John Tomlinson, *Cultural Imperialism: A Critical Introduction* (London: Pinter Publishers, 1991).

6. Charles R. Acland, *Screen Traffic: Movies, Multiplexes, and Global Culture* (Durham, N.C.: Duke University Press, 2003), p. 26.

7. http://www.imdb.com, accessed 25 January 2005.

8. Peter S. Grant and Chris Wood, *Blockbusters and Trade Wars: Popular Culture in a Globalized World* (Vancouver, B.C.: Douglas & McIntyre, 2003), pp. 118–19.

9. Bill Grantham, *'Some Big Bourgeois Brothel': Contexts for France's Culture Wars with Hollywood* (Luton, U.K.: University of Luton Press, 2000), p. 87.

10. One of the reasons that Japan has historically been able to keep a hold on its market is because of the high cultural discount on foreign programming. See Colin Hoskins, Stuart McFadyen, and Adam Finn, *Global Television and Film: An Introduction to the Economics of the Business* (Oxford: Clarendon Press, 1997), p. 33.

11. Hans Mommaas, "The Politics of Culture and World Trade," in Annemoon van Hemel, Hans Mommaas, and Cas Smithuijsen, eds., *Trading Culture: GATT, European Cultural Policies and the Transatlantic Market* (Amsterdam: Boekman Foundation, 1996), p. 12.

12. Scott Robert Olsen suggests that American cultural products easily blend into other cultures because their manifest narrative structures are transparent, by which he means that audiences can project indigenous values, beliefs, rites, and rituals into the texts. "Hollywood Planet: Global Media and the Competitive Advantage of Narrative Transparency," in Robert C. Allen and Annette Hill, *The Television Studies Reader* (London: Routledge, 2004), p. 214.

13. Jeanette Steemers, *Selling Television: British Television in the Global Marketplace* (London: British Film Institute, 2004), p. 4.

14. See Máire Messenger Davies and Roberta E. Pearson, "To Boldly Bestride the World Like a Colossus: Shakespeare, *Star Trek* and the European TV Market," in Ib Bondebjerg and Peter Golding, *European Culture and the Media* (Bristol, U.K.: Intellect Books, 2004), pp. 65–90.

15. See, for example, Ien Ang, *Watching Dallas: Soap Opera and the Melodramatic Imagination* (London: Methuen, 1985); Tamar Liebes and Elihu Katz, *The Export of Meaning: Cross Cultural Readings of Dallas*, 2nd ed. (Oxford: Polity Press, 1993).

16. On the global distribution of non-American media, see Stuart Cunningham and Elizabeth Jacka, *Australian Television and International Mediascapes* (Cambridge: Cambridge University Press, 1996). Also see John Sinclair, Elizabeth Jacka, and Stuart Cunningham, eds., *New Patterns in Global Television: Peripheral Vision* (Oxford: Oxford University Press, 1996), and Joseph Straubhaar, "Beyond Media Imperialism: Asymmetrical Interdependence and Cultural Proximity," *Critical Studies in Mass Communication*, 8 (1991), pp. 39–59.

17. Andrew Ross, *No Respect: Intellectuals and Popular Culture* (New York: Routledge, 1989), p. 7.

18. For more on this, see Michael Woolf, "The Magic Kingdom: Europe in the American Mind," in Philip John Davies, ed., *Representing and Imagining America* (Keele, U.K.: Keele University Press, 1996).

19. Allen J. Scott, "A New Map of Hollywood: The Production and Distribution of American Motion Pictures," *Regional Studies*, 36 (2002), pp. 957–75, specifically p. 970.

20. European Audiovisual Observatory, "Press Release: The Imbalance of Trade in Films and Television Programmes between North America and Europe Continues to Deteriorate," 9 April, 2000, http://www.obs.coe.int/about/oea/pr/desequilibre.html. The European Audiovisual Observatory's compilation of statistics about media flow is another reason for our focus upon Europe, because there is no comparable source for other geographic regions.

21. Milly Buonanno, ed., *Continuity and Change: Television Fiction in Europe* (Luton, U.K.: University of Luton Press, 2000), p. xi.

22. This is in contrast to newsstands in any midsize city in, for example, Italy or the Netherlands, which stock newspapers from all over Western Europe.

23. The United States and Japan are the primary producers of video games. The European Union Commission has already taken cognizance of the importance of video games, passing a resolution "with the intention of securing the communication of European cultural values through interactive media, especially computer games": Simon Egenfeldt-Nielsen, "The EU Commission Starts the Game," *Game Research*, http://www.game-research.com/art_eu_com.asp, accessed 14 January 2005.

24. Steemers, *Selling Television*, p. 32.

25. Milly Buonanno, "Eurofiction: Comparative Analysis of the Results of the Seventh Year of Research on European Fiction," in *Television Channels: Program Production and Distribution*, vol. 5 of *Yearbook 2003: Film, Television, Video and Multimedia in Europe* (Strasbourg: European Audiovisual Observatory, 2003), p. 65.

26. Anna Herold, *European Public Film Support within the WTO Framework*, (Strasbourg: European Audiovisual Observatory, 2003), p. 2.

27. For a further analysis of the importation of these films into the United States and the elite response, see Roberta Pearson and William Uricchio, "Italian Spectacle and the U.S. Market," in Roland Cosandey and Francois Albera, eds., *Images across Borders* (Lausanne: Editions Payot Lausanne, 1995), pp. 95–105.

28. Douglas Gomery, *Shared Pleasures: A History of Movie Presentation in the United States* (London: BFI, 1992), p. 181.

29. Barbara Wilinsky, *Sure Seaters: The Emergence of Art House Cinema* (Minneapolis: University of Minnesota Press, 2001), pp. 31–32.

30. Gomery, p. 189.

31. Gomery, p. 181.

32. Wilinsky, p. 3.

33. Gomery, p. 193.

34. Wilinsky, p. 135.

35. David Waterman and Krishna Jayakar, "The Competitive Balance of the Italian and American Film Industries," *European Journal of Communication*, 15 (2000), p. 508.

36. Jeffrey Miller, *Something Completely Different: British Television and American Culture* (Minneapolis: University of Minnesota Press, 2000), p. xii.

37. Ibid., p. 21.

38. Ibid., p. 75.

39. Ibid., p. 87.

40. Ibid., p. 89.

41. Ibid., p. 91.

42. Steemers, *Selling Television*, pp. 13–14.

43. Jeanette Steemers, "Selling British Television on the Global Stage: The Challenge of Exporting British Television Drama," paper delivered at the annual conference of the Media and Cultural Studies Association, University of Lincoln, U.K., January, 2005.

44. The best source for statistics on European film and television, the European Audiovisual Observatory (Council of Europe), is primarily (and understandably) concerned with the circulation of European media within Europe and how best to protect the domestic market from imports (i.e., Hollywood). Unfortunately, it offers little data on the circulation of European products outside of the Union, partly because of the

difficulty of establishing in a precise manner the receipts of European media exports. European producers are just as concerned about distribution within the European Union as to the North American and other markets. See Wolfgang Closs, "Analysing Case Studies of European Film Success," The Strasbourg European Film Forum (Strasbourg: European Audiovisual Observatory, 2001): http://www.obs.coe.int/online_publication/reports/forum2001_report.html, accessed 27 October 2004.

45. Solon Consultants, *Audiovisual Industry: Trade and Investment Barriers in Third Country Markets* (Final Report DG1 Market Access Unit, November 1998), p. 35. Report prepared for the EU.

46. European Audiovisual Observatory, *Yearbook 2003: Film, Television, Video and Multimedia in Europe* (Strasbourg: European Audiovisual Observatory, 2003): p. 35.

47. Waterman and Jayakar, p. 502. In the last ten years, the highest-grossing foreign films in the United States have typically originated in Asia, such as *Crouching Tiger, Hidden Dragon* (2000, $128 million) and Jet Li's *Hero* (2004, $53 million).

48. Toby Miller, p. 76; Steemers, p. 104.

49. Jonathon D. Levy, "Evolution and Competition in the American Video Marketplace," in Albert Moran, ed., *Film Policy: International, National, and Regional Perspectives* (London: Routledge, 1996), p. 55.

50. Steemers, p. 142.

51. Steemers, p. 143.

52. BBC Broadcast Limited, *BBC Broadcast Helps BBC America with Its Spring Clean* (London: BBC Ventures Press Office, 24 March 2004). Press release.

53. Steemers, p. 106.

54. Films of "foreign" origin are subjectively measured but in this case are non-English, first released outside of the United States, include at least two of the stars, director, or writer who are of another nationality, or have a story or setting that reflects that nationality. In the case of English-language film (i.e., from the United Kingdom, Australia, or Canada), the picture's above- and below-the-line talent must be a majority of the originating nationality and reflect related stories and themes. For example, *Bend It Like Beckham*, although it achieved some popularity in North America, is classified as a British film. This week, foreign offerings include films from Australia, New Zealand, China, Japan, Brazil, India, and Canada.

55. Solon Consultants, p. 25.

56. Steemers, p. 109.

57. André Lange, *The Ups and Downs of European Cinema* (European Audiovisual Observatory, August 2001). Prepared for the Council of Europe.

58. Waterman and Jayakar, p. 504.

59. Barry Litman, *The Motion Picture Mega-Industry* (Boston: Allyn & Bacon, 1998): pp. 277, 59.

60. Hoskins et al., p. 61.

61. Toby Miller, p. 151.

62. "Average Hollywood Movie Costs Tops $100 Million" (Reuters Newswire, 24 March 2004). Accessed at http://www.backstage.com/backstage/news/article_display .jsp?vnu_content_id=1000471132.

63. William Paul, "The K-Mart Audience at the Mall Movies," *Film History*, 6 (1994), pp. 487–501, reprinted in Gregory A. Waller, ed., *Moviegoing in America: A Sourcebook in the History of Film Exhibition* (Oxford: Blackwell Publishers, 2002), p. 289.

64. Toby Miller, p. 48.

65. Levy, p. 55.

66. Steemers, p. 109.

67. Solon Consultants, p. 28.

68. Steemers, p. 111.

69. North America uses the National Television Standards Committee (NTSC) standard, which displays up to 525 lines of resolution. Most of Western Europe uses the Phase Alternating Line (PAL) standard, which offers up to 625 lines of resolution. But France, Russia, parts of Greece, and Eastern Europe operate on the Sequential Colour with Memory, or SECAM (the acronym for the French "Sequential Couleur avec Memoire").

Chapter 8

1. Aaron Friedberg, *The Weary Titan: Britain and the Experience of Relative Decline, 1895–1905* (Princeton: Princeton University Press, 1988), p. 300.

2. The centrality of hegemonic power does not mean that globalization is reducible to the set of strategic and security concerns associated with great power status. Although the focus of this chapter is on military strategy and although I believe that security concerns are important, they are part of the story, not its entirety.

3. Paul Kennedy, *The Rise and Fall of the Great Powers* (London: Unwin Hyman, 1988).

4. Bruce Mazlish, *The New Global History* (New York and Oxford: Routledge, 2006), p. 9.

5. Andrew Bacevich, *American Empire: The Realities and Consequences of U.S. Diplomacy* (Cambridge, Mass.: Harvard University Press, 2002).

6. "Key figures" are Donald Rumsfeld, Richard Cheney, and Paul Wolfowitz.

7. While a careful reading of the report (*The National Security Strategy of the United States of America*, Washington, D.C.: The White House, September 2002) suggests that the principal danger envisaged was China, the notion of the export of liberty through military preponderance can be directly translated into the global war on terrorism.

8. Michael Vlahos, *The Blue Sword: The Naval War College and the American Mission, 1919–1941* (Newport, R.I.: Naval War College Foundation, 1980).

9. Gabriel Kolko, *The Politics of War: The World and United States Foreign Policy, 1943–1945* (New York: Pantheon, 1968); Melvyn Leffer, *A Preponderance of Power: National Security, the Truman Administration, and the Cold War* (Stanford: Stanford University Press, 1992).

10. Of course it was never quite this simple. There was confusion about whether the Soviet Union, "international communism," or all forms of popular insurgency was the principal enemy. The development of the doctrine of containment was not a foregone conclusion and, in any case, the interpretation of quite what "containment" meant was a much-debated issue. Moreover, there were considerable anxieties, as well as serious debate, about the military means to implement the strategy.

11. Gabriel Kolko, *Century of War: Politics, Conflicts, and Society since 1914* (New York: New Press, 1994).

12. Andrew Krepinevich, *The Army and Vietnam* (Baltimore: Johns Hopkins University Press, 1986).

13. The reasons for this remain a matter of debate, but the decision to rely on indigenous forces supplemented by American Special Forces showed a maturation in counterinsurgency thinking.

14. Robert Kagan, *Of Paradise and Power: America and Europe in the New World Order* (New York: Knopf, 2003); Charles Kupchan, *The End of the American Era: U.S. Foreign Policy and the Geopolitics of the Twenty-First Century* (New York: Knopf, 2002).

15. G. John Ikenberry, ed., *America Unrivaled: The Future of the Balance of Power* (Ithaca, N.Y.: Cornell University Press, 2002).

16. Paul Bracken, *Fire in the East: The Rise of Asian Military Power and the Second Nuclear Age* (New York: HarperCollins, 1999).

17. G. John Ikenberry, *After Victory: Institutions, Strategic Restraint, and the Rebuilding of Order after Major Wars* (Princeton, N.J.: Princeton University Press, 2001).

18. The evidence for this proposition is still controversial. There seems to be some considerable empirical support for the democracy part of the hypothesis. The evidence for the trade part is less compelling. For my assessment of the evidence, see Ian Roxborough, "War and Militarism," in George Ritzer, ed., *Handbook of Social Problems* (London: Sage, 2004).

19. Richard Haass, *The Reluctant Sheriff: The United States after the Cold War* (New York: Council on Foreign Relations, 1997).

20. Power-projection capability is the ability to sustain military operations in a distant region. This depends on logistic capabilities and on the ability to overcome whatever antiaccess resistance might be established by local powers. As such, power-projection capabilities are relative and dynamic.

21. United States Commission on National Security/21st Century, *New World Coming: American Security in the 21st Century* (Washington, D.C., 1999).

22. The National Security Strategy argues (p. 31) that "The war on terrorism is not a clash of civilizations. It does, however, reveal the clash inside a civilization, the battle for the future of the Muslim world."

23. In this optic, the notion that radical Islam (or even Islam) is the principal enemy fits well with a belief that modernization and globalization require a certain degree of secularization and a separation of church and state.

24. The solution to this conundrum is not to argue that there are features intrinsic to the belief system of Islam that predispose that religion toward terrorism and jihad. All religions are sufficiently elastic and malleable that they can be interpreted as mandating a wide range of conduct. Christianity, for example, has been seen variously as mandating pacifism (as in the literalness with which Quakers take the injunction not to kill) and as justifying crusades to extirpate unbelievers. So it is with Islam. A proper understanding of the role of religion in terrorism should not start with the religious texts but should rather ask why certain groups at particular times and places choose a militant interpretation of their religion. It is sociology, rather than theology, that provides us with the answers we need. To say this, however, is not to dismiss the role of religion. Certain kinds of religious beliefs, particularly those of a Manichean and apocalyptic kind, add fuel to the fire of terrorism. These beliefs, and the groups and institutions that propagate them, need to be countered by systematic efforts to provide an alternative, more tolerant, and more reasonable worldview. This applies as much to Christianity or any other religion as it does to Islam. It should be recalled that prior to the attacks of September 11, 2001, the most dramatic incidents involving loss of life in the United States—the Oklahoma City bombing and the Branch Davidian siege at Waco, Texas—each involved apocalyptic beliefs flourishing on the wilder fringes of Christianity. The enemy of a tolerant, reasonable society is religious intolerance and unreason, whether the believers adhere to Islam, Christianity, or any other religion. A sociological analysis of the reasons for militant religiosity of the kind that sometimes spills forth in terrorism is required.

25. This is by no means necessarily a bad approach. It is possible for America to pressure other states to repress terrorists. The central difficulty with the statecentric approach is the conceptual myopia that it often brings with regard to the best methods of dealing with nonstate actors.

26. It cannot be said that there is any evidence that current American strategists share a similar agreement about the central strategic challenge to the United States.

27. Mancur Olson, *The Rise and Decline of Nations: Economic Growth, Stagflation, and Social Rigidities* (New Haven, Conn.: Yale University Press, 1984).

28. Friedberg, *The Weary Titan*, p. 139.

29. There is now a large body of literature on contemporary U.S. civil–military relations. See Peter Feaver, ed., *Soldiers and Civilians: The Civil-Military Gap and American National Security* (Cambridge, Mass.: MIT Press, 2001).

30. The British Empire did better in this respect. Political officers were assigned to colonial troops, and the Indian Civil Service trained colonial administrators. As Niall Ferguson has noted, the United States could learn a lesson or two here. ("The Empire Slinks Back," *New York Times*, April 27, 2003.)

Chapter 9

1. Niall Ferguson, *Empire: The Rise and Demise of the British World Order and the Lessons for Global Power* (New York: Basic Books, 2002); also, Ferguson, *Colossus: The Price of America's Empire* (New York: The Penguin Press, 2004).

2. James Kurth, "First War of the Global Era: Kosovo and U.S. Grand Strategy," in Andrew J. Bacevich and Eliot A. Cohen, eds., *War over Kosovo: Politics and Strategy in a Global Age* (New York: Columbia University Press, 2001), pp. 63–96.

3. See, for example, Andrew J. Bacevich, *The American Empire: The Realities and Consequences of U.S. Diplomacy* (Cambridge, Mass.: Harvard University Press, 2002); the five articles in the special issue on "An American Empire?" of *The Wilson Quarterly*, Summer 2002; and the diverse collection of articles gathered in Andrew J. Bacevich, ed., *The Imperial Tense: Prospects and Problems of American Empire* (Chicago: Ivan R. Dee, 2003).

4. Some portions of the next sections have been published in my "Confronting the Unipolar Moment: The American Empire and Islamic Terrorism," *Current History* (December 2002), pp. 403–07.

5. Michael Mandelbaum, *The Ideas That Conquered the World: Peace, Democracy, and Free Markets in the Twenty-First Century* (New York: Public Affairs, 2002).

6. Samuel P. Huntington, *The Clash of Civilizations and the Remaking of World Order* (New York: Simon & Schuster, 1996); Roger Scruton, *The West and the Rest: Globalization and the Terrorist Threat* (Wilmington, Del.: ISI Books, 2002).

7. National Commission on Terrorist Attacks Upon the United States, *The 9/11 Commission Report: Final Report of the National Commission on Terrorist Attacks Upon the United States* (New York: W.W. Norton, 2004).

8. *The National Security Strategy of the United States of America* (Washington, D.C.: The White House, 2002).

9. The strategy of unilateral preemption was not really unprecedented in the history of American foreign policy. It was a method used by the United States on several occasions in the nineteenth and early twentieth centuries. See John Lewis Gaddis, *Surprise, Security, and the American Experience* (Cambridge, Mass.: Harvard University Press, 2004).

10. The development of the administration's focus upon Iraq is discussed in Bob Woodward, *Plan of Attack* (New York: Simon & Schuster, 2004); James Fallows, "Bush's Lost Year," *The Atlantic Monthly* (October 2004), pp. 68–84; and Chaim

Kaufmann, "Threat Inflation and the Failure of the Marketplace of Ideas: The Selling of the Iraq War," *International Security* (Summer 2004), pp. 5–48.

11. Walter Russell Mead, *Special Providence: American Foreign Policy and How It Changed the World* (New York: Alfred A. Knopf, 2002).

12. The concept of the "democratic peace" is based on the observation that, historically, liberal democracies have not gone to war with one another.

13. I have discussed these transformations in my "First War of the Global Era: Kosovo and U.S. Grand Strategy," in Bacevich and Cohen, *War over Kosovo.*

14. A useful and detailed account of foreign–policy making in the Clinton administration is given by David Halberstam, *War in a Time of Peace: Bush, Clinton, and the Generals* (New York: Scribner's, 2001).

15. Stefan Halper and Jonathan Clarke, *America Alone: The Neo-Conservatives and the Global Order* (New York: Cambridge University Press, 2004).

16. Francis Fukuyama, "The Neoconservative Moment," *The National Interest* (Summer 2004), especially pp. 65–66.

17. The classic exposition was Russell F. Weigley, *The American Way of War: A History of United States Military Strategy and Policy* (Bloomington, Ind.: Indiana University Press, 1973).

18. An earlier and shorter version of the next sections has been published in my "Iraq: Losing the American Way," *The American Conservative* (March 15, 2004), pp. 10–16.

19. Weigley, *The American Way of War*, Chapters 6–7.

20. Harry G. Summers Jr., *On Strategy: A Critical Analysis of the Vietnam War* (Novato, Calif.: The Presidio Press, 1982) and *On Strategy II: A Critical Analysis of the Gulf War* (New York: Dell Publishing, 1992).

21. Halberstam, *War in a Time of Peace.*

22. Peter J. Boyer, "The New War Machine: How General Tommy Franks Joined Donald Rumsfeld in the Fight to Transform the Military," *The New Yorker* (June 30, 2003), pp. 55–71.

23. A major exponent of the neoconservative way of war is Max Boot. See his "The New American Way of War," *Foreign Affairs* (July/August 2003), pp. 41–58, and his *The Savage Wars of Peace: Small Wars and the Rise of American Power* (New York: Basic Books, 2002).

24. Ibid., Chapters 6–7, 10.

25. James Fallows, "Blind into Baghdad," *The Atlantic Monthly* (January/February 2004), pp. 53–74.

26. Ibid., pp. 72–73.

27. The misconception and mistakes of the U.S. occupation authorities in Baghdad during 2003–2004 are extensively described by William Langewiesche, "Welcome

to the Green Zone: The American Bubble in Baghdad," *The Atlantic Monthly* (November 2004), pp. 60–88.

28. Ibid., pp. 72–73, 88.

Chapter 10

1. Cf. William Korey, *NGOs and the Universal Declaration of Human Rights: "A Curious Grapevine"* (New York: St. Martin's Press, 1998).

2. Subsequent to the conference that served as the background for this present volume, Richard Haass published his book, *The Opportunity: America's Moment to Alter History's Course* (New York: Public Affairs, 2006), which takes a similar position.

3. In an incisive analysis, Jason Ralph, in "Between Cosmopolitan and American Democracy: Understanding US Opposition to the International Criminal Court," *International Relations*, 17 (2003), pp. 195–212, illustrates how the commitment to democracy of the United States works to justify its opposition to the International Criminal Court while allowing America to claim the role of being the moral arbitrator for the world.

4. The ways of the divinity, however, are passing strange, and there appear to be elements in American Christianity that might point in the direction of favoring global citizenship.

5. Cf., for example, Martin Shaw, "The Historical Sociology of the Future," *Review of International Political Economy*, 5 (Summer 1998), pp. 321–26.

6. For a more extended discussion of this subject, see my article, "The Hi-jacking of Global Society," *The Journal of Civil Society*, 1 (May 2005), pp. 5–17.

Index